"Transformation" and "revival" have becume .. conversation for those who consider themselves as followers of Jesus. However, very few of us are proactively growing in the kind of lifestyle that reflects the image of our Lord. Chris Vennetti provides a clear road map to anyone desiring authentic personal revival that will lead to family, community and national transformation. I highly recommend *Journey into the Spirit Empowered Life* for such a time as this and to such a person as YOU!

Dai Sup Han, Founder/National Facilitator, Prayer Surge NOW!, Serving with Youth With A Mission

As president of Every Home for Christ International, a global mission's ministry with over 4,000 staff worldwide, I have the privilege of knowing and serving some incredible men and women of God. These men and women have one thing in common: they are totally surrendered to Christ, walking daily in the power of the Holy Spirit, and living out a Spirit-empowered life. Chris Vennetti's *Journey into the Spirit Empowered Life* will help you discover and cultivate just such an empowered lifestyle. Through practical steps, probing questions, and insightful teachings, this book will guide you into the deeper things of the Spirit so that you, too, can see the Lord moving in and through you in mighty ways.

Dr. Dick Eastman, International President, Every Home for Christ International

Chris is on an amazing journey. Actually it is an impossible journey - but it is a journey that embraces the heart of the God of the impossible. Chris is inviting us to join him on this journey as together we discover God's love, joy and the amazing plans He has for our lives. I encourage you to join Chris on this adventure into the heart of God as you read, *Journey Into the Spirit Empowered Life.*

Tom Victor, President, The Great Commission Coalition (Kingwood, TX)

For anyone that is hungry for pursuing a deeper place in the Lord, Chris Vennetti's book can help you to dig until you find that One precious pearl of hope. As you interact with the scriptures, the Holy Spirit and the reading of this Spirit filled compilation, you will be spiritually empowered to raise your hands and shout out loud, "Here I am Lord, send me!"

Rickie Bradshaw, Pastor/Consultant, Union Baptist Association, Sentinel Group (Int'l Fellowship of Transformation Partners)

Excellent writing with a great desire to move people forward and to live fully for Jesus. *Journey Into the Spirit Empowered Life* reminds me of CS Lewis in Mere Christianity where he talks of the renewed horse not just being able to jump higher but a horse that can fly because it has sprouted wings and can soar!

Ruth Mangalwadi, Co-Author *The Legacy of William Carey, A Model for the Transformation of a Culture*

Chris has written a gracious but needed challenge; a call to the radical lifestyle we cannot ignore as we read the scriptures. He has summarized this journey well:

A truly Spirit-Empowered person is someone with a lifestyle that is radically consecrated to Jesus Christ, and who has learned to live in a place of wholehearted faith in the character, will and ways of God.

May the Lord use this teaching to transform our view of the Christian life, expand our vision of authentic discipleship, and drive us back to scripture in a way that results in Spirit-led, scripture-fed expressions of God's love in and through our Lord and Savior Jesus Christ.

Phil Miglioratti, National Pastors' Prayer Network

Chris calls the reader to a deep place of radically following Jesus. After all is this not the place that we are to live as Christians? It is a call to follow Jesus unreservedly with full surrender. To give up what so many of us have held on to for too long, the control of our own lives and destinies.

As you read *Journey into the Spirit Empowered Life*, I pray that God will speak loudly to you. That He will continue to draw you to a place of complete surrender and the deepest place of dependence upon this unbelievable God that we love, follow and serve. May this book that contains a message from the Lord to us in these days, call you to a sweet place of abiding in God's presence in your life.

I pray that God will use this book in your life to help you be a transforming influence on those in your family, community and nation. May God use this book to cause you to allow Him to walk in and through you to bring about a lifestyle and fruit that will help establish God's kingdom through you on earth as it is in heaven.

Milton Monell, Director of Global Prayer, a ministry of Campus Crusade for Christ, International

Journey into the Spirit Empowered Life is a book that provides a roadmap to connect us with the plan and purpose of God to see our personal lives ignited with love and passion for Him, resulting in the cumulative overflow of renewal in our homes and cities. We teach what we know, but we reproduce who we are. Author Chris Vennetti, has penned this book as an overflow of his lifelong commitment to see the glory of God his heavenly Father manifested here on earth as the waters cover the sea. Every child of God needs to read this book to align their plans and purposes with that of the One who wants to live His Life through us. (Gal. 2:20.)

Paul Benjamin Sr., Founder & President, Central Florida Dream Center & the Love Sanford Project Inc.

Journey into the Spirit Empowered Life comes from an author who is speaking from personal experience and striving to live what he preaches. This book will help you understand how to let Jesus live your life for you and live His life through you to impact your community and disciple the nations. It exposes our need and yet encourages us to move into a destiny only GOD could offer us. For those longing for transformation this is a book to be read, absorbed and followed.

Chris Leeper, Pastor, New Beginnings Christian Fellowship (El Cajon, CA)

Chris has a passionate heart to reach people with the gospel of Jesus Christ. This well-written account of his journey and calling will stir you to consider what you can do to be a part the Great Commission and adventure that we are all called to fulfill. **Steve Homcy, Pastor, Director of Adult Ministries, Church of the Redeemer (Gaithersburg, MD)**

I'm really excited about Chris's book, *Journey Into the Spirit Empowered Life*. We have been praying together for years and what Chris writes has been the subject of his prayers for as long as I've known him. Chris writes with an understanding of what is on the Father's heart and this is what makes his book such a gift to the Church and a necessary tool for such a time as this! **Carlos Sarmiento, Director, Orlando House of Prayer**

We are living in exciting times when God is stirring his people to believe for a great outpouring of the Holy Spirit upon the earth. Chris Vennetti is a revival forerunner. In his book, *Journey into the Spirit Empowered Life,* Chris calls us to the purposes of God for our lives, our families, our cities, and our nations. This book will stir the fire within and call you to be all that God has created you to be! **Roger Hackenberg, Pastor, Hope Community Fellowship**

Journey Into the Spirit Empowered Life gives hope to those who have been wounded and inspiration to become a genuine disciple of Jesus Christ.

Tomas Lares, Executive Director, Florida Abolitionist, NDP Task Force

God knows how His kingdom is established in the world and He let His servant Chris understand His wisdom through various life experiences with Him. This book of wisdom gives us the hope that if we will only walk with the Holy Spirit and obey Him in everyday life, God's kingdom will come into our nation. I pray that this book will be a trumpet sound to the ears of His people, "Awaken and determine to die to yourselves and live unto Jesus!"

TC Kim, Facilitator, Transform USA (Colorado Springs, CO)

Journey into
the
Spirit Empowered Life

A Guide to Personal, Family & Community Transformation

Chris Vennetti

Acknowledgements

First of all I am grateful to the Father, Jesus Christ and the Holy Spirit for their sacrificial love that has captured my heart and changed the course of my life.

Secondly I would like to thank my beautiful and patient wife, Rebecca for her love and support during the process of bringing this project together. In many ways this book is the culmination of the last 15 years worth of pursuing God, and she has been with me during nearly every one of the highs and lows of this journey. I am also grateful for our four children, Jeremiah, Joshua, Joel and Ruth whose lives have brought so much meaning to my life, and who have helped shape me into who I am today.

I am eternally grateful to my earthly parents, Janet and Jim who have prayed for me virtually every day of my life and who I owe far more than I will ever know. Thanks to Dan and Kristina, my brother and sister-in-law in Sweden for their love, prayers and support throughout our various life adventures.

Thanks to my wife's family who has journeyed with us, Dixie and Mike, Traci, Gregg, Beth, Chuck and Kevin.

Special thanks to Brandon Mead for his patience in helping with the manuscript to make sure that everything was prepared and formatted properly even when this project proved to be more work than anticipated! Special thanks to Josh Daniel for your willingness to help design the book cover and the time spent getting everything just right.

Last but not least, many thanks to the friends, family and fellow ministers of the Gospel who have supported our family throughout the years of the journey that is described in this book. Thank you for being who you are as you have made untold contributions towards shaping our family and the lives of those around us!

Table of Contents

Introduction

THEN MOSES STRETCHED OUT HIS HAND OVER THE SEA; AND THE LORD SWEPT THE SEA BACK BY A STRONG EAST WIND ALL NIGHT AND TURNED THE SEA INTO DRY LAND, SO THE WATERS WERE DIVIDED. THE SONS OF ISRAEL WENT THROUGH THE MIDST OF THE SEA ON THE DRY LAND, AND THE WATERS WERE LIKE A WALL TO THEM ON THEIR RIGHT HAND AND ON THEIR LEFT.

EXODUS 14:21-22

In obedience to God, Moses stretched out his hand and the Red Sea parted. Hundreds of thousands of men, women and children were freed as one man followed the direction of the living God. It may seem like just a story to us, but not that long ago the Living God broke through the impossibilities of man and set a nation free to worship Him. In a very similar way, God is now looking for a people who will become consumed with His agenda to set captives free.

A Longing for Something Deeper

In the heart of many people across the earth there is a pronounced longing for something more than what they are currently experiencing in their spiritual journey. There is a sincere desire among many to really know the God who created them. This book is written for all those who sincerely desire to explore a deeper relationship with God.

There are others who have had some form of a relationship with God for years, and yet they too have a desire

1

for greater fruitfulness in their labors. As followers of Jesus Christ they believe that Jesus is the Son of God who lived, died, and rose again for the forgiveness of their sins and to purchase them as a people for Himself. They acknowledge that He has sent His Holy Spirit to indwell each of us who have surrendered our lives to Him. Yet many Christ-followers are equally aware that there is something more to a relationship with God than what we are currently experiencing. We know that our marriages and families should be experiencing more of God's redemptive power. We have a longing for our local church to have greater impact. We even at times catch a glimpse of the fact that God desires all men to be saved and the nation's discipled in His ways.

This book is an attempt to lay out God's heart desire for every one of His followers. We will share a Biblical background behind what we mean by the discipleship of nations, and God's original intent in giving the Gospel of Jesus Christ to mankind. We will hear testimonies of how Spirit-Empowered followers of Jesus Christ are being used of God to help disciple nations. We will then get hands on and learn about the practical components of a Spirit-Empowered lifestyle, and how this can be implemented in our personal lives, families, sphere of influence and even in entire regions. Could there be a greater adventure than this?

There's only one catch. In order to enter into more of Christ's Life, we must first let go of more of our lives. The more we die to ourselves, the more we will experience the reality of His Life.

THE BRIDE BELONGS TO THE BRIDEGROOM. THE FRIEND WHO

ATTENDS THE BRIDEGROOM WAITS AND LISTENS FOR HIM, AND IS FULL OF JOY WHEN HE HEARS THE BRIDEGROOM'S VOICE. THAT JOY IS MINE, AND IT IS NOW COMPLETE. HE MUST BECOME GREATER; I MUST BECOME LESS." JOHN 3:29-30 (NIV)

It is my hope and prayer that as you interact with the scriptures in this book, and as you interact with the Spirit of God, that He will lead you to a deeper place in Him than you have ever experienced before. Not only that, but I pray that as you experience God in this way that He will take you deeper and deeper into Himself all the days of your life.

This book is written with the vision to equip millions of Spirit-Empowered followers of Jesus Christ in order to disciple every nation in His ways. It is our prayer that Jesus Christ will receive all the glory and honor that He deserves in the nations of the earth. He wants to disciple the nations through us. Will you let Him use you to be a part of His work?

May we each be counted among those who accept the invitation to enter more deeply into the Spirit-Empowered Life.

In His Service,

Chris Vennetti

Disciple Nations International

Please contact us should God place it on your heart to be a part of raising Spirit-Empowered followers of Jesus Christ in your city/nation.

Contact Information:

www.dninternational.org   Email: office@dninternational.org

3

Goal of Reading This Book

Pursuit of Greater Wisdom and Not Greater Head Knowledge

WISDOM SHOUTS IN THE STREET,

SHE LIFTS HER VOICE IN THE SQUARE;
AT THE HEAD OF THE NOISY STREETS SHE CRIES OUT;
AT THE ENTRANCE OF THE GATES IN THE CITY SHE UTTERS HER SAYINGS:
"HOW LONG, O NAIVE ONES, WILL YOU LOVE BEING SIMPLE-MINDED?
AND SCOFFERS DELIGHT THEMSELVES IN SCOFFING
AND FOOLS HATE KNOWLEDGE?
TURN TO MY REPROOF,
BEHOLD, I WILL POUR OUT MY SPIRIT ON YOU;
I WILL MAKE MY WORDS KNOWN TO YOU."

PROVERBS 1:20-23

FOR WISDOM IS BETTER THAN JEWELS; AND ALL DESIRABLE THINGS CANNOT COMPARE WITH HER.

PROVERBS 8:11

The Western world has been so shaped by Greek thought that many have come to believe that the end goal of learning something new is the acquisition of further mental information. Therefore, all too often we choose to consume a great deal of information that remains in our minds but does not affect our daily practice. Apparently this is not unique to our day in time because Jesus Himself referred to this error.

4

"THEREFORE EVERYONE WHO HEARS THESE WORDS OF MINE AND ACTS ON THEM, MAY BE COMPARED TO A WISE MAN WHO BUILT HIS HOUSE ON THE ROCK. AND THE RAIN FELL, AND THE FLOODS CAME, AND THE WINDS BLEW AND SLAMMED AGAINST THAT HOUSE; AND YET IT DID NOT FALL, FOR IT HAD BEEN FOUNDED ON THE ROCK. EVERYONE WHO HEARS THESE WORDS OF MINE AND DOES NOT ACT ON THEM, WILL BE LIKE A FOOLISH MAN WHO BUILT HIS HOUSE ON THE SAND. THE RAIN FELL, AND THE FLOODS CAME, AND THE WINDS BLEW AND SLAMMED AGAINST THAT HOUSE; AND IT FELL—AND GREAT WAS ITS FALL."

MATTHEW 7:24-27

God's Word defines foolishness as hearing His Word but failing to put it into practice. Wisdom is putting into practice what God has said. Therefore receiving God's truth into our minds is just the first step in acquiring real wisdom. We must then allow what we have heard to become part of our understanding. As we understand this new truth from God at a deeper level, and begin to put it into practice, only then do we begin to step into Biblical wisdom.

We need to make a decision at the beginning of our journey through this book. Will we merely read this book thinking that greater head knowledge will produce life change? Or will we submit to what the Bible says about wisdom, and take the time to allow what we read here to move from our minds, into our daily practice?

For this book to be of real value, let us begin by asking God to shift our goal, so that instead of aiming to merely read a new book, or acquire more head knowledge, we would have a heart to pursue wisdom. To acquire wisdom is going to take

5

more time than to merely obtain more head knowledge. This is the reason far too many have settled for less. Let us make a concerted effort to allow God to push us past the place where we are satisfied with the status quo, and where life transformation is our only goal in reading through this book.

To assist you in your pursuit of wisdom, we have included a section at the end of each chapter that has discussion questions, action points and prayer points. We believe that as you take the time to talk about, and pray into what you have read, this will lead you to the place of putting it into practice. As you persevere in moving further in your journey with God, His Spirit will take what you are putting into practice, and cause it to become part of your lifestyle.

Guide for Small Group Facilitators

Though it is possible to go through this book alone, we highly encourage you to consider going through it with others, so that as you process through each chapter God can take the content even deeper into your heart. At the end of each chapter we have included several items with the hope of helping this book become a practical application guide. In encouraging you to invite others to join with you on this journey, we hope that this will be a tool that God is able to use to do a deep and lasting work in your life.

At the end of each chapter there is a short section that includes:

Discussion Questions: These questions are there to help you process individually, as well as in a corporate setting.

Action Points: Too often we can learn something intellectually, but fail to make the practical adjustments in our lives that will lead to long-term transformation. It is our hope that these action points will help you to cross a very practical line to implement what you are learning. If you are going through this as a small group, you may consider using these action points as a means of seeking to hold each other accountable to the things that God has been speaking to you as you go through the book.

Prayer Points: We believe that though we may discuss something using our minds, it is often only as we bring things to God in prayer that we come to really take hold of them in our hearts. These prayer points are just an initial guide that we hope will launch you into deep times of prayer so that each section of the book becomes a part of your daily life.

Small Group Format

We would suggest leaving approx. 2 hours per meeting in order to process through 1-2 chapters of the book.

- You may consider beginning the group with a time of worship and prayer to focus everyone's hearts on Jesus.

- The discussion questions are valuable in processing through the book as a group. As a facilitator you will want to encourage open interaction rather than attempting to be the primary one sharing. Often it may be necessary to attempt to draw out quieter members so that everyone has an opportunity to share.

- For the action points section, you may consider breaking up into smaller accountability groups of 2 or 3. If you are in a mixed group, since it is often easier to share more deeply in environments with all men or all women, consider breaking up into smaller groups to allow for deeper transparency and accountability.

- You will also want to leave time to pray for each other.

Some of what is shared during the group may be confidential as those within the group are processing through deep wounds or struggles with sin. We would encourage you to regularly announce to the group that this is a safe environment to be open and honest and that their confidential confessions will stay within the group.

Personal Preparation

As a group facilitator you will want to be prepared and refreshed in the material yourself so that you can share it with the others. A good goal would be to ask God to do a deep work in your own heart as you read through the book so that as you are sharing this material it comes from a place of personal experience rather than mere head knowledge.

Commitment to the Group

It is important to stick with the book all the way through in order to get the maximum benefit. At the beginning of the group you may consider holding an introductory meeting in which you share about the book and why you believe it would be valuable to go through it. Then you may consider asking participants to make a commitment to remain with the group.

You may consider looking at the back of the book to see how you might go through the 30 Day Challenge as a group. For those overseeing a ministry, the back of the book provides instruction on how we can assist you with a congregation-wide launch of *Journey into the Spirit Empowered Life*.

Moving Forward

When the book is completed then what? As the group facilitator, begin praying early on about the next steps that God would have you take after you have completed *Journey into the Spirit Empowered Life*. Some within your group may be led to take this study into their sphere of influence. (for example, a teacher may see how they could start a Spirit Empowered group at their local school, a CEO may begin a group at their place of work, a member of a church may see how this could begin to spread throughout the rest of the church body.) Be praying into how God would have you transition from reading this book, to spreading this message to your sphere of influence.

My Story

I was born in Washington, D.C. to Jim and Janet Vennetti. Two years after my birth, my brother Dan was born, and our family of four started off on the journey of life. From an early age, I had seen my life as a precious gift. One reason for this was the fact that my father is a former priest and my mother a former nun. Had God not intervened in their lives, and called them to marriage, I would not exist. I was also born after many years of prayer as my parents had endured the pain of numerous miscarriages prior to my birth. Being the first born after such pain, and such prayer, has always been something in the back of my mind.

At a time in the nation of America where many people experience moving from state to state, our family spent the first 18 years of my life in Rockville, Maryland. For better or for worse, this allowed my friendships there to become lasting ones. You would think that in a loving environment, surrounded by two godly examples that my heart would have been given over to the things of God. Instead, though I was raised with much talk about the Lord, and many church services, something was missing in my heart. Oddly enough, the security of my home, and the goodness of my parent's lives, actually caused me to push away from truly following God. I wanted to be my own person. I wanted to be independent. This is the true hallmark of the sinful nature within us all.

Public school had its challenges and left me with virtually no Godly influence outside of my own home. In high school, I fought the urging of my parents to attend youth group activities. I insisted that I did not know anybody there, and this was excuse enough in my book. This unwillingness to get involved with other Christians was to cost me dearly in college. I had no spiritual foundation on which to stand. My faith had never truly transferred from my parents to me. Throughout these years I had one friend who attended occasional Christian services with me, but for the most part, neither of us really knew God, and neither of us knew how to walk closely with Him.

My junior year in high school, I visited a college campus in Virginia several times before choosing to attend the university. It was the uplifting Christian environment I had experienced during those visits that eventually caused me to make my choice. Strange how we can live one way, yet in our heart of hearts know that we want something deeper with God. After making my selection, I was later to find out that this school was well known for two key areas outside of academics: "partying" and "beautiful women". Of course, my friends took the liberty of informing me of this prior to my departure.

I fought the temptations of drink and women for a time, but without any real fellowship with other believers, the roots of my Christian heritage seemed to crumble around me as I was faced with such a daily assault on my faith. The mindset of those living without God slowly became my mindset. The goals and dreams of those without God began to plant dark seeds in my heart.

Outside of the occasional times of visiting my parents, nearly four years went by without setting foot in a church service. In my heart of hearts, I knew something was missing in my life, but now I wasn't even sure how to get out of the web in which I was entangled. It took the hand of God to reach in and pull me out of my filth.

Several months before my college graduation, I found myself working part-time at an ABC-affiliate television station. The atmosphere was not just ungodly, but openly demonic. As these dark influences pulled at my soul, a desire began to spark in my heart to get involved with the Christian fellowship on campus. At that time, I was double majoring, and working at the television station in the evenings. This hectic schedule did not even allow God to have any leftovers. Yet the desire to taste of His life continued to mount. Clearly this was God, as I had not even attended anything Christ-centered for years. I felt I needed to quit my job because I was working the same night as the campus meetings. Against all human logic, I did just that.

God has His ways of bringing us to Himself, even if He uses our own selfish motives to do it. The night I went back to the campus ministry was the last night to sign up for a spring break trip that they were taking down to Panama City, Florida. To be honest, I simply wanted to have a good time on spring break, but nobody I knew had any money. I had been working and saving to go somewhere exotic yet all my partying friends had already used up the money that they had.

That evening, as I stood in a room full of people who were worshipping God, I knew I needed to do something about my present spiritual state. I decided to sign up for the trip even though I did not know anyone else in the group. This had been my hang-up for as long as I could remember. I wasn't necessarily against the things of God; I just had no other Christian friends, and felt more comfortable with the unbelievers I knew.

During spring break, all I can say is that God did a miracle. A complete and total revolution of my life occurred! One evening, I was randomly selected to preach the Gospel to a hotel room full of people who were doing the very things I had been doing just days earlier. The alcohol was flowing freely as a girl from our Christian group asked them if they would "turn the music down" because I had something I wanted to tell them. As I stood up I had no idea what to say, yet out of my mouth flowed one of the clearest, most powerful presentations of the necessity of Christ's forgiveness that I have ever given in over a decade of ministering to others. As I finished sharing, I knew that I didn't even know what I shared with them in my natural mind. It actually felt like God had reached His hand down and spoken to them through me. It was this experience that revolutionized my life. It wasn't the fine speech of a trained minister that arrested my heart. It took a personal experience with God to bring me through to the place that I knew He was really alive.

Days later, we were given some free time to enjoy ourselves at the resort, and instead I found myself leaving our group and going down the beach to share the Gospel with total strangers. A liberty and a life had come into me that I had never known in all my years of Christian experience. For the first time there was a power over sin and a power to live for God. I was truly a new creation in Christ!

Upon returning to the university I didn't know what to do. Everything was different now. None of my friends could understand what had happened to me. Even I couldn't understand what had happened.

The next weekend I was scheduled to leave for a flight to Hartford, Connecticut to interview with ESPN. This was a desire I had had for as long as I could remember. (For those unfamiliar with ESPN, this is one of America's largest sports television channels.) In the interview, I was offered a position as a video editor, the very thing I had wanted to become. Yet, for the first time in a long time, I knew I needed to let God lead me, so I told them that I had to think about it, which really meant I had to pray about it.

Interestingly enough, just before leaving for the trip I had reached under my bed and pulled out a book entitled "Is That Really You God?" in which a man by the name of Loren Cunningham had one supernatural experience with God after another. I had first read this book in high school and it had planted seeds of faith in me that if God could speak to this man with such intimacy He could speak to me as well. Once again I was reading the testimonies in this book and while looking out the window of the plane I paused and asked God for a sign. This book gave me the faith to believe that if it was really His will for me to turn down ESPN He would just have to speak to me with such clarity that I couldn't miss it. I told Him that unless He gave me a sign I was going to take the job. (Now, I'm not recommending we put God to a test like this, but I honestly didn't know what else to do at the time.)

14

On my return trip, I had to drive several hours from Washington, D.C. to get back to the university. By this point I had completely forgotten about the prayer I had prayed about wanting a sign. As I was driving I had the strongest sense that I needed to pull off the road at the next exit. I looked at my gas tank, and it was full. I had no reason to get off at that exit. Yet I found myself turning the wheel, and on I went traveling down an unknown road in the middle of the countryside.

Shortly thereafter, I began to feel that I needed to make a right hand turn onto a specific side street. Instead I resisted this as a crazy thought and continued driving down the road wondering what I was doing. The moment I passed that road I knew I needed to turn around. I eventually came back to the road and turned onto it. It was a small gravel pathway winding around what looked like private property. I envisioned a man with a shotgun at the end of the driveway telling me to get off his property.

As I passed trees and various hills, I soon noticed that this road was leading up to a large building. The closer I got, the more the thought came, "Could this be a CHURCH building?" As crazy as this seemed, I began to realize that this was exactly what it was. For a few moments I sat in the parking lot in stunned silence. Knowing now that it was God who had led me here, but completely uncertain of what He wanted me to do next. The only thing I could think of was to go up to the door and explain what had just happened, and ask them if they had any employment opportunities available. It was Sunday afternoon around 1:30 pm and there were still a few cars left in the parking lot following their church service.

15

I went up to the front door but it was locked. I knocked and stood there but there was still no answer. I went around the entire building knocking and waiting for a response, but no one ever came out. I wrote down the address and the name of the church on a piece of paper and got back into my car. I didn't know what to do. I knew God had brought me here, but I kept saying, "God, I don't know what I am supposed to be getting from all this?" I must have sat in the parking lot for 20 minutes before proceeding to leave with the thought that perhaps God would eventually reveal to me why He had brought me here.

I pointed my car back toward the road and headed out. Driving in a bit of a stupor, I wound around the small gravel path, before heading out to the main road. For whatever reason, I looked up at the sun, and without any clouds in the sky, it seemed to me to be more glorious than it had ever been before. At that moment, I looked down and there to the left of the car was a huge wooden sign which read: "You Are Now Entering the Mission Field" – right then and there God spoke into my mind, "You asked for a sign, *there it is!*"

I slammed on the brakes of my car and sat there in awe. I don't know how long I sat there, but I was aware, in a way I had never been before, that God was real, and that He had a purpose for my existence which was far greater than all the plans I had been making for myself.

After fasting from food for several days I did what I knew I needed to do. I called ESPN and told the man who interviewed me, "I don't know if you can understand this, but God has told me to turn down this job so I am being obedient to Him." I didn't really know what else to say.

Looking back on it, I realize just how much God's grace carried me through it all. I had no other options. I had already left my position with the previous television station which was to be the stepping-stone to this dream job. Now I had nothing in the physical realm to lean on. I was, for the first time, in a humanly impossible situation. And as is always the case when we step out in faith, God came through!

Within several weeks, God led me to apply for a position with a mission's organization. I ended up going through a discipleship program that planted good seeds in my heart that are still bearing fruit today. During this school, for the first time I got to know God and not just know about Him. He became everything to me. Our team went to the Philippines for a two-month outreach, and I found myself preaching in prisons and high schools, helping lead Bible studies in villages, serving and sacrificing for handicapped children. Coming out of the village at night I would look up at the stars and stand in amazement at a God who loved me enough to patiently bear with me for decades. This God who never gave up on me, came to me with such love and mercy that I was now living a life that I could never have imagined.

Today, nearly 15 years after the events described in this story I am married to a wonderful Godly woman named Rebecca. We have four children, Jeremiah, Joshua, Joel and Ruth. God has seen fit to use our lives in some 20-30 different nations and to help give oversight to Disciple Nations International, a ministry based out of Orlando, FL (USA). We can testify that our God is a faithful God. We will never surrender something to Him and regret it. Our only regrets will be those things we held onto and did not trust Him with.

It is our prayer and desire that this book will be used by God's Spirit to bring about a greater manifestation of His Life on the earth. We pray that He will lead you into deeper intimacy in your relationship with Jesus Christ!

Section 1: God's Plan for Individuals & Nations

Chapter 1: New Life in Christ

HOWEVER, YOU ARE NOT IN THE FLESH BUT IN THE SPIRIT, IF INDEED THE SPIRIT OF GOD DWELLS IN YOU. BUT IF ANYONE DOES NOT HAVE THE SPIRIT OF CHRIST, HE DOES NOT BELONG TO HIM.

ROMANS 8:9

Before we go into a discussion on what it means to live a life empowered by God's Spirit, we must first determine whether or not we have the Spirit of God living in us. As you read in "My Story" I myself would have told you that I was a Christian for many years, but I lacked the reality of having been born again by the Spirit of God. The Word of God says that the things of God are veiled to the minds of those who do not have the Spirit of God (2 Cor. 4:3), therefore, I believe God desires to give each reader of this book an opportunity to begin your journey with Jesus Christ today if you have not done so already.

To truly enter into God's Kingdom, there is a need for a real repentance from the way you have lived in the past and to enter into a submission to Jesus Christ as your new Master. This is not merely words that we say with our lips, but it is within our hearts that God's Spirit brings us to the place where from that point forward we surrender the entirety of our lives to Him.

"THEREFORE LET ALL THE HOUSE OF ISRAEL KNOW FOR CERTAIN THAT GOD HAS MADE HIM BOTH LORD AND CHRIST—THIS JESUS WHOM YOU CRUCIFIED."

NOW WHEN THEY HEARD THIS, THEY WERE PIERCED TO THE HEART, AND SAID TO PETER AND THE REST OF THE APOSTLES, "BRETHREN,

WHAT SHALL WE DO?" PETER SAID TO THEM, "REPENT, AND EACH OF YOU BE BAPTIZED IN THE NAME OF JESUS CHRIST FOR THE FORGIVENESS OF YOUR SINS; AND YOU WILL RECEIVE THE GIFT OF THE HOLY SPIRIT.

ACTS 2:36-38

The repentance that is called for is a full and complete surrender of our past sins in exchange for the Life of Christ. We are effectively saying that we are forever giving Jesus Christ our old, sinful life, and we are now taking up His new sinless Life. We are giving Him permission to be the Lord of our life. This is a covenant relationship, similar to the covenant that a husband and wife enter into on the day of their wedding. As a follower of Jesus Christ, our baptism is like the wedding ceremony, in which we publicly declare our allegiance to Jesus Christ.

Why Would We Surrender Our Lives to Jesus Christ?

We are sinners and destined for eternal separation from God

WHEN THE WOMAN SAW THAT THE TREE WAS GOOD FOR FOOD, AND THAT IT WAS A DELIGHT TO THE EYES, AND THAT THE TREE WAS DESIRABLE TO MAKE ONE WISE, SHE TOOK FROM ITS FRUIT AND ATE; AND SHE GAVE ALSO TO HER HUSBAND WITH HER, AND HE ATE. THEN THE EYES OF BOTH OF THEM WERE OPENED, AND THEY KNEW THAT THEY WERE NAKED; AND THEY SEWED FIG LEAVES TOGETHER AND MADE THEMSELVES LOIN COVERINGS.

THEY HEARD THE SOUND OF THE LORD GOD WALKING IN THE GARDEN IN THE COOL OF THE DAY, AND THE MAN AND HIS WIFE HID THEMSELVES FROM THE PRESENCE OF THE LORD GOD AMONG THE

TREES OF THE GARDEN.

GENESIS 3:6-8

FOR ALL HAVE SINNED AND FALL SHORT OF THE GLORY OF GOD.

ROMANS 3:23

From the first man and woman on the planet to today, mankind has lived in sinful rebellion against the Great Creator God, hiding from His Presence. God's Word says that all mankind has sinned and fallen short of God's glory. This means that there is not a man, woman or child on earth who was not born with a sinful heart. We are all born with a heart that is prone to living in rebellion against the God who created us. We see the manifestation of this sinful heart every day through decisions we make to go with our pride, our selfishness, our own will and ways. There are big and small ways we see our sinful heart manifested. Even small children can be seen to have a sinful heart as everything in their world revolves around them. "Me" and "mine" are some of the most common first words. To us this sinful nature may not appear to be that big of a deal.

Sin Is a Big Problem

FOR AS THE HEAVENS ARE HIGHER THAN THE EARTH, SO ARE MY WAYS HIGHER THAN YOUR WAYS AND MY THOUGHTS THAN YOUR THOUGHTS.

ISAIAH 55:9

We may think, "So what if I'm a little selfish or prideful at times, everyone is like that and some are even worse. I'm no

Hitler or Stalin." That's the perspective of someone who has lived in a sinful world and has only seen the best and worst of what mankind is able to offer. God's perspective is far different from ours. God sees sinful man as living in complete and utter rebellion against His rightful place as the King of the universe. Every time we make a decision to trust ourselves instead of Him, and do what we want to do, in our pride and unbelief, we effectively raise a sword and declare war against God being God.

We may not see it that way. We may think we are just living as all other human beings live. Those who are religious may even think they are pleasing to God through their adherence to various religious rituals, but the Creator of the universe looks right through all our outward acts and sees our prideful, selfish and unbelieving hearts. We are an abomination to Him as long as we hold onto our sin. We have no hope of being rescued from hell if we continue to hold onto our lives.

YOU WERE DEAD IN YOUR TRESPASSES AND SINS, IN WHICH YOU FORMERLY WALKED ACCORDING TO THE COURSE OF THIS WORLD, ACCORDING TO THE PRINCE OF THE POWER OF THE AIR, OF THE SPIRIT THAT IS NOW WORKING IN THE SONS OF DISOBEDIENCE. AMONG THEM WE TOO ALL FORMERLY LIVED IN THE LUSTS OF OUR FLESH, INDULGING THE DESIRES OF THE FLESH AND OF THE MIND, AND WERE BY NATURE CHILDREN OF WRATH, EVEN AS THE REST.

EPHESIANS 2:1-3

Paul writes in Ephesians that in our very nature, we are "children of wrath." We are born with a nature that cannot save itself, but is daily heaping up greater judgment against us for the Day of God's Judgment on all those who have lived in rebellion to His rightful Rule (Romans 2:5).

The Creator God Has Made Only One Way for Sinful Mankle to Be Restored into a Right Relationship with Him

For God so loved the world, that He gave His only begotten Son, that whoever believes in Him shall not perish, but have eternal life.

John 3:16

Jesus said to him, "I am the way, and the truth, and the life; no one comes to the Father but through Me."

John 14:6

Let it be known to all of you and to all the people of Israel, that by the name of Jesus Christ the Nazarene, whom you crucified, whom God raised from the dead—by this name this man stands here before you in good health. He is the stone which was rejected by you, the builders, but which became the chief corner stone. And there is salvation in no one else; for there is no other name under heaven that has been given among men by which we must be saved."

Acts 4:10-12

God has made only one way for us to be restored to Him. The religious world would tell us that there are many roads back to God. Whether it is through one of the world religions, or through their various requirements on their human adherents, they place the burden on mankind to make ourselves right with God. They believe that through enough religious rituals they can somehow be forgiven of their sins and be restored. The Bible teaches that the Creator God has made only one provision for mankind to be restored into right relationship with Him, and that is through the shed blood of His Son Jesus Christ who paid the price for our sins. He took into His own body the punishment that we deserved.

All mankind's efforts to try to please God through religious ritual simply go to show how low a view of God that we have. To think of God as such a small being that we could somehow measure up to His holiness through our own "good deeds" is spiritual blindness. We are blind to the level of just how inherently sinful we are. Just how selfish and prone to treat ourselves as god. We do not even begin to grasp His holiness when we believe that there is something we could do on earth to earn our way into His Kingdom. There is no way for mankind to make ourselves holy enough to be pleasing to God. If that were the end of the story, then we would all be destined for hell. Since God is this holy, the only hope that fallen man had was for God Himself to reach down into our sinful state, and rescue us by somehow making us as holy as He is holy.

Jesus Christ is God's Provision for Mankind

AGAIN THE HIGH PRIEST WAS QUESTIONING HIM, AND SAYING TO HIM, "ARE YOU THE CHRIST, THE SON OF THE BLESSED ONE?" AND JESUS SAID, "I AM; AND YOU SHALL SEE THE SON OF MAN SITTING AT THE RIGHT HAND OF POWER, AND COMING WITH THE CLOUDS OF HEAVEN." TEARING HIS CLOTHES, THE HIGH PRIEST SAID, "WHAT FURTHER NEED DO WE HAVE OF WITNESSES?

MARK 14:61-63

In the book of Mark we see Jesus being questioned by the high priest and He clearly stated, "I am the Messiah". The Messiah is the Savior of all of humanity. His statement was the reason that the high priest got so upset, that a mere man called himself God.

WHEN THEY CAME TO THE PLACE CALLED THE SKULL, THERE THEY CRUCIFIED HIM AND THE CRIMINALS, ONE ON THE RIGHT AND THE OTHER ON THE LEFT...JESUS, CRYING OUT WITH A LOUD VOICE, SAID, "FATHER, INTO YOUR HANDS I COMMIT MY SPIRIT." HAVING SAID THIS, HE BREATHED HIS LAST.

LUKE 23:33, 46

Jesus Christ is God's Son. He lived a perfect life and He died for the sins of all mankind. He is the only One able to save us from our sin nature and give us His divine nature. No other god can save us from our sins. No other religion or religious ritual is acceptable in the eyes of the Creator God. Human ritual is nothing but mankind's vain attempt to measure up to God's holiness. We cannot even come close no matter how hard we try. There is no salvation in anyone but Jesus Christ.

BUT THOMAS, ONE OF THE TWELVE, CALLED DIDYMUS, WAS NOT WITH THEM WHEN JESUS CAME. SO THE OTHER DISCIPLES WERE SAYING TO HIM, "WE HAVE SEEN THE LORD!" BUT HE SAID TO THEM, "UNLESS I SEE IN HIS HANDS THE IMPRINT OF THE NAILS, AND PUT MY FINGER INTO THE PLACE OF THE NAILS, AND PUT MY HAND INTO HIS SIDE, I WILL NOT BELIEVE."

AFTER EIGHT DAYS HIS DISCIPLES WERE AGAIN INSIDE, AND THOMAS WITH THEM. JESUS CAME, THE DOORS HAVING BEEN SHUT, AND STOOD IN THEIR MIDST AND SAID, "PEACE BE WITH YOU." THEN HE

26

SAID TO THOMAS, "REACH HERE WITH YOUR FINGER, AND SEE MY HANDS; AND REACH HERE YOUR HAND AND PUT IT INTO MY SIDE; AND DO NOT BE UNBELIEVING, BUT BELIEVING." THOMAS ANSWERED AND SAID TO HIM, "MY LORD AND MY GOD!" JESUS SAID TO HIM, "BECAUSE YOU HAVE SEEN ME, HAVE YOU BELIEVED? BLESSED ARE THEY WHO DID NOT SEE, AND YET BELIEVED."

JOHN 20:24-29

The cross was God's greatest way of expressing His Love for us. Jesus Christ lived to die for us. God the Father willingly allowed His Son to be killed so that you and I could receive forgiveness for our sins and re-enter a life of intimate relationship with Him.

HE WHO HAS FOUND HIS LIFE WILL LOSE IT, AND HE WHO HAS LOST HIS LIFE FOR MY SAKE WILL FIND IT.

MATTHEW 10:39

Jesus is saying here that in order to enter into His Life, we must give up our lives. It is not enough to just mentally believe that Jesus Christ is God's Son, we must surrender the entirety of our lives to Him. If we hold onto our lives, we will lose them forever at the end of our days. Even many of those who claim to be "Christian" are presently destined for hell because they have placed their hope in religious ritual (Church attendance, Bible reading, saying certain prayers etc.) but they have failed to surrender the entirety of their lives to Jesus Christ to be saved.

It is only as a deep and real surrender of our lives takes place that a new life enters into us. This new life is the Life of

Jesus Christ Himself. We are a new creation, the old is gone and the new has come (2 Cor. 5:17). There are no words to describe the glorious new Life that Jesus offers to us. Only those who have entrusted their entire lives to Him can truly know what takes place and how He begins to change our heart desires to come into agreement with His heart desires. How new and glorious is this Life in Christ!

Going to church services does not mean that we have been brought into this new life. Reading our Bibles does not guarantee that we have entered into this new life. Saying certain prayers is no guarantee. This is a matter of our hearts entering into a deep and real covenant relationship with the Creator God through the shed blood of His Son Jesus Christ. It is only the deep and real surrender of our old life, and a complete entrusting of ourselves to Jesus that causes us to be born anew into Christ's Kingdom.

The Necessity of Being Born Again

JESUS ANSWERED AND SAID TO HIM, "TRULY, TRULY, I SAY TO YOU, UNLESS ONE IS BORN AGAIN HE CANNOT SEE THE KINGDOM OF GOD."

JOHN 3:3

Do you know that you know you have been born again? Are you absolutely certain that the Spirit of God has come to live inside of you? If you are not certain, it may be helpful to ask others you know who walk closely with Jesus to tell you if they have seen evidence of God's Spirit living in and through you. You do not want to have a false sense of security when it comes to this issue. Eternal life and death are on the line.

28

Testimony

I attended church for over 20 years before experiencing what it means to be born again. I prayed prayers of asking Jesus Christ to "come into my heart" but the reality was that I had not yet truly surrendered my life to Him. I was still holding onto it in various ways. As far as I remember, no one warned me of my precarious spiritual position. I thought that I was okay.

Eventually, God's Spirit led me to a point in my life where I knew, I either surrender the entirety of my life to Christ, or I could very well be going to hell, even though I had prayed and read the Bible since I was a child. In that place of true surrender to Jesus Christ, all I can say is that within one week I had had more powerful encounters with God than I had had in over twenty years worth of religion.

I believe that there are many others like me who are lacking spiritual power in their lives due to the fact that they have never truly surrendered their lives to Jesus Christ. They may be "Christian", attend church services, read their Bibles, and pray, but in their heart of hearts their lives are still their own. Therefore they are still children of wrath and destined for hell unless they repent and surrender their lives to Jesus Christ.

I invite you to allow the Holy Spirit to search your heart right now. Go ahead and give Him full permission to reveal to you whether or not you have truly surrendered your life to the Lordship of Jesus Christ.

"NOT EVERYONE WHO SAYS TO ME, 'LORD, LORD,' WILL ENTER THE KINGDOM OF HEAVEN, BUT HE WHO DOES THE WILL OF MY FATHER

WHO IS IN HEAVEN WILL ENTER. MANY WILL SAY TO ME ON THAT DAY, 'LORD, LORD, DID WE NOT PROPHESY IN YOUR NAME, AND IN YOUR NAME CAST OUT DEMONS, AND IN YOUR NAME PERFORM MANY MIRACLES?' AND THEN I WILL DECLARE TO THEM, 'I NEVER KNEW YOU; DEPART FROM ME, YOU WHO PRACTICE LAWLESSNESS.'

MATTHEW 7:21-23

Jesus spoke of those who prophesied, cast out demons and even performed miracles in His Name, but did not enter the Kingdom of God. Allow God's Spirit to go beyond any assumptions you have made about your salvation. You want the truth about your salvation to be made clear to you. This is a matter of life and death. He is the Great Physician, and if you are presently spiritually dead, you want to know it now. If there is still breath in your body then there is still time for repentance that leads to eternal life (Acts 11:18).

If you are spiritually dead He is the only One capable of bringing you to life. Give Him as much time as you need to in order for it to be made clear to you where you are at with Him. The fruit of your life should resemble the fruit of the life of Jesus Christ. If it does not, either you have not yet given Him your life, or you have fallen back into holding onto your life. In either case, you have a spiritual emergency on your hands. You must deal with this now. Do not delay another minute or hour.

Testimony

For me it took coming to the place where I said to Jesus in all honesty, "From this point forward the rest of my life is Yours. You can do with it whatever You want." Something took place in that moment that has changed the course of my life ever since. After over 20 years of being a part of religious services this was the moment of my spiritual birth.

Rather than attempting to list particular words for your prayer time, I would suggest that you simply go to God in all honesty and surrender the entirety of your being to Him. Confess any past or current sins that come to your heart to share with Him. Choose to forgive anyone that you may be holding unforgiveness against. Allow God's Spirit to bring you into a place of true repentance in which you actually agree to turn away from your sinful way of life once and for all. You have lived as His enemy. You have lived as though you are god and He is not. This is a very serious situation. This is not a light prayer. This is admitting that the entirety of your life has been in the wrong and that you have lived in utter rebellion of His rightful leadership of your life. From this moment on you are inviting Him to lead everything in your life. It will no longer be your life but His.

Enter into a time of prayer and confess your sin and your desire for Jesus Christ to be the Lord of your life. Go as long as it takes until you have entered into a real communion with Him where your life has been exchanged for His. If this takes minutes, hours, days, or weeks – go until this surrender has been deeply secured. He Himself will bring confirmation to you that you are now really His child.

For all who are being led by the Spirit of God, these are sons of God. For you have not received a spirit of slavery leading to fear again, but you have received a spirit of adoption as sons by which we cry out, "Abba! Father!" The Spirit Himself testifies with our spirit that we are children

OF GOD. *ROMANS 8:14-16*

Prayer Time: We would highly encourage you to stop here and take time in prayer to surrender the entirety of your life to Jesus. Please take as much time as you need to. You may consider putting the book down and just going to God to express your heart to Him now.

A Brand New Life

"RABBI, WE KNOW THAT YOU HAVE COME FROM GOD AS A TEACHER; FOR NO ONE CAN DO THESE SIGNS THAT YOU DO UNLESS GOD IS WITH HIM." JESUS ANSWERED AND SAID TO HIM, "TRULY, TRULY, I SAY TO YOU, UNLESS ONE IS BORN AGAIN HE CANNOT SEE THE KINGDOM OF GOD."

JOHN 3:2-3

THEREFORE IF ANYONE IS IN CHRIST, HE IS A NEW CREATURE; THE OLD THINGS PASSED AWAY; BEHOLD, NEW THINGS HAVE COME.

2 COR. 5:17

FOR HE RESCUED US FROM THE DOMAIN OF DARKNESS, AND TRANSFERRED US TO THE KINGDOM OF HIS BELOVED SON, IN WHOM WE HAVE REDEMPTION, THE FORGIVENESS OF SINS.

COLOSSIANS 1:13-14

If you just surrendered the entirety of your past, present and future to Jesus Christ, you are now a child of God. You have been transferred from the kingdom of darkness to the Kingdom of light. The scriptures tell us that even the angels in heaven rejoice over one sinner who repents (Luke 15:10). By exchanging your life for the life of Christ, you have made the greatest decision that you will ever make in your earthly life.

This is just the beginning of your journey with God and not the end. There is an adventure awaiting you as you begin to journey deeper into a real knowing of who He is. There will be many battles to face, and obstacles to overcome, but you do not need to fear because He has promised to be with you always even to the very end of the age (Matthew 28:20). As long as you do not forsake Him He will not forsake you (2 Timothy 2:11-13).

For those of you who crossed the line of full surrender to Jesus Christ, you can be assured that the Spirit of God now lives inside you. During the rest of this book we will be exploring what it means for us to have God Himself dwelling within us. We will look at how this supernatural reality should affect our lives, our family relationships, and our sphere of influence. We hope you will join us on this journey into the Spirit-Empowered Life!

Discussion Questions:

1. Have you ever truly surrendered the entirety of your life to Jesus Christ? (If not, are you ready to surrender your life to Him now?)

2. Based on the scriptures we looked at, how do you know that God's Spirit has come to live inside you? (Romans 8:14-16, 2 Cor. 5:17) What has been your experience of God's Life being lived in and through you?

3. Have you ever struggled to overcome sin? Do you believe that some of this struggle is because you are still

attempting to live the Christian life in your own strength? (Explain/Discuss)

Action Point:

Bring your current spiritual state before God and ask for His insight. If you have yet to fully surrender your life to Jesus Christ take the time to process through this decision now. Don't leave from this section until you have crossed a real line of decision to allow Jesus to have all of you.

Prayer Focus:

For this chapter, we are encouraging you to enter for the first time (or re-enter) a place of total surrender of your life to Jesus Christ. Make that the singular focus of this time of prayer. Take however long you need to for this to become the reality of your heart.

Chapter 2:
Defining the Spirit-Empowered Life

AND IN THE FOURTH WATCH OF THE NIGHT HE CAME TO THEM, WALKING ON THE SEA. WHEN THE DISCIPLES SAW HIM WALKING ON THE SEA, THEY WERE TERRIFIED, AND SAID, "IT IS A GHOST!" AND THEY CRIED OUT IN FEAR. BUT IMMEDIATELY JESUS SPOKE TO THEM, SAYING, "TAKE COURAGE, IT IS I; DO NOT BE AFRAID."

PETER SAID TO HIM, "LORD, IF IT IS YOU, COMMAND ME TO COME TO YOU ON THE WATER." AND HE SAID, "COME!" AND PETER GOT OUT OF THE BOAT, AND WALKED ON THE WATER AND CAME TOWARD JESUS.

MATTHEW 14:25-29

At the command of Jesus, Peter, an ordinary human being, walked on water. Is it possible that in our day and time that God is calling His children to a life so far above the norm that it will seem as though we are walking on water? Those who claim Jesus Christ as their Lord have been called to walk on top of waves, trials, difficulties, set backs, wounds, and fears that ordinary people live in slavery to.

Could it be that God intends for the lifestyle of every follower of Jesus to be so far above average that it is actually impossible to live the "Christian" life apart from Him? Can you imagine yourself living such a humanly impossible life? Can you believe that the God who created the universe actually wants to live His Life in and through you?

35

JESUS SAID TO HIS DISCIPLES, "TRULY I SAY TO YOU, IT IS HARD FOR A RICH MAN TO ENTER THE KINGDOM OF HEAVEN. AGAIN I SAY TO YOU, IT IS EASIER FOR A CAMEL TO GO THROUGH THE EYE OF A NEEDLE, THAN FOR A RICH MAN TO ENTER THE KINGDOM OF GOD." WHEN THE DISCIPLES HEARD THIS, THEY WERE VERY ASTONISHED AND SAID, "THEN WHO CAN BE SAVED?" AND LOOKING AT THEM JESUS SAID TO THEM, "WITH PEOPLE THIS IS IMPOSSIBLE, BUT WITH GOD ALL THINGS ARE POSSIBLE."

MATTHEW 19:23-26

If it is impossible to please God through our human efforts to live a good life then it is clear that God must have another plan. In fact, His plan is so radical that we often minimize it. God Himself has promised to come and live inside of us so that we will have a completely different life. A Spirit-Empowered Life!

God's Standard for Every Member of His Kingdom

"I SAY TO YOU, AMONG THOSE BORN OF WOMEN THERE IS NO ONE GREATER THAN JOHN; YET HE WHO IS LEAST IN THE KINGDOM OF GOD IS GREATER THAN HE."

LUKE 7:28

How can this be true? Think of the life and ministry of John the Baptist. He lived out of a place of radical surrender to God. He even laid down his physical life for his faith. Yet Jesus tells us that the least member of His Kingdom is greater than John. Has this been your experience? Have you seen the Body of Christ operating at the standard that Jesus raised for us?

36

As shocking as this is, Jesus had something even more surprising to say:

"TRULY, TRULY, I SAY TO YOU, HE WHO BELIEVES IN ME, THE WORKS THAT I DO, HE WILL DO ALSO; AND GREATER WORKS THAN THESE HE WILL DO; BECAUSE I GO TO THE FATHER."

JOHN 14:12

Jesus Himself stated that you will do even greater works then He did. This is the Word of God. This is pure truth. Therefore, if you are failing to experience the reality of God's standard then you must ask God's Spirit in what way you are not fulfilling His requirements. Surely our lack of fruitfulness is not a lack of desire on God's part. Instead, there is something in us or around us that is keeping us from experiencing the type of fruitfulness that He intends for us to live in.

Meditate on these two scriptures until they grip your heart with a Divine Jealousy to see this fruitfulness worked in and through you. God wants this fruitfulness even more than you do because it gives great honor and glory to His Name (John 15:8).

What is meant by the term "Spirit-Empowered"?

In order to enter into a discussion on what we mean by a Spirit-Empowered Life, there are two simple questions that help to reveal what we are talking about.

1. What percentage of your typical day is self-led? Meaning, how much of your typical day is led by your own mind, will and emotions?

2. What percentage of your typical day is truly Holy Spirit-led? Meaning, what percentage of the day is lived in a place of being completely dead to your own thinking, will and emotions and instead led by God's Spirit?

This lifestyle can be summed up very simply by recognizing that it is a life lived from one moment to the next with a purposeful choice to keep in step with exactly what God's Spirit is asking of us (Galatians 5:25). What this lifestyle looks like and how we practically begin to live in this way are some of the things that we want to examine. You can be sure that this is not humanly possible, but only the Holy Spirit can lead us into this reality.

FOR THOSE WHOM HE FOREKNEW, HE ALSO PREDESTINED TO BECOME CONFORMED TO THE IMAGE OF HIS SON, SO THAT HE WOULD BE THE FIRSTBORN AMONG MANY BRETHREN.

ROMANS 8:29

AND DO NOT GET DRUNK WITH WINE, FOR THAT IS DISSIPATION, BUT BE FILLED WITH THE SPIRIT.

EPHESIANS 5:18

According to the Word of God, we have been predestined to be conformed into the image of Jesus Christ. We have been given a clear command by God to "be filled with the Spirit." In order to push past the religious baggage that surrounds this terminology, we must go back and re-examine God's original intention in sending His Holy Spirit to those who believe in His Son Jesus Christ. Instead of simply holding up our denomination's understanding of God's Spirit, or our good and bad experiences with this discussion from the past, we must go back to the Word of God with fresh eyes in order to see what God intended when He told us to "be continuously filled" with His Spirit.

The standard of a Spirit-Empowered Life supercedes any doctrinal differences between evangelicals and charismatics. It refers to a life that is being constantly filled with God's Spirit. It is a life that has so died to our will that we are filled with the life of God Himself. In this way, we are truly a vessel, or Body, for Jesus Christ to fulfill His eternal purposes through us.

God's Purpose in Sending Us the Holy Spirit

I WILL ASK THE FATHER, AND HE WILL GIVE YOU ANOTHER HELPER, THAT HE MAY BE WITH YOU FOREVER; THAT IS THE SPIRIT OF TRUTH, WHOM THE WORLD CANNOT RECEIVE, BECAUSE IT DOES NOT SEE HIM OR KNOW HIM, BUT YOU KNOW HIM BECAUSE HE ABIDES WITH YOU AND WILL BE IN YOU. "I WILL NOT LEAVE YOU AS ORPHANS; I WILL COME TO YOU. AFTER A LITTLE WHILE THE WORLD WILL NO LONGER SEE ME, BUT YOU WILL SEE ME; BECAUSE I LIVE, YOU WILL LIVE ALSO. IN THAT DAY YOU WILL KNOW THAT I AM IN MY FATHER, AND YOU IN ME, AND I IN YOU."

JOHN 14:16-20

THE HELPER, THE HOLY SPIRIT, WHOM THE FATHER WILL SEND IN MY NAME, HE WILL TEACH YOU ALL THINGS, AND BRING TO YOUR REMEMBRANCE ALL THAT I SAID TO YOU.

JOHN 14:26

PETER SAID TO THEM, "REPENT, AND EACH OF YOU BE BAPTIZED IN

*THE NAME OF JESUS CHRIST FOR THE FORGIVENESS OF YOUR SINS;
AND YOU WILL RECEIVE THE GIFT OF THE HOLY SPIRIT."*

ACTS 2:38

The Holy Spirit is a Person. He has a mind, will, and emotions. He has been sent to bring to our remembrance everything that Jesus has taught us. He can be pleased and joyful and He can also be grieved (Luke 10:21, 1 Thes.1:6, Isaiah 63:10, Eph 4:30). He speaks to and through men and women who have surrendered themselves to Him (Mark 13:11, Acts 13:2, 21:11, 2 Peter 1:21).

*(JESUS SPEAKING) "IF YOU THEN, BEING EVIL, KNOW HOW TO GIVE
GOOD GIFTS TO YOUR CHILDREN, HOW MUCH MORE WILL YOUR
HEAVENLY FATHER GIVE THE HOLY SPIRIT TO THOSE WHO ASK HIM?"*

LUKE 11:13

God willingly gives the Holy Spirit to indwell those who have given their lives to Jesus Christ. In sending us the Person of the Holy Spirit, God's primary intention was to establish a completely new type of humanity. We are a new creation due to the fact that God Himself now indwells our physical bodies (1 Cor. 6:19, 2 Cor. 5:17, Gal. 6:15). The new creation life has nothing to do with our trying harder to be a good person, but in learning to die so that He can live His Life through us.

*DO NOT GRIEVE THE HOLY SPIRIT OF GOD, BY WHOM YOU WERE
SEALED FOR THE DAY OF REDEMPTION.*

EPHESIANS 4:30

It is possible to grieve the Holy Spirit and resist Him from having full control of our lives. Instead, God is looking for a people who will truly surrender every way in which they have lived for themselves. In this way, the literal life of God is released to flow in and through them to a lost and dying world.

I HAVE BEEN CRUCIFIED WITH CHRIST; AND IT IS NO LONGER I WHO LIVE, BUT CHRIST LIVES IN ME; AND THE LIFE WHICH I NOW LIVE IN THE FLESH I LIVE BY FAITH IN THE SON OF GOD, WHO LOVED ME AND GAVE HIMSELF UP FOR ME.

GALATIANS 2:20

Based on the Word of God, His primary heart-level intention in sending us His Spirit was so that we would die to ourselves to such a degree that it is no longer us who live but it is truly Jesus Christ Himself living through us.

I AM THE VINE, YOU ARE THE BRANCHES; HE WHO ABIDES IN ME AND I IN HIM, HE BEARS MUCH FRUIT, FOR APART FROM ME YOU CAN DO NOTHING.

JOHN 15:5

Have you ever stopped to think about what Jesus meant when He said we could do "nothing" apart from Him? Clearly there is much that we can do apart from Him. We can sin recklessly apart from Him, we can raise our family apart from Him, we can even do "ministry" apart from Him, yet He calls these things "nothing". Somehow in God's valuation of our lives, unless we are walking in deep intimacy with Him everything that we are doing amounts to nothing. He is speaking of a life so fully surrendered to the Person of the Holy

Spirit that we do not even seek to speak words unless the Father has given them to us to speak.

Do you not believe that I am in the Father, and the Father is in Me? The words that I say to you I do not speak on My own initiative, but the Father abiding in Me does His works.

John 14:10

In John 14 Jesus was modeling for us what it means to be wholly guided by God. Jesus was not willing to even speak a word unless it was His Father living His Life through Him. The question now comes, "Does God really expect *me* to live in this way? And if so, why have I not met anyone who comes even close to what you are describing?" The answer to the first question is "Yes" as we will see in 1 John 2:6. The answer to the second question is a sad one and part of the reason why this book was written.

The one who says, "I have come to know Him," and does not keep His commandments, is a liar, and the truth is not in him; but whoever keeps His word, in him the love of God has truly been perfected. By this we know that we are in Him: the one who says he abides in Him ought himself to walk in the same manner as He walked.

1 John 2:4-6

The Word of God states that if we are claiming to be a follower of Jesus Christ, then our lives should be lived in the same manner that Jesus lived. This is an incredibly high standard, yet this is God's heart intention for every one of His children. Though we may not have seen this standard modeled for us, it is the standard that the Word of God lays out for us. John states that this is how we know that we are in Him, as our lives are lived in the same manner that Jesus lived.

Has this been our understanding of the Gospel, or have we settled for religious rhetoric without the reality of the Life of God flowing in us and through us? Is it possible that many of us have minimized the heart intention of God in sending us His Spirit, bringing it down to various religious activities (going to church, reading the Bible, & being "nice") when instead, He desires His children to have His Life literally flowing through them?

The Holy Spirit Makes the New Covenant a Reality

AND THE HOLY SPIRIT ALSO TESTIFIES TO US; FOR AFTER SAYING,

"THIS IS THE COVENANT THAT I WILL MAKE WITH THEM
AFTER THOSE DAYS, SAYS THE LORD:
I WILL PUT MY LAWS UPON THEIR HEART,
AND ON THEIR MIND I WILL WRITE THEM,"

HEBREWS 10:15-16

We are told that in the New Covenant we will not have to try through our own efforts to obey the law, but that God's Spirit will fulfill the law through us as we surrender and trust Him.

FOR WHAT THE LAW COULD NOT DO, WEAK AS IT WAS THROUGH THE FLESH, GOD DID: SENDING HIS OWN SON IN THE LIKENESS OF SINFUL FLESH AND AS AN OFFERING FOR SIN, HE CONDEMNED SIN IN THE FLESH, SO THAT THE REQUIREMENT OF THE LAW MIGHT BE FULFILLED IN US, WHO DO NOT WALK ACCORDING TO THE FLESH BUT ACCORDING

TO THE SPIRIT.

ROMANS 8:3-4

It is our belief, that by raising the true standard of a Holy Spirit empowered life that God's global church will begin to rise up into the fullness that God intended from the very beginning and which we have seen expressed at various times in Church history. As more and more believers in Jesus Christ learn to live out a Spirit-Empowered lifestyle they will be used of God to disciple their families, their local congregations, and their spheres of influence in the will and ways of Jesus Christ.

Raising the Standard of a Spirit-Empowered Life

A truly Spirit-Empowered person is someone with a lifestyle that is radically consecrated to Jesus Christ, and who has learned to live in a place of wholehearted faith in the character, will and ways of God. As a result of their surrender and faith in God's Spirit, they progressively experience victory over everything that hinders the advancement of Christ's Kingdom. This victorious lifestyle supernaturally leads to evangelism, discipleship and an unconditional love for God and others.

This book will discuss various components to living out a Spirit-Empowered Life:

- **A Lifestyle of Deep intimacy with God** (Through the Word, worship, prayer etc.)
- **A Lifestyle of a Prayer Warrior** –Interceding for the purposes of God
- **A Lifestyle of a Soul Winner** – Seeking opportunities to witness Jesus Christ to everyone that God brings our way

- **A Lifestyle of Discipleship** – Which takes the time to model and mentor what God has taught us in a depth of relationship with others
- **A Lifestyle of Sending** – In which we empower others to go and establish Spirit-Empowered disciples in their families, and sphere of influence

This type of equipping is a proactive approach to disciple every facet of society. It begins with the already existent Body of Christ in any region of the world, and moves out to those God transforms through their Spirit-Empowered lives. When we take even one soul who is living this type of lifestyle, and encourage them to establish this way of life in their families, and in their sphere of influence, extraordinary fruit results because it is not a human strategy but the Spirit of God living through them to disciple the nations! This lifestyle helps to activate every member of the Body of Christ in a region to become a true ambassador of Jesus Christ to their sphere of influence (2 Cor. 5:20).

The implementation of establishing this type of lifestyle is already producing tremendous fruit in the nations of China, India, Uganda, Argentina, Taiwan, as well as in other parts of Asia, Africa, Europe and the America's.

The discipleship of the nations is God's work, not ours. Only as we die to ourselves will He have the freedom to live His life through us. We believe it is time for the nations to believe God to raise up millions of Spirit-Empowered followers of Jesus Christ. Millions of souls gripped with a deep and real intimacy with their Creator God. Millions of souls who have chosen to live as Prayer Warriors and daily call forth the will of heaven to come on the earth. Millions of Soul Winners who will take the love and Life of Jesus Christ to those who do not know Him. Millions of Disciple-makers who will raise up the next generation of souls given radically over to Jesus Christ and then send them to do the same. Will you join with us?

The Whole Body of Christ Needed

GUARD, THROUGH THE HOLY SPIRIT WHO DWELLS IN US, THE TREASURE WHICH HAS BEEN ENTRUSTED TO YOU.

2 TIMOTHY 1:14

The Person of the Holy Spirit orchestrates all of the work of God on the earth. We need Him if any of our labors for Christ are going to be effective. Therefore, we believe that this call is to the entire Body of Christ. The heartbeat of a Spirit-Empowered life is not doctrinally within a single denomination, but it is based on foundational principals that are applicable for all followers of Jesus Christ worldwide. We invite everyone called by the Name of the Lord Jesus Christ to participate in this work of raising up Spirit-Empowered followers in the nations.

You Have a Role to Play in Your Nation

Will you choose to allow God's Spirit to begin to work more deeply in your own life and sphere of influence?

"IF YOU SHOULD SAY IN YOUR HEART, 'THESE NATIONS ARE GREATER THAN I; HOW CAN I DISPOSSESS THEM?' YOU SHALL NOT BE AFRAID OF THEM; YOU SHALL WELL REMEMBER WHAT THE LORD YOUR GOD DID TO PHARAOH AND TO ALL EGYPT." DEUT. 7:17-18

We believe that our God is jealous for the nations of the earth. We believe that He wants the nations to be turned wholeheartedly to Jesus. We believe that He is looking for a people who will step out in faith and believe Him for that which is humanly impossible (Matthew 19:26)!

HE MADE FROM ONE MAN EVERY NATION OF MANKIND TO LIVE ON ALL THE FACE OF THE EARTH, HAVING DETERMINED THEIR APPOINTED TIMES AND THE BOUNDARIES OF THEIR HABITATION, THAT THEY WOULD SEEK GOD, IF PERHAPS THEY MIGHT GROPE FOR HIM AND FIND HIM, THOUGH HE IS NOT FAR FROM EACH ONE OF US.

ACTS 17:26-27

Based on Acts 17, is there a redemptive purpose in why God has allowed your nation to exist? Is it possible that Jesus wants to bring such a move of His Spirit to your nation that it begins to touch the outermost parts of the earth? Is it possible that you have a role to play in your nation rising up into God's original purpose?

THEN THEY WILL REBUILD THE ANCIENT RUINS,
THEY WILL RAISE UP THE FORMER DEVASTATIONS;
AND THEY WILL REPAIR THE RUINED CITIES,
THE DESOLATIONS OF MANY GENERATIONS. ISAIAH 61:4

Discussion Questions:

1. What has your view been of the Holy Spirit in the past? Did you view Him as a Person? If so, in what way?
2. What has been your day to day experience in learning to allow God's Spirit to live His Life through you?
3. In what areas would you say that you have room to grow in giving God's Spirit greater control?

Action Step:

"MY SHEEP HEAR MY VOICE, AND I KNOW THEM,
AND THEY FOLLOW ME." JOHN 10:27

Ask God for one practical action step that you can take to help you grow in your understanding of His Spirit Living in and through you. Write this down, and by God's grace, choose to pray about this and put it into practice. Watch what God does as you obey Him.

_____

_____

_____

_____

Prayer Focus:

Holy Spirit I ask that You would reveal Yourself to me in a deeper way than I have ever known before. I ask that You would teach me what it means for You to be in control of my thoughts, speech and actions. I open up my heart to You and I ask that You would fill me with Your Life. Teach me how to turn more and more of my life over to You. (Continue to pray as God leads you.)

Chapter 3:
Make Disciples of All Nations

What is God's vision for nations? What level of faith does He have for them?

In order to know what to have faith for, it is essential that we gain a deeper understanding of exactly what God's will is for nations. Do you believe that Jesus Christ wants to manifest His Kingdom on the earth? Do you believe He has been given authority to do this? How much more authority does Jesus need before His Kingdom can be manifested on the earth?

JESUS CAME UP AND SPOKE TO THEM, SAYING, "ALL AUTHORITY HAS BEEN GIVEN TO ME IN HEAVEN AND ON EARTH. GO THEREFORE AND MAKE DISCIPLES OF ALL THE NATIONS, BAPTIZING THEM IN THE NAME OF THE FATHER AND THE SON AND THE HOLY SPIRIT, TEACHING THEM TO OBSERVE ALL THAT I COMMANDED YOU; AND LO, I AM WITH YOU ALWAYS, EVEN TO THE END OF THE AGE."

MATTHEW 28:18-20

We see from Jesus' final words before His departure from the earth that He has the desire and the faith to believe that **entire nations** will become His disciples. He has the faith to believe that entire nations will be taught all of His commandments and begin to walk in them. We must have a deep revelation that this is what God wants so that we will have the necessary faith to believe for what He believes.

The Greek word for disciple is "mathéteuó" and it is referring to helping someone become a matured, growing disciple (literally, "a learner," a true Christ-follower). (Ref: Helps Word Studies) Jesus is saying that His Church is to go forth and make the nations His students, instructing entire nations to put into practice everything He taught us. In this way the Kingdom of God is to be established on the earth as it is in heaven:

"PRAY, THEN, IN THIS WAY: 'OUR FATHER WHO IS IN HEAVEN, HALLOWED BE YOUR NAME. 'YOUR KINGDOM COME. YOUR WILL BE DONE, ON EARTH AS IT IS IN HEAVEN.'

MATTHEW 6:9-10

If God has faith for nations, what constitutes a "nation"?

While there are many technical ways that we can describe a nation based on a common language, culture, ethnicity, history etc...but here we just want to mention 5 key institutions that are mentioned in the Word of God as having been created by God, and which help to form the foundation of any nation.

5 Institutions of a Nation:

- **Marriage & Family** (Genesis 2:18-24, Deut. 6:6-9)
- **Business/Financial Stewardship/Resource Allocation** (Genesis 2:15, Deut. 8:18, 28:12)
- **Government** (Romans 13:1)
- **Belief System** – (Education, media, the arts...) (Deut. 4:14, Matthew 28:20, Exodus 31:3, Acts 19:23-27)
- **Priesthood/Spiritual elders** (Exod. 19:5-6, 1 Peter 2:4-9)

If we are serious about obeying Jesus' command to disciple our nation, then we must proactively believe God's Spirit to establish the lifestyle of His Kingdom in each of these spheres of society.

Has your nation become a disciple of Jesus Christ?

Has this level of discipleship already been accomplished in our nation? Have we systematically broken down every facet of society and begun to make them a learner and student of the will and ways of Jesus Christ? Have our families, our government, our businesses, our educational system, our media and television, and our local congregations been thoroughly instructed in all the commandments of Jesus to such a degree that they are implementing His way of life? If we have failed to see this take place up until this time then there is still much work to be done.

We hope that this revelation of nations will show us that God's goal for His Body is for more than planting churches on the fringe of society. He desires to see every way in which our nation's culture is living in rebellion against Him to be uprooted and removed, and to be replaced by the culture of His Kingdom. This may not always be seen in the physical realm, as His Kingdom often advances through the blood of the martyrs, but it is His desire for His Name to be made known throughout society.

"FOR THE EARTH WILL BE FILLED WITH THE KNOWLEDGE OF THE GLORY OF THE LORD, AS THE WATERS COVER THE SEA."

HABAKKUK 2:14

How much does the water cover the ocean floor? Is there just a little water covering the bottom of the ocean or is the ocean floor absolutely submerged in a massive amount of water? (Scientists have stated that the average depth of the ocean is 3,682 meters (12,080 ft)!) The Word of God speaks of a time when the earth will be filled with the knowledge of God's glory as the waters cover the sea. Let us join our faith with the faith of God and believe Him for this in our day.

What is God's heart towards the lost? Is He content that billions are perishing and going to an eternal hell?

FIRST OF ALL, THEN, I URGE THAT ENTREATIES AND PRAYERS, PETITIONS AND THANKSGIVINGS, BE MADE ON BEHALF OF ALL MEN, FOR KINGS AND ALL WHO ARE IN AUTHORITY, SO THAT WE MAY LEAD A TRANQUIL AND QUIET LIFE IN ALL GODLINESS AND DIGNITY. THIS IS GOOD AND ACCEPTABLE IN THE SIGHT OF GOD OUR SAVIOR, WHO DESIRES ALL MEN TO BE SAVED AND TO COME TO THE KNOWLEDGE OF THE TRUTH.

1 TIMOTHY 2:1-4

Paul instructs us that it is God's desire for **all mankind** to be saved and to come to a knowledge of the truth about His Son Jesus Christ. Knowing this should give us great boldness in our witness for Christ. As Christ's ambassadors we should live with the certainty of God's blessing as we step out in obedience to His command to make disciples of all nations. If God Himself is for us, who can be against us? (Romans 8:31)

Does God have the faith to see your nation become a disciple of Jesus Christ?

Testimonies from the Nations

In order to take a step closer to the faith that God has for our nation it is helpful to hear testimonies of what God is doing in other parts of the world. Since He is no respecter of persons (Acts 10:34-35), we can believe that if He will do this in one part of the earth, that He is willing to do this where we live too. All that is required is for us to align our lives with His Spirit in such a way that He is loosed to produce similar fruit in and through our lives.

Testimony from Mongolia

The Mongolian Church doesn't use the name Baptist, Methodist etc...they like to use the name "Mongolian Church". God has placed in the heart of the Body of Christ in Mongolia to unite around a vision to see 10% of the country become true disciples of Jesus Christ over the course of the next several years. (Today the percentage is between 2-3%) This would mean hundreds of thousands of souls coming to know Jesus in a short period of time.

God has raised up a 24-7 prayer movement in which churches from across the capital city are praying day and night for a move of God's Spirit. They have recruited 90% of the Body of Christ in the capital city to be a part of this. One coordinator oversees the capital (9 districts), one coordinator the countryside (21 districts). Each week they have a management board of the Prayer Movement to hear God's direction about what He wants to happen next.

There are many testimonies coming in as people understand that the Kingdom of God will not advance without a deep dependency on God's Spirit.

Testimony from Indonesia

Known globally as the nation with the largest Muslim population, Indonesia is experiencing a powerful prayer revival. Five million Christians are participating in non-stop prayer throughout hundreds of cities while focusing their prayers on the government, media, youth and social and religious issues of concern.

Prayer organizers have commissioned multi-story buildings throughout the country for this interdenominational initiative where living quarters have been put in place for intercessors. At these prayer sites, participants take four-hour shifts with the option to rest in order to recharge for their next prayer shift.

Recently over 100,000 Christians, including 20,000 trained child intercessors and 20,000 youth, gathered at a stadium in the nation's capital city, Jakarta, for a large-scale prayer meeting that was televised live in over 300 other cities throughout the country. God is on the move in Indonesia!

Testimony from China

In 1948 some have estimated that there were only about 1 million Christ-followers in China. Revival broke out in the rural areas of China and started to move to cities like Shanghai. Much of this revival was fueled by the blood of the martyrs and the lives of those who were willing to give up everything for the Kingdom of Jesus Christ. Today there are estimated to be 75-110 million Christ-followers in China. Each day an estimated 35,000 souls come to know Jesus Christ! China now has one of the highest populations of Christians anywhere in the world.

It is no coincidence that during this same period of explosive church growth, that the lifestyle of the believers has been one of radical surrender and faith in God. Many have willingly laid down their lives to see the Gospel begin to penetrate all aspects of society. Today, what we are seeing is unprecedented in church history, but it should be remembered that this has not come without a high price. There were those like Hudson Taylor and many others who pioneered laying the foundation of the Gospel at a time when few were receptive.

Testimony from Uganda

The nation of Uganda has been through many difficulties over the years. As a result, the Body of Christ in Uganda is a real encouragement for any nation to believe that if we will simply persist in the will and ways of God, there is no nation or people group that cannot become a disciple of Jesus Christ.

The pattern was simple. His people humbled themselves, prayed, sought His face, and turned from their wicked ways. His powerful response to their humility has caused many to travel halfway around the world to see the handiwork of God.

Over a period of 24 years (1962-1986) Uganda faced 10 dictatorships, and bloodshed after bloodshed. In 1971 Idi Amin came into power as an Islamic dictator determined to kill those who were in positions of influence. Members of the Body of

Christ were often arrested, tortured and some were even killed for their faith. Things got so bad that the only safe place to pray was in the jungles at night.

Time and time again, as the level of prayer in the Body of Christ was raised, their prayers gave birth to change in the physical realm. Finally after all these struggles, a new president came into power in 1986, and peace and freedom of worship were restored. Those who lived in Uganda at this time say that each time peace would be restored, the Body of Christ would go back to sleep in their prayer lives, and then another judgment would hit the nation.

In 1986 when a more lasting peace took place, churches were growing numerically, and new ministries were coming up in many locations. But an unseen enemy of sexual compromise and disease was beginning to grow in the nation. By the early 1990's the World Health Organization declared Uganda to be the nation worst hit worldwide with HIV/AIDS (Estimates of 34-36% of their population). Clearly, even though there was numerical growth, the church had failed to instruct its members on the importance of marriage and family discipleship.

The government actually came to the Christian pastors to let them know about the AIDS pandemic, and it is reported that they stated, "We need your Jesus to intervene, otherwise this nation will collapse." The report indicated that if things continued in this way that the entire economy would fall apart and that the only ones remaining would be the very old and the very young.

At first the mood of the pastors was one of great discouragement, "Why is it always Uganda? What have we done against God?" But at this time a young pastor stood up and stated, "If we turn our backs on God what hope do we have? He has been faithful in the past, and if we will seek Him in this situation, He will be faithful again!" God used this statement to rekindle faith in the hearts of the pastors to seek God.

Seeking God for a Way Forward

It was during this season of seeking God in prayer and fasting that the Lord revealed a strategy to take the nation back for His Kingdom. It involved mobilizing everyone called by the Name of the Lord and challenging them to a lifestyle that was radically given over to Jesus Christ. It involved challenging individuals to raise prayer for the nation in their personal lives, in their families, in the local congregations, and then out into society. The Lord spoke to them that if they would partner with Him in instituting a "net of prayer" across the nation that He would fish their nation out of troubled waters.

God instructed them not to disregard any sector of His Church but to go out and share this vision with everyone who claimed Jesus throughout the nation. The Lord spoke to them that He has many people who serve His purposes, even in parts of the Church that they would not have expected, and they were to reach out to every denomination and sector of His Church. At first it was not easy attempting to gather the Body of Christ as many were focused on what they were already doing and there were many divisions from the past to fight through. But in time God gave them the grace to reach out to Christ-followers in virtually every denomination across the nation and to cast vision for uniting together in prayer on behalf of the nation.

National Level Fruit

The testimonies that came out of Uganda following the efforts made to unite the Body of Christ and establish a Spirit-Empowered lifestyle are nothing short of astounding! Individuals experienced the revival of God in their personal relationship with Jesus. Among the families who sought to establish this type of lifestyle in their homes, there were many reports of marriages being restored and brought back from the brink of divorce. Love for husbands and wives deepened as it had never been before. Families began to truly take up the task of discipling their children in the home and seek God daily in His Word, worship and prayer. Eventually this lifestyle of radical abandonment to Christ spread throughout every sector of life: businesses, the educational system, media and the government.

Today it is stated that virtually every business in Uganda's capital city, Kampala, has a corporate gathering of Christ-followers who are proactively discipling their workplace. In just the radio alone a dramatic turn around took place. Where it had been illegal to have any Christian broadcasting, the spiritual atmosphere has so changed that it is popular to listen to Gospel music and times of preaching. Today, virtually all of the 140 radio stations in the nation have some form of Gospel programming in order to keep their audience. Even Al Jazeera, the Islamic network, on Sunday mornings puts on Gospel programming because they know that if they don't they will not have an audience to watch their programs.

Amazingly, in time it is reported that the percentage of HIV/AIDS dropped from 34%-36% down to only 6%. Uganda is the only nation in Africa to see such a dramatic turnaround. During this season of national prayer, God gave them a strategy in which the Church partnered with the Government to go into the schools and encourage the students to a lifestyle of sexual purity. The combination of raising the level of prayer across the nation, alongside receiving a practical strategy from God for the youth of the nation, caused many young people to make a commitment to remain pure until marriage. There were also supernatural healings of those who had been stricken with AIDS. In one congregation alone they have seen over 70 documented cases of AIDS being healed by the power of Jesus Christ.

Some years later, the Lord led the Body of Christ into a season of 14 days of National Repentance for the sins of the past. During this time, the First Lady of the nation, Janet Museveni, heard about what was going on and she broke down in tears and said, "This is God! Whatever I need to do in order to assist this I am willing." She was then used of the Lord to share this with the President.

At the national gathering there were representatives from Parliament, the military, police, church officials – all repenting on behalf of the ways in which they had sinned against God. Then the time came when the President showed up at the meetings. He heard how the previous presidents had covenanted the nation to other gods. Even before they had finished speaking, he arose from his seat, came forward and handed the flag of the nation over to representatives of the Body of Christ. Handing over the flag was like handing over the power of the nation to the Church. In a later national gathering the President and First Lady stood as the nation of Uganda was covenanted to the Lordship of Jesus Christ for the next one thousand years.

As you can see, our God is more than able to disciple nations, if He will simply find a people who are willing to join Him in His work.

Will you begin to believe God to move in a similar way in your nation?

Think about the obstacles that Uganda faced: An Islamic dictator closing down church buildings and arresting pastors, murdering hundreds of thousands of people. Other dictators following him, bloodshed after bloodshed, failing economy, failing educational system, and being declared the nation worst hit worldwide with HIV/AIDS. Today, Uganda is viewed as a model of AIDS prevention even among secular sources, and they presently have a Christian population of approx. 84%. While Uganda is not an earthly utopia, and they are not without difficulties, God has proven that as His people set their hope in Him, He is more than able to establish His Kingdom on earth as it is in heaven.

Testimony from Taiwan

Taiwan had a predominately Buddhist (35%), Taoist (33%) and non-religious (18%) population with only a small percentage of Christians (approx. 2.6%). About four years ago there were only a few congregations that fully committed to implement this lifestyle in their personal lives, and in their families. As they persevered in this, dramatic personal and family testimonies began to arise and other ministries started to become involved with this vision.

Over the next several years the work spread to over 1,000 congregations across the nation who began to equip people in a lifestyle of radical abandonment to Jesus. At this point the message began to impact so many people that they started to have large regional meetings where most of the time was taken to share one encouraging testimony after another. The pastors across the nation also started to gather once a month for two days of fasting, prayer, and encouragement in the vision of seeing this lifestyle spread across the land. There are dramatic stories of marriages being restored, and prodigal sons and daughters returning to Jesus. Virtually everyone has a story of an unsaved family member, friend, or acquaintance who has come to Christ through the Spirit-Empowered lifestyle of those around them.

After the families began to experience revival, they were then challenged to impact their society. The Body of Christ began to take this lifestyle out into their places of work, into the government, and into the schools. In a relatively short period of time, there began to be regional meetings with hundreds of marketplace professionals who had started up corporate worship gatherings in their places of work and as a result were experiencing dramatic change. Many souls came to Christ, and the spiritual atmosphere began to shift in different workplaces. One of the national Christian television networks began to broadcast the meetings so that believers across the nation were made aware of what was happening. What had previously been unheard of was now becoming a reality right before their eyes.

Today between 1,000-2,000 congregations are working together towards a goal of seeing tens of thousands equipped in a Spirit-Empowered lifestyle across the nation. Due to the change that this lifestyle has already brought to the Body of Christ, ministers in the nation now believe that they are in a position to seek to unite 75%-100% of the 4,000 congregations in the nation and go for a harvest of one million souls. Already in just 4 years, hundreds of thousands have come to Christ as the percentage of Christ-followers is reported to have nearly doubled from 2.6% to 5% and is still growing. As the Body of Christ began to take seriously their responsibility to disciple the nation in the will and ways of Jesus Christ, God is moving across the land in answer to these prayers. This began in their personal lives as they allowed God to teach them what it meant to remain in a Spirit-Empowered lifestyle, and then moved on to their families, and then out to the world around them.

Since God is moving this way all over the nations, will you believe Him to move so powerfully in your nation that His redemptive destiny begins to come to pass right before your eyes!

"YOU ARE THE LIGHT OF THE WORLD. A CITY SET ON A HILL CANNOT BE HIDDEN; NOR DOES ANYONE LIGHT A LAMP AND PUT IT UNDER A BASKET, BUT ON THE LAMPSTAND, AND IT GIVES LIGHT TO ALL WHO ARE IN THE HOUSE."

MATTHEW 5:14-15

Discussion Questions:

1. Based on Matthew 28:18-20 what is God's vision for the nations? (Share this in your own words)
2. What level of faith does God have to fulfill His vision for the nations?
3. Share anything that encouraged you or stood out to you in the testimonies from the various nations. (Mongolia, Indonesia, China, Uganda, Taiwan)
4. What do you think God wants to do in your nation?
5. How could you see yourself being a part of what God desires to do in your nation?

Action Step:

* Write down your answer to the final discussion question about God's heart for your nation, and your role in what He wants to do in your nation. Put this in a place that you will see it regularly and as God's Spirit leads you, begin to make this a specific prayer target.

_____

_____

_____

_____

* As an extra action point, you may consider beginning to study revivals that have taken place in the past as a means of stirring your faith to believe God for great things in your nation.

Prayer Focus:

We want to join our faith with God's faith for the nations:

Father, I thank You and praise You that there is nothing impossible for You! I thank You that all the nations of the earth are like a drop of water in a bucket compared to You. I choose to trust You with the nation that You have placed me in. I choose to believe that You will use me here for Your glory. Show me my role in Your much larger vision of discipling this nation. (Continue to pray into this as God's Spirit leads you.)

Section 2: Hindrances to Kingdom Advancement

Chapter 4: The Battle to Establish God's Kingdom on the Earth

We would be remiss if we simply painted a beautiful picture of establishing a Spirit-Empowered lifestyle in our personal lives, families and sphere of influence, but did not mention the blood, sweat and tears that will likely be necessary in order to see this take place. In most cases, due to the fact that we are entering enemy occupied territory and seeking to establish Christ's Kingdom, there will be a fierce battle.

There is a very real spiritual battle whenever we seek to see a literal establishment of Christ's Kingdom on the earth. This is the case whether the battle is within your personal life, your family life, or your sphere of influence. The larger the territory you are going for, the larger the battle. The last thing that Satan and his demons want is for you to live wholeheartedly for the Lord Jesus Christ in this Spirit-Empowered lifestyle. There will be a real battle to get you to be pushed back and settle for a lifestyle that is far from what God intends.

A good visual picture of the battle that is before us is found by looking at Joshua as he and the Israelites entered into the Promised Land. There were great victories, such as at the city of Jericho. But then this victory was followed by a pricey compromise by Achan that cost many lives (Joshua 7:5). Shortly after that, they failed to rely on God's counsel and got involved with a covenant with the Gibeonites that they should not have made (Joshua 9:14-16).

As they moved across the Promised Land and learned to rely upon God's wisdom, they were victorious time and time again. It was not an overnight process but one that took years, before the whole land began to come into their hands. Establishing a Spirit-Empowered Lifestyle in our personal life, family, and sphere of influence is not a quick fix, but a God-given means of seeing the Kingdom of God advance in any land. Though it may be a battle, we can trust our God to give us strength, and insight in how to overcome. He is faithful. If we rely upon Him, there is no weapon formed against us that will prosper (Isaiah 54:17).

Know Your Enemy

What are the enemies that would seek to come against us?

AND YOU WERE DEAD IN YOUR TRESPASSES AND SINS, IN WHICH YOU FORMERLY WALKED ACCORDING TO THE COURSE OF THIS WORLD, ACCORDING TO THE PRINCE OF THE POWER OF THE AIR, OF THE SPIRIT THAT IS NOW WORKING IN THE SONS OF DISOBEDIENCE. AMONG THEM WE TOO ALL FORMERLY LIVED IN THE LUSTS OF OUR FLESH, INDULGING THE DESIRES OF THE FLESH AND OF THE MIND, AND WERE BY NATURE CHILDREN OF WRATH, EVEN AS THE REST.

EPHESIANS 2:1-3

In Ephesians chapter 2 Paul identifies three primary hindrances or "battlefields" to the establishment of Christ's Kingdom on the earth.

- **The flesh** (sin nature)
- **The course of this world** (world's system)

- **The prince of the power of the air** (Satan and his demons)

The schemes of the enemy that Paul mentions here are the three main hindrances to the advancement of the will of God on earth. If we are to overcome them we must identify any way in which we are still in bondage to them and begin to allow the Person of the Holy Spirit to set us free, so that we may be effective in helping to set others free.

Each battlefield is applicable within our personal lives, families, sphere of influence, and local congregation as well as in our region. The Spirit of God not only desires to reveal any way in which we are still in bondage but He expects us to trust Him to overcome these forces of darkness.

HE WHO HAS AN EAR, LET HIM HEAR WHAT THE SPIRIT SAYS TO THE CHURCHES. TO HIM WHO OVERCOMES, I WILL GRANT TO EAT OF THE TREE OF LIFE WHICH IS IN THE PARADISE OF GOD.

REV. 2:7

HE WHO HAS AN EAR, LET HIM HEAR WHAT THE SPIRIT SAYS TO THE CHURCHES. HE WHO OVERCOMES WILL NOT BE HURT BY THE SECOND DEATH.

REV. 2:11

Overcoming these hindrances is not optional it is essential. The Spirit of God expects us to trust Him to overcome every one of these hindrances to such a degree, that not only are we free ourselves, but we are in a position to push back the spiritual forces in the heavenly realm and carry Christ's

Kingdom back into the world's system to impact it for the glory of God.

Hindrances to the Establishment of God's Kingdom on the Earth:

Battlefield #1: The Flesh/Sin Nature/Human Nature

The heart of our sin nature is the twin roots of pride and unbelief. This is a pride in our own estimation of our character, our will and our ways and unbelief in God's character, will and ways. The sin nature is our human understanding and ways being exalted above God's understanding and ways.

The "Worldly" Flesh

There are two primary ways in which our sin nature will seek to manifest itself. One manifestation of our human pride and unbelief is openly against God. It is a life that has cast off moral restraints and is living for the pleasures of this temporary life. We will call this the "worldly" flesh, and it is highlighted in the following scriptures:

BELOVED, I URGE YOU AS ALIENS AND STRANGERS TO ABSTAIN FROM FLESHLY LUSTS WHICH WAGE WAR AGAINST THE SOUL.

1 PETER 2:11

BUT IF YOU ARE LED BY THE SPIRIT, YOU ARE NOT UNDER THE LAW. NOW THE DEEDS OF THE FLESH ARE EVIDENT, WHICH ARE: IMMORALITY, IMPURITY, SENSUALITY, IDOLATRY, SORCERY, ENMITIES, STRIFE, JEALOUSY, OUTBURSTS OF ANGER, DISPUTES, DISSENSIONS, FACTIONS, ENVYING, DRUNKENNESS, CAROUSING, AND THINGS LIKE THESE, OF WHICH I FOREWARN YOU, JUST AS I HAVE FOREWARNED

69

YOU, THAT THOSE WHO PRACTICE SUCH THINGS WILL NOT INHERIT THE KINGDOM OF GOD. GALATIANS 5:18-21

Paul is very clear in the book of Galatians that if we do not learn what it means to repent and trust the Spirit of God to overcome our flesh, then we "will not inherit the kingdom of God." (vs. 21)

DO YOU NOT KNOW THAT THOSE WHO RUN IN A RACE ALL RUN, BUT ONLY ONE RECEIVES THE PRIZE? RUN IN SUCH A WAY THAT YOU MAY WIN. EVERYONE WHO COMPETES IN THE GAMES EXERCISES SELF-CONTROL IN ALL THINGS. THEY THEN DO IT TO RECEIVE A PERISHABLE WREATH, BUT WE AN IMPERISHABLE. THEREFORE I RUN IN SUCH A WAY, AS NOT WITHOUT AIM; I BOX IN SUCH A WAY, AS NOT BEATING THE AIR; BUT I DISCIPLINE MY BODY AND MAKE IT MY SLAVE, SO THAT, AFTER I HAVE PREACHED TO OTHERS, I MYSELF WILL NOT BE DISQUALIFIED.

1 COR. 9:24-27

When we speak of our "worldly" flesh we are referring to a lifestyle that is lived for our primary human appetites. As children of God, we must believe God's Spirit to teach us how these human desires are to be brought into submission to His Spirit. While human appetites have in fact been given to us from God, the problem comes when we start seeking to fulfill these desires in a way that is contrary to the will and ways of God. For example: Having sex outside of marriage is one way that the flesh seeks to pervert God's good desires, and fulfill them in a way that is outside of His will.

Paul expresses a balanced understanding of our human desires:

I KNOW HOW TO GET ALONG WITH HUMBLE MEANS, AND I ALSO KNOW HOW TO LIVE IN PROSPERITY; IN ANY AND EVERY CIRCUMSTANCE I HAVE LEARNED THE SECRET OF BEING FILLED AND GOING HUNGRY, BOTH OF HAVING ABUNDANCE AND SUFFERING NEED. I CAN DO ALL THINGS THROUGH HIM WHO STRENGTHENS ME.

PHILIPPIANS 4:12-13

Some of our human appetites include:

- A desire for food (1 Cor. 10:30-31, Mark 7:18-19, Phil.3:19)

- A desire for financial provision / security (Deut. 8:18)

- A desire for self-worth / self recognition (2 Cor. 5:17)

- A desire for sexual & physical pleasure/enjoyment (Genesis 1:28, Matthew 5:27-30, 1 Cor. 7:3-5)

THEREFORE, SINCE CHRIST HAS SUFFERED IN THE FLESH, ARM YOURSELVES ALSO WITH THE SAME PURPOSE, BECAUSE HE WHO HAS SUFFERED IN THE FLESH HAS CEASED FROM SIN, SO AS TO LIVE THE REST OF THE TIME IN THE FLESH NO LONGER FOR THE LUSTS OF MEN, BUT FOR THE WILL OF GOD. FOR THE TIME ALREADY PAST IS SUFFICIENT FOR YOU TO HAVE CARRIED OUT THE DESIRE OF THE GENTILES, HAVING PURSUED A COURSE OF SENSUALITY, LUSTS, DRUNKENNESS, CAROUSING, DRINKING PARTIES AND ABOMINABLE IDOLATRIES. IN ALL THIS, THEY ARE SURPRISED THAT YOU DO NOT RUN WITH THEM INTO THE SAME EXCESSES OF DISSIPATION, AND THEY MALIGN YOU; BUT THEY WILL GIVE ACCOUNT TO HIM WHO IS READY TO JUDGE THE LIVING AND THE DEAD.

1 PETER 4:1-5

71

The "Religious" Flesh

*THIS IS THE ONLY THING I WANT TO FIND OUT FROM YOU: DID YOU
RECEIVE THE SPIRIT BY THE WORKS OF THE LAW, OR BY HEARING
WITH FAITH? ARE YOU SO FOOLISH? HAVING BEGUN BY THE SPIRIT,
ARE YOU NOW BEING PERFECTED BY THE FLESH?*

GALATIANS 3:2-3

As Paul mentions here in Galatians, the flesh is not merely the obvious "bad things" done in our human lusts, but we can even fall into attempting to do the work of God in our own pride and unbelief. We will call this the "religious" flesh. It is just as detestable to God as the worldly flesh, because it has the same root of pride in our ways and unbelief in God.

In fact, in some ways the religious flesh is even more dangerous than the worldly flesh, because it holds up a mask of godliness and causes us to think that this is how we are to live as followers of Christ. When pastors and ministers have fallen into living in their religious flesh, they poison the souls of many others. They model with their lifestyle that it is acceptable to be a follower of Christ, yet live in our flesh. They may have all the right words of religion, but just like the Pharisees of old, they miss the heart of God, and live by their own power and not the power of God's Spirit.

The religious flesh is our human will power and understanding, seeking to live a "Christian" life apart from God. This subtle form of our sin nature is prevalent in vast portions of the global Body of Christ. So many souls are striving in all their human energies to seek to live out a life that is pleasing to God.

72

The Religious Flesh Leads to Self-Righteousness

One problem with living in our religious flesh is that we have a tendency to set a standard of what we believe to be a "godly life". After setting this standard, if we start to believe that we are succeeding, we can begin to become self-righteous in our interactions with others. We can become convinced that we are pleasing to God in our own efforts. Therefore, we may start to look down on others that we do not believe are following God with the same passion that we have.

> *NOW THESE THINGS, BRETHREN, I HAVE FIGURATIVELY APPLIED TO MYSELF AND APOLLOS FOR YOUR SAKES, SO THAT IN US YOU MAY LEARN NOT TO EXCEED WHAT IS WRITTEN, SO THAT NO ONE OF YOU WILL BECOME ARROGANT IN BEHALF OF ONE AGAINST THE OTHER. FOR WHO REGARDS YOU AS SUPERIOR? WHAT DO YOU HAVE THAT YOU DID NOT RECEIVE? AND IF YOU DID RECEIVE IT, WHY DO YOU BOAST AS IF YOU HAD NOT RECEIVED IT?*

> *1 COR. 4:6-7*

Paul writes to remind us, *"What do you have that you did not receive?"* If we have anything that is truly valuable in the eyes of God, if we have any hunger or desire for Him, then it is entirely due to His unmerited favor! In this way, we have no right to boast about being more godly or spiritual than another person. If there is anything that is truly good in our lives, then it has come from God and not from us.

The Religious Flesh leads to Condemnation

> *THEREFORE THERE IS NOW NO CONDEMNATION FOR THOSE WHO ARE IN CHRIST JESUS. FOR THE LAW OF THE SPIRIT OF LIFE IN CHRIST*

JESUS HAS SET YOU FREE FROM THE LAW OF SIN AND OF DEATH.

ROMANS 8:1-2

The flipside of self-righteousness occurs when someone seeks to live the Christian life in their own strength but they fail to measure up to the standard that they have set for themselves. This failure to live the Christian life in their own strength causes them to feel like they never measure up. In this place of self-condemnation we can come to view God as always displeased with us. We lose sight of His delight in us, we lose sight of His love for us, and we feel that we are destined to never fulfill what He has called us to.

Self condemnation is not God's will for His children. He desires for us to know how He delights in us as a loving father delights in his children. He wants us to know His love, His mercy and His supernatural power to overcome every temptation to sin. Jesus has called us to a life of freedom and not condemnation.

KNOWING THIS, THAT OUR OLD SELF WAS CRUCIFIED WITH HIM, IN ORDER THAT OUR BODY OF SIN MIGHT BE DONE AWAY WITH, SO THAT WE WOULD NO LONGER BE SLAVES TO SIN; FOR HE WHO HAS DIED IS FREED FROM SIN. NOW IF WE HAVE DIED WITH CHRIST, WE BELIEVE THAT WE SHALL ALSO LIVE WITH HIM.

ROMANS 6:6-8

Whether we have a tendency to go with self-righteousness, or a tendency to fall into condemnation, God's solution is totally different than what we might think. He is not asking us to try harder to overcome. He is calling us to die more deeply to our human striving. He tells us that He never intended for us to try to live the Christian life on our own. Instead, He says, *"Come to Me, all who are weary and heavy-laden, and I will give you rest. Take My yoke upon you and learn from Me, for I am gentle and humble in heart, and you will find rest for your souls."* (Matthew 11:28-29)

In order to overcome our religious flesh, we must take the time to seek to enter more deeply into a place of real surrender to Jesus Christ. We must learn to die to our religious flesh by no longer attempting to live the Christ-Life in our own strength and efforts, but instead to learn what it means to trust God's Spirit to live His Life on our behalf.

THEREFORE I URGE YOU, BRETHREN, BY THE MERCIES OF GOD, TO PRESENT YOUR BODIES A LIVING AND HOLY SACRIFICE, ACCEPTABLE TO GOD, WHICH IS YOUR SPIRITUAL SERVICE OF WORSHIP.

ROMANS 12:1

Battlefield #2: The System / "Course of this world"

AND YOU WERE DEAD IN YOUR TRESPASSES AND SINS, IN WHICH YOU FORMERLY WALKED ACCORDING TO THE COURSE OF THIS WORLD.

EPHESIANS 2:1-2

There is a "course" or system of human relationships and beliefs that surround us. This system is shaped by our sphere of influence. If we are in a community of Christ-followers who have been equipped with a Biblical worldview, then these relationships and beliefs will likely be conducive to seeing the Kingdom of God established. If we are in an environment that is filled with relationships and beliefs that are contrary to the Kingdom of Jesus Christ, then this belief system may be a strong hindrance to our obedience to God. God's Spirit has given us a responsibility to see the culture of the Kingdom of Jesus Christ established in the system of life that surrounds us.

In every nation, there is a culture or way of life that causes the people of that nation to live and act in certain ways. This course of life is evident in the following institutions of society:

Family

Our family relationships can be one of the greatest motivators toward following God. This was God's intention (Deut. 6:6-9). These relationships and the written and unwritten laws within our home will either push us closer to Christ, or they will seek to hinder us from Him. In faith we must believe God to break every hindrance.

Marketplace/business

The business relationships and the written and unwritten laws within our place of work can propel us closer to Christ, or cause us to shrink back due to the fear of man, fear losing our job etc. If we really seek to establish Christ's Kingdom in our workplace we will need to rely on God's Spirit to overcome the obstacles that may be there.

Mindset Molders (Education, media, arts...)

The mindset of a nation has a very powerful effect on how the people of that territory will live their lives. Some of the key ways a national mindset is shaped is through the educational system, the media, arts and entertainment. If we desire to disciple our nation in the will and ways of Jesus Christ then we must proactively ask God's Spirit for His wisdom on how to use these powerful tools to shape the believe system of the land.

Sadly, it is becoming a global crisis in the Body of Christ that those within the Church and even those in leadership positions are being shaped by the values promoted by television and films that are being produced by those without faith in Jesus Christ. In virtually every nation there is now some version of a global culture that is driven by temporary desires and pleasures.

As followers of Jesus Christ, we must continuously ask God's Spirit to keep our hearts and minds free from the influence of the kingdom of darkness that these mindset molders may seek to push upon us. We will likely need to take drastic measures to ensure that ungodly values coming from the television and media do not infiltrate our homes. As we are set apart from these influences, we are then in a position of authority to ask God to show us how we can make a difference in this area of our world. For some it might be to pray for those who help to shape the school system, or the key leaders in media, while others may have the opportunity to make a hands-on difference. As long as the Church allows for compromise with ungodly media, it has little to no authority to call others to come out and be free.

Personal Testimony:

A short while after returning from Africa and seeing their hunger for the things of God, the Spirit of God began to deal with me about watching television. He asked me a simple question, "Why do you need to be entertained?" As I thought about this question I realized that my real answer was, "Because my life is still about myself. I like to be entertained because it gives me temporary pleasure." The fact of the matter was that I would allow myself to be entertained even by things that I knew were displeasing to God.

Within a relatively short period of time God gently led me to turn off the television and begin to take that same time in order to invest it in the Word of God, worship and prayer. This extra time was also spent with my family to cultivate an environment of worship, prayer and the Word of God. The benefits of making this decision to remove the television from our lives, and invest that time in the eternal purposes of God have already reaped untold benefits. Only God knows what difference this will make on the Day of Judgment.

Government

THE PLAN SEEMED GOOD TO PHARAOH AND TO ALL HIS OFFICIALS. SO PHARAOH ASKED THEM, "CAN WE FIND ANYONE LIKE THIS MAN, ONE IN WHOM IS THE SPIRIT OF GOD?"

THEN PHARAOH SAID TO JOSEPH, "SINCE GOD HAS MADE ALL THIS KNOWN TO YOU, THERE IS NO ONE SO DISCERNING AND WISE AS YOU. YOU SHALL BE IN CHARGE OF MY PALACE, AND ALL MY PEOPLE ARE TO SUBMIT TO YOUR ORDERS. ONLY WITH RESPECT TO THE THRONE WILL I BE GREATER THAN YOU." SO PHARAOH SAID TO JOSEPH, "I HEREBY PUT YOU IN CHARGE OF THE WHOLE LAND OF EGYPT."

GENESIS 41:37-41 (NIV)

TO THESE FOUR YOUNG MEN GOD GAVE KNOWLEDGE AND UNDERSTANDING OF ALL KINDS OF LITERATURE AND LEARNING. AND DANIEL COULD UNDERSTAND VISIONS AND DREAMS OF ALL KINDS. AT THE END OF THE TIME SET BY THE KING TO BRING THEM INTO HIS SERVICE, THE CHIEF OFFICIAL PRESENTED THEM TO NEBUCHADNEZZAR. THE KING TALKED WITH THEM, AND HE FOUND NONE EQUAL TO DANIEL, HANANIAH, MISHAEL AND AZARIAH; SO THEY ENTERED THE KING'S SERVICE.

DANIEL 1:17-19 (NIV)

There are Biblical testimonies, as well as testimonies throughout human history of times when an earthly government began to align itself with the will and the ways of God. This has often served as a powerful testimony to the nations of the need to seek God. At other times, when those in government have been against God's will and ways, this has led to some of the greatest atrocities that have ever occurred on the face of the earth. Therefore, we can understand why Paul admonished the Church to pray for those in positions of earthly authority.

FIRST OF ALL, THEN, I URGE THAT ENTREATIES AND PRAYERS, PETITIONS AND THANKSGIVINGS, BE MADE ON BEHALF OF ALL MEN, FOR KINGS AND ALL WHO ARE IN AUTHORITY, SO THAT WE MAY LEAD A TRANQUIL AND QUIET LIFE IN ALL GODLINESS AND DIGNITY. THIS IS GOOD AND ACCEPTABLE IN THE SIGHT OF GOD OUR SAVIOR, WHO DESIRES ALL MEN TO BE SAVED AND TO COME TO THE KNOWLEDGE OF THE TRUTH.

1 TIMOTHY 2:1-4

Clearly the written and unwritten laws of the government have a powerful effect on the land. If the government formally sanctions a law that is against the will of God, it has a powerful effect on the people of the nation. This causes people to come to believe that this type of law is okay even if it is in opposition to God. We should be diligent to pray for those in authority, and believe God to bring them into a saving relationship with His Son Jesus.

Called to Honor Not Criticize

EVERY PERSON IS TO BE IN SUBJECTION TO THE GOVERNING AUTHORITIES. FOR THERE IS NO AUTHORITY EXCEPT FROM GOD, AND THOSE WHICH EXIST ARE ESTABLISHED BY GOD...FOR BECAUSE OF THIS YOU ALSO PAY TAXES, FOR RULERS ARE SERVANTS OF GOD, DEVOTING THEMSELVES TO THIS VERY THING. RENDER TO ALL WHAT IS DUE THEM: TAX TO WHOM TAX IS DUE; CUSTOM TO WHOM CUSTOM; FEAR TO WHOM FEAR; HONOR TO WHOM HONOR. ROMANS 13:1,6-7

HONOR ALL PEOPLE, LOVE THE BROTHERHOOD, FEAR GOD, HONOR THE KING. 1 PETER 2:17

The Word of God clearly indicates that it is God who has allowed our rulers and that we are to submit to and honor them with our thoughts, words and actions. In contradiction to God's clear instructions, there is a crisis of epidemic proportions within the Body of Christ when it comes to honoring our earthly leaders. For some reason it appears that the vast majority of believers feel justified slandering those who have been placed in positions of authority over them.

When dealing with earthly leaders, many believers have falsely entered into a mode of criticism that is very earthly and unspiritual. In this way we deny the Word of God, and we walk by sight rather than in the awareness that we are in a battle against spiritual forces and not flesh and blood. If we ever get caught in a trap of blaming the darkness for being dark, we have lost sight of God's perspective. Instead of human criticism, we would do much better to observe the Word of God and choose to honor our leaders and pray for them out of a heart of love and compassion. God loves even His enemies and He expects us to love all mankind as He does.

Model the Difference

FOR THE SCEPTER OF WICKEDNESS SHALL NOT REST UPON THE LAND OF THE RIGHTEOUS, SO THAT THE RIGHTEOUS WILL NOT PUT FORTH THEIR HANDS TO DO WRONG.

PSALM 125:3

Instead of criticizing what we believe is wrong or corrupt in our government, God may be using this sense of urgency to call some of us to rise up and take an active role in being a part of the solution at a local, regional or national level. There are many instances throughout the Bible (for example, Joseph, Daniel, Shadrach, Meshach, Abednego, Sergius Paulus a governor in Rome, Cornelius a Roman centurion) and throughout Church history, where God used men and women to bring His Kingdom ways into earthly governments. Our God is no respecter of persons. He is more than willing to reach out to those who are open to Him in the sphere of government. May we believe God to establish godly leaders in every sector of our government.

The System of Worship / Priesthood (Holy vs. Unholy)

The relationships and written and unwritten laws of the system of worship in a nation powerfully affect the type of spirituality that is practiced in the land. Those who practice a spirituality that does not include the teachings of Jesus will often have laws and relationships set up to oppose the advancement of the Kingdom of God. At the same time, even the Church itself, if we are not careful, can begin to come under the influence of some of the ways of the Kingdom of darkness. That may be through blatant compromise with the world's ways of seeking temporary pleasure, or it may be in the form of religion that lacks a depth of intimacy with Jesus Christ.

As the Body of Christ is rightly positioned, walking in a depth of intimacy with Jesus, and working together as a united Church to advance Christ's Kingdom, it is possible to see the Kingdom of God begin to uproot and remove long held strongholds that the enemy has had in the land. Where there had been worship to false gods, it is possible to see this removed and restored with worship to King Jesus.

In some nations the predominant religion is Islam, Buddhism or Hinduism and you can see how this shapes the belief system and way of life of the entire nation. Within the church our battle is not so much against an external "false religion" but the schemes that the devil has used to set up a false religious system within the Church.

A Form of Godliness That Denies God's Power

AND HE SAID TO THEM, "RIGHTLY DID ISAIAH PROPHESY OF YOU HYPOCRITES, AS IT IS WRITTEN: 'THIS PEOPLE HONORS ME WITH

THEIR LIPS, BUT THEIR HEART IS FAR AWAY FROM ME. 'BUT IN VAIN DO THEY WORSHIP ME, TEACHING AS DOCTRINES THE PRECEPTS OF MEN.'   MARK 7:6-7

There are many ways that something can appear to honor God on the outside but be done from a heart that is far from God. Here are some common characteristics of the religious system:

- Exaltation of the traditions of man above the commandments of God

- Concerned with our own kingdoms and not God's Kingdom.

- Mirrors the world's system but with a religious appearance. Within this religious worldliness we see the pursuit of fame, fortune, power, pleasure etc.

- Tries to prevent God from moving, often due to the fact that God's ways are not humanly understandable.

THEREFORE THE CHIEF PRIESTS AND THE PHARISEES CONVENED A COUNCIL, AND WERE SAYING, "WHAT ARE WE DOING? FOR THIS MAN IS PERFORMING MANY SIGNS. IF WE LET HIM GO ON LIKE THIS, ALL MEN WILL BELIEVE IN HIM, AND THE ROMANS WILL COME AND TAKE AWAY BOTH OUR PLACE AND OUR NATION."

JOHN 11:47-48

In this passage Jesus had clearly raised a man from the dead (Lazarus). Yet the blindness of the religious system was so great that this miracle is the reason that they decided they must kill Him. Jesus was moving in ways that were contrary to the religious system and they got upset about it and wanted to stop Him. Even today, the religious system seeks to prevent

God from moving in the way that He wants to. This is a clear sign of something not being of the Lord.

"BEWARE OF PRACTICING YOUR RIGHTEOUSNESS BEFORE MEN TO BE NOTICED BY THEM; OTHERWISE YOU HAVE NO REWARD WITH YOUR FATHER WHO IS IN HEAVEN."

MATTHEW 6:1

- Focused on the outward rather than the heart (Saul vs. David)

"AND WHEN YOU ARE PRAYING, DO NOT USE MEANINGLESS REPETITION AS THE GENTILES DO, FOR THEY SUPPOSE THAT THEY WILL BE HEARD FOR THEIR MANY WORDS." MATTHEW 6:7

- Going through the religious motions in our prayer life, worship, reading of God's Word. Lack of real life and passion in our relationship with God.
- Failure to disciple our families because we are so preoccupied with our own lives/ministry that we miss our first mission field.

Advancing the Kingdom of Jesus Christ into the Spheres of Society

If we are going to see our nation discipled into the ways of Jesus Christ, it is going to take more than being separated from the bad laws and influence of the world's system. Once our hearts and minds have been liberated from the wicked way the enemy has sought to twist these elements of society, then as the people of God, we must head back into the places of influence in our society and instruct them in the ways of Christ's Kingdom. As the ways of Christ's Kingdom come into our

84

families, our workplaces, the government, the media, and education then we will see Jesus Christ exalted in ways we may never have thought possible.

If we are to be successful in discipling our nation, then we must ask God's Spirit to show us how to shift the "course of life" in these institutions away from the kingdom of darkness, and towards the will and ways of God. We are to exalt the way of life that Jesus Christ instructed us in such a way that it begins to uproot and remove the elements of darkness in our current way of life and replaces them with His way of life.

Battlefield #3: Spiritual forces of darkness

FOR OUR STRUGGLE IS NOT AGAINST FLESH AND BLOOD, BUT AGAINST THE RULERS, AGAINST THE POWERS, AGAINST THE WORLD FORCES OF THIS DARKNESS, AGAINST THE SPIRITUAL FORCES OF WICKEDNESS IN THE HEAVENLY PLACES.

EPHESIANS 6:12

As followers of Jesus Christ, we are aware that there is a very real enemy who seeks to oppose us. It is our privilege and responsibility to take our stand against Satan and his demons. These spiritual forces are working to influence the belief system around us (Ephesians 2:2). They are seeking to provoke our flesh against us. They are working hard to get us to give into them, so that they can have some legal ground within our lives to steal, kill and destroy us (John 10:10). Peter describes them like a roaring lion looking for someone to devour.

THEREFORE HUMBLE YOURSELVES UNDER THE MIGHTY HAND OF GOD, THAT HE MAY EXALT YOU AT THE PROPER TIME, CASTING ALL

YOUR ANXIETY ON HIM, BECAUSE HE CARES FOR YOU. BE OF SOBER SPIRIT, BE ON THE ALERT. YOUR ADVERSARY, THE DEVIL, PROWLS AROUND LIKE A ROARING LION, SEEKING SOMEONE TO DEVOUR. BUT RESIST HIM, FIRM IN YOUR FAITH.

1 PETER 5:6-9

We can see the manifestation of different spiritual forces in our cities. There are some places where it is very clear that the people of the land have given themselves over to a spirit of lust. This spiritual deception is manifested in the physical realm through seductive advertisements and stores that seek to lure people to buy the latest and greatest products, urging us to pursue temporary pleasures. It is clear in other places that a false religious spirit is controlling the area. The people who live there may not have the same temptation to give into lust, but their minds are being blinded in a different way by a spirit that appears very religious, but keeps them from surrendering their lives to Jesus Christ.

EVEN IF OUR GOSPEL IS VEILED, IT IS VEILED TO THOSE WHO ARE PERISHING, IN WHOSE CASE THE GOD OF THIS WORLD HAS BLINDED THE MINDS OF THE UNBELIEVING SO THAT THEY MIGHT NOT SEE THE LIGHT OF THE GOSPEL OF THE GLORY OF CHRIST, WHO IS THE IMAGE OF GOD.

2 COR. 4:3-4

Darkness Can Be Pushed Back

Whenever an individual begins to surrender their lives to Jesus Christ and trust His Spirit, territory is taken back for the Kingdom of God. An individual heart is becoming a vessel of

Christ's Kingdom. If a family chooses to surrender and trust Jesus Christ, darkness will be pushed back and God's Kingdom will be established in their home. As the people of God in any territory begin to surrender to Jesus and trust His Spirit in their local congregations, they are beginning to loose the grip of darkness over the territory. As the Body of Christ is living in this way and as they begin to unite across denominational lines, and pray targeted prayers at a regional level, there is great authority in the spiritual realm to see darkness over entire regions pushed back and the Kingdom of Jesus Christ advance.

May we be faithful in the role God that has given us to help set our region free from the forces of darkness. May we humble ourselves underneath God's mighty hand. May we proactively turn away from any way in which we have allowed our lives to come into agreement with the kingdom of darkness. In this way, the legal ground that we had surrendered to the enemy is broken. As this repentance goes deep into every area of our lives, we will then have the strength to stand up and resist the devil in the power of the Lord Jesus Christ and he will flee from us. As we are set free, we will then be in a position to help set our families free and our sphere of influence free. Praise God!

SUBMIT THEREFORE TO GOD. RESIST THE DEVIL AND HE WILL FLEE
FROM YOU. JAMES 4:7

Overcoming Darkness and Advancing Christ's Kingdom

We can see from this chapter that our job is not an easy one. In fact, it is humanly impossible to even set ourselves free, let alone to see our families, our sphere of influence, or our state or nation enter into the ways of Jesus Christ. God has not told us that we have to figure out these layers of darkness and overcome them on our own. Instead, He has stated that He will overcome them on our behalf as we give ourselves completely over to Him. He has said that He will fight on our behalf when we keep in step with His Holy Spirit.

As we prepare to face the many battles that will come against us, we can once again see the vital importance of learning what it means to remain in a Spirit-Empowered lifestyle. It is very evident that we must allow God's Spirit to establish this lifestyle in us, so that we will be able to stand our ground against all the enemy's schemes.

FINALLY, BE STRONG IN THE LORD AND IN THE STRENGTH OF HIS MIGHT. PUT ON THE FULL ARMOR OF GOD, SO THAT YOU WILL BE ABLE TO STAND FIRM AGAINST THE SCHEMES OF THE DEVIL.

EPHESIANS 6:10-11

May we make a choice today to ask God's Spirit to begin to set us free from these hindrances, so that we can be an effective instrument in His hands to bring His eternal Kingdom to others. As we allow God's Spirit to have greater and greater possession of us, we will be prepared to meet any challenge that may come against us.

FOR GOD, WHO SAID, "LIGHT SHALL SHINE OUT OF DARKNESS," IS THE ONE WHO HAS SHONE IN OUR HEARTS TO GIVE THE LIGHT OF THE KNOWLEDGE OF THE GLORY OF GOD IN THE FACE OF CHRIST. BUT WE HAVE THIS TREASURE IN EARTHEN VESSELS, SO THAT THE SURPASSING GREATNESS OF THE POWER WILL BE OF GOD AND NOT FROM OURSELVES. 2 COR. 4:6-7

Discussion Questions:

1. In what way have you seen your flesh (your pride and unbelief) seeking to keep you from living wholeheartedly for God? How do you believe God would have you deal with this?

2. Think about the relationships and beliefs in your family, workplace, education, media, government, Church. In what way have you seen the belief system around you seeking to keep you from living wholeheartedly for God? How do you believe God would have you deal with this?

3. In what way have you experienced spiritual forces of darkness seeking to hold you back from living wholeheartedly for God? How do you believe God would have you deal with this?

4. Do you believe that God's Spirit can set you free from each of these hindrances? Why or why not? (Explain/Discuss)

Action Points:

- Ask the Holy Spirit to identify any way that these hindrances still have a hold on your life. Write down anything that He reveals to you.

Sin nature/human nature_____

_____

The System / "Course of Life"_____

_____

Spiritual forces_____

Take these revelations from God's Spirit as specific, urgent prayer requests before the Lord. Seek God until the grip of sin, the belief system, and the enemy has been broken off your life and you are free to run into the purposes that Jesus Christ has for you. If you are having difficulty breaking free from these hindrances on your own, invite other mature Christ-followers to assist you in praying through to victory.

- Ask God's Spirit if there is any way that you have lived in self-righteousness in your relationship with Him and with others. If He shows you that you have, be quick to confess this sin of religious pride to Him, and ask Him to lead you into a deep and real repentance.

- Ask God's Spirit if there is any way that you have lived in self-condemnation. If He shows you that you have ask the Holy Spirit to show you how He sees you. Allow His love for you to fill your heart and change your perspective on how He views you. He does not want His children living in condemnation, but joy, hope, life and freedom.

- Ask God's Spirit to reveal to you any way that He wants you to be a part of praying through the areas of darkness that are seeking to hold back your family, sphere of influence, local congregation and region.

Prayer Focus:

We want to focus our prayers on humbling ourselves underneath God's mighty hand and resisting Satan so that he will flee from us.

Lord Jesus, we come in faith to You! We acknowledge that You are high above every enemy that would seek to set itself up against Your purposes in our lives. We humble ourselves before You and acknowledge that this battle is Yours. We trust You to go out to battle on our behalf and to give us wisdom in this daily fight that takes place around us. Protect us, support us and fight for us. Push back every form of darkness that has been coming against us, so that we will be fully effective for Your Kingdom purposes. (Continue to pray into this as God's Spirit directs you.)

Chapter 5: Understanding and Overcoming Woundedness

FOR IF YOU FORGIVE OTHERS FOR THEIR TRANSGRESSIONS, YOUR HEAVENLY FATHER WILL ALSO FORGIVE YOU. BUT IF YOU DO NOT FORGIVE OTHERS, THEN YOUR FATHER WILL NOT FORGIVE YOUR TRANSGRESSIONS.

MATTHEW 6:14-15

These are strong words by Jesus on a topic that affects everyone on the planet. We have devoted a whole chapter to overcoming woundedness because of how prevalent this is, and because of the serious consequence that Jesus spoke about if we hold onto unforgiveness in our hearts. Jesus stated plainly that we ourselves will not be forgiven if we fail to forgive others for the ways in which they have sinned against us.

Jesus never walked in woundedness. When we look at His life we never see Him giving into self-pity, unforgiveness, or rage for the way people were treating Him. In the natural He faced great opposition, being contradicted by His own creation, eventually being mocked, beaten and murdered by those He came to save. While He was grieved and upset at times by the pride and unbelief of the people, we do not see Him stepping into unforgiveness. The scriptures are abundantly clear that He never once went with woundedness, forgiving even those who crucified Him (Luke 23:34).

Though we may know this as a historical fact, have we ever asked ourselves the question, "Why did Jesus never give into woundedness? How was He able to rise above the temptation to give into woundedness from the hurtful actions of those around Him?"

Where do the wounds in our souls come from?

Very simply, wounds that affect our souls stem from times when we believe that someone has sinned against us. This sin may be committed with an intention of deliberately harming us. At other times wounds can take place due to something that we have perceived as a sin, when in fact the offender did not intentionally sin against us, and may not even be aware that they have caused us any harm.

An example of a perceived sin would be when two people are communicating and one makes a statement in which they intended no harm, but due to mishearing what was said, the other person takes an offense. Wounds can take place when we are insulted and it offends our pride or when someone did not trust us with something that we believe we were capable of. We may have felt dishonored by something that was said or done and this can plant a seed of unforgiveness in our hearts. Satan of course will be quick to seek to stir up thoughts of anger and unforgiveness. If we are not quick to forgive those who offend us, and in turn ask God's Spirit to heal our wound, then this seed of darkness can quickly grow into a debilitating unforgiveness and woundedness in our hearts.

When we look at the life of Christ, the key to Jesus' continuous victory over woundedness was that He never once gave into unforgiveness when He was sinned against. He never once chose to give into sin (pride in Himself and unbelief in God). He maintained a straight course, forgiving those who sinned against Him, and never once allowing for pride in His heart.

"I HAVE TOLD YOU THESE THINGS, SO THAT IN ME YOU MAY HAVE PEACE. IN THIS WORLD YOU WILL HAVE TROUBLE. BUT TAKE HEART! I HAVE OVERCOME THE WORLD."

JOHN 16:33 (NIV)

BELOVED, DO NOT BE SURPRISED AT THE FIERY ORDEAL AMONG YOU, WHICH COMES UPON YOU FOR YOUR TESTING, AS THOUGH SOME STRANGE THING WERE HAPPENING TO YOU; BUT TO THE DEGREE THAT YOU SHARE THE SUFFERINGS OF CHRIST, KEEP ON REJOICING, SO THAT ALSO AT THE REVELATION OF HIS GLORY YOU MAY REJOICE WITH EXULTATION.

1 PETER 4:12-13

Jesus promised us a life in which we would be sinned against. He promised us a life of being hated by all mankind. He Himself suffered rejection, humiliation and physical persecution, and He told us that we too would face similar difficulties. Perhaps this is one reason why He spoke about the vital importance of living a lifestyle of constant forgiveness and of praying blessing for our enemies. The apostles faced tremendous difficulties even to the point of despairing of their lives (2 Cor. 1:8). Yet somehow, in the midst of all our trials and persecutions, we are called to die to our pride and walk in real heart level forgiveness.

If we are to face such rejection, a good question to ask would be, "How many people within the Body of Christ have been properly equipped to handle the daily offenses that take place in life?" Beyond just knowing in our minds that we should "forgive those who have sinned against us", how many Christ-followers are truly prepared to face the daily onslaught that comes against our faith in the form of various offenses? For far too many, this has been the unexpected battleground that has caused us to be defeated in our walk with God.

Offenses May Come Through:

1. **Our Sin Nature**
2. **The World's System/Religious System**
   a. Spiritual leadership
   b. Marriage/parents/family
   c. Workplace
   d. Government
   e. Mindset molders (Education, media, arts...)
3. **Demonic Influence**

Many of the offenses that come against us are tied in some way to our sin nature. Therefore we will take a more extended look at how our sin nature hinders us from walking in freedom from offense. By putting to death the root of our sin nature, we can begin to experience freedom from unforgiveness in all areas of our lives no matter where the offense may be originating from, even if we did nothing to deserve what was done to us.

Our Sin Nature Often Magnifies the Sins Committed against Us

A man who is physically dead cannot be wounded nor feel pain. He is dead and all his sense of pain in the physical realm is gone. Even if his hand was harshly cut off he would have no reaction. Take this same man before he had died, and cut off his hand, and his reaction will be quite different!

In a very similar way, when we have died to ourselves, and fully surrendered our will and our way to God, then when offense comes against us, our reaction will be greatly diminished. To the degree that we have died to our pride, we will find that God can lead us to a place where we have little to no reaction at all just as Jesus did. Our simple response to being offended when we have truly died to ourselves will be to immediately choose to forgive them for their offense and move forward.

THE MIND SET ON THE FLESH IS HOSTILE TOWARD GOD; FOR IT DOES NOT SUBJECT ITSELF TO THE LAW OF GOD, FOR IT IS NOT EVEN ABLE TO DO SO, AND THOSE WHO ARE IN THE FLESH CANNOT PLEASE GOD.

ROMANS 8:7-8

Due to the fact that every human being has been born with a sin nature that is filled with pride and unbelief, when we are sinned against, if we do not choose to surrender our pride to God, then we will have a strong tendency to magnify the sin that took place against us. What may only have been an ant hill suddenly becomes Mount Everest when we talk about the offense with others. Our pride was offended and we did not like it.

If we allow our pride to dwell on the offense then we will have the tendency to blow it completely out of proportion. In time, if we do not forgive the offender and repent of the way we chose to go with our pride, then we are headed towards bondage. While we may think that our pride and unforgiveness are protecting us from future wounds, in reality, this reaction to being offended is only causing us to remain victims to those around us.

Deeper Surrender Allows Us to Overcome

We do not need to allow for this magnification of the offenses that come against us. We can choose to die to ourselves to such a degree that we no longer live (Gal. 2:20). If we will choose to die, this cuts off our sin nature from having the freedom to intensify the offenses that take place against us. Then it is simply a matter of choosing to forgive those who have sinned against us and our hearts remain whole and unaffected by those who would seek to offend us.

This is not to say that it is easy to remain in this place of being dead to ourselves when someone is shooting fiery darts of accusation. It does mean that by the empowerment given to us by God's Spirit, we have the freedom to choose to not go with our sin nature. We have the freedom to choose to forgive those who have offended us.

This should be wonderful news for all of those who have dwelled too long in a place of past wounds, wondering how we can ever be healed and restored. Jesus Christ is willing and able to heal you. Even right now this process can begin by choosing to forgive those who have wounded you. As you release forgiveness to them this opens the door for God's Spirit to forgive and heal you.

DO NOT JUDGE SO THAT YOU WILL NOT BE JUDGED. FOR IN THE WAY YOU JUDGE, YOU WILL BE JUDGED; AND BY YOUR STANDARD OF MEASURE, IT WILL BE MEASURED TO YOU.

MATTHEW 7:1-2

YOU HAVE HEARD THAT IT WAS SAID, 'YOU SHALL LOVE YOUR NEIGHBOR AND HATE YOUR ENEMY.' BUT I SAY TO YOU, LOVE YOUR ENEMIES AND PRAY FOR THOSE WHO PERSECUTE YOU, SO THAT YOU MAY BE SONS OF YOUR FATHER WHO IS IN HEAVEN; FOR HE CAUSES HIS SUN TO RISE ON THE EVIL AND THE GOOD, AND SENDS RAIN ON THE RIGHTEOUS AND THE UNRIGHTEOUS.

MATTHEW 5:43-45

What happens when our "enemies" end up being those we love? What happens when friends or family or fellow church members prove to be among those who sin the most grievously against us? What if my offender is someone that I have to be around every day? These same principals still apply. Jesus never said, "Love your enemies unless they end up being someone you never thought would be your enemy. Love your enemies unless they sin against you twenty times a day."

We have truly been called to a humanly impossible life. Jesus Himself faced the fact that one of His closest companions betrayed Him to the death. There will likely be times in our lives when those we count on the most will sin grievously against us.

Let us take on the attitude that Jesus had, that this is another opportunity for God to be glorified. We cannot control how those around us will act, but we can choose how we will respond to them. Even if your friend or family member may presently appear to be your enemy, your response of love, forgiveness, and remaining dead to your pride, will give great glory and honor to your heavenly Father.

THEN PETER CAME AND SAID TO HIM, "LORD, HOW OFTEN SHALL MY BROTHER SIN AGAINST ME AND I FORGIVE HIM? UP TO SEVEN TIMES?" JESUS SAID TO HIM, "I DO NOT SAY TO YOU, UP TO SEVEN TIMES, BUT UP TO SEVENTY TIMES SEVEN. MATTHEW 18:21-22

In His Word, Jesus gave us instructions on how we are to respond even if we are sinned against by the same person over seven hundred times a day. The solution to healing and wholeness is right in front of our eyes if we will simply put it into practice.

Easily Offended

BUT EVERYONE MUST BE QUICK TO HEAR, SLOW TO SPEAK AND SLOW TO ANGER. JAMES 1:19

LOVE IS PATIENT, LOVE IS KIND AND IS NOT JEALOUS; LOVE DOES NOT BRAG AND IS NOT ARROGANT, DOES NOT ACT UNBECOMINGLY; IT DOES NOT SEEK ITS OWN, IS NOT PROVOKED, DOES NOT TAKE INTO ACCOUNT A WRONG SUFFERED, DOES NOT REJOICE IN UNRIGHTEOUSNESS, BUT REJOICES WITH THE TRUTH; BEARS ALL THINGS, BELIEVES ALL THINGS, HOPES ALL THINGS, ENDURES ALL THINGS. LOVE NEVER FAILS.

1 COR. 13:4-8

Some of us may wonder why we become so easily offended. In the past we may have been able to endure great offense with ease. Now it seems that even the littlest sin against us cause us to blow up in anger and frustration. The Word of God tells us that love is what gives us the grace to suffer long with those who offend us.

Therefore, if we find that we are getting easily irritated, this is a sure sign that we have lost sight of God's love for us and His love for those around us. Instead of attempting to not be easily offended in our own strength, recognize that you are probably in need of a recharge of God's love for you. As you meditate on the love Jesus has for you, He will restore a willingness to bear the offenses of others.

Church Hurt

THEN ONE OF THE TWELVE, NAMED JUDAS ISCARIOT, WENT TO THE CHIEF PRIESTS AND SAID, "WHAT ARE YOU WILLING TO GIVE ME TO BETRAY HIM TO YOU?" AND THEY WEIGHED OUT THIRTY PIECES OF SILVER TO HIM.

MATTHEW 26:14-15

Jesus can relate to being betrayed by a close companion. We all know the story of Judas, but one thing that we may forget is that prior to his betrayal, Judas was a member of the disciples and someone that Jesus had shared His life with. Judas ate with Jesus, fellowshipped with Him, saw His miracles and listened to His teachings. This was a person that Jesus had poured his life into morning and night for years.

NOW HE WHO WAS BETRAYING HIM GAVE THEM A SIGN, SAYING,

"WHOMEVER I KISS, HE IS THE ONE; SEIZE HIM." IMMEDIATELY JUDAS WENT TO JESUS AND SAID, "HAIL, RABBI!" AND KISSED HIM. AND JESUS SAID TO HIM, "FRIEND, DO WHAT YOU HAVE COME FOR."

MATTHEW 26:48-50

JESUS ALSO ASKED, "JUDAS, ARE YOU BETRAYING THE SON OF MAN WITH A KISS?"

LUKE 22:48

Do you hear Jesus' words? He called Judas his friend. He asked him, "Are you betraying the Son of Man with a kiss?" Look at the level of relationship they had for Judas to select a kiss as the means of identifying Jesus. Jesus had modeled to Judas a deep intimacy with God, a supernatural power over demons and sicknesses, a love for people that caused Him to weep with their pain, and in spite of all this, Judas not only betrayed Him, but handed Him over to be killed for money. This is not to say that the person we may have been offended by in the Church is equivalent to Judas, but we can see through Jesus' relationship with Judas that He can relate to our pain.

It is one thing to be hurt by those who have no knowledge of God, but what if an offense takes place against us by a fellow brother or sister in Christ? What if the person who has offended us is even in a leadership role in Christ's Body? How are we to respond?

I know that I have personally found it easier to understand the offenses that I have received from those who do not have a relationship with God, but have at times struggled to forgive those who I believe should know better than to do what they did. I have found the enemy right there to accuse my fellow brothers and sisters to me and seek to get me to hold onto unforgiveness against them.

We must jealously guard our hearts against any unforgiveness no matter who the source was of our offense. We do not need to understand why someone offended us. Our response must be a choice to forgive. Even if our offense came through a leader in Christ's Church we have no justification in the eyes of God to hold that sin against them. We must choose to forgive. Our own soul depends on it, and we will find that when we choose to forgive them that we will be set free ourselves.

Life Altering Offenses

Some offenses may be as simple as a statement that offends our pride. Other offenses such as physical and sexual abuse, adultery and murder, can seek to alter and destroy the rest of our lives. Does the Word of God provide any solace to someone who has lost a loved one because of another person's wickedness? Does God offer hope to those who have been abused to the degree that they don't even believe that they will ever be able to function normally again?

PEACE I LEAVE WITH YOU; MY PEACE I GIVE TO YOU; NOT AS THE WORLD GIVES DO I GIVE TO YOU. DO NOT LET YOUR HEART BE TROUBLED, NOR LET IT BE FEARFUL.

JOHN 14:27

FOR JUST AS THE SUFFERINGS OF CHRIST ARE OURS IN ABUNDANCE, SO ALSO OUR COMFORT IS ABUNDANT THROUGH CHRIST. 2 COR. 1:5

God offers us a peace and a comfort that goes beyond human understanding. Jesus set the example for us as He chose to forgive His murderers in the midst of His agony on the cross (Luke 23:34). Stephen also publicly forgave those who were stoning him to death:

> *WHEN THEY HAD DRIVEN HIM OUT OF THE CITY, THEY BEGAN STONING HIM; AND THE WITNESSES LAID ASIDE THEIR ROBES AT THE FEET OF A YOUNG MAN NAMED SAUL. THEY WENT ON STONING STEPHEN AS HE CALLED ON THE LORD AND SAID, "LORD JESUS, RECEIVE MY SPIRIT!" THEN FALLING ON HIS KNEES, HE CRIED OUT WITH A LOUD VOICE, "LORD, DO NOT HOLD THIS SIN AGAINST THEM!" HAVING SAID THIS, HE FELL ASLEEP. ACTS 7:58-60*

Choosing to forgive our offenders in situations that defy all human decency is by no means easy. In fact this is humanly impossible, but by the grace that God's Spirit provides us, it is possible to forgive even the vilest offenses. In some cases, it is only as we recognize our own need for forgiveness that we will have the grace to forgive those who have offended us in this way. (For help in seeing with this perspective consider reading and meditating on Matthew 18:21-35.)

The Great Danger – Getting Offended with God

There is a tremendous danger lurking in the shadows for those who have not been properly equipped to handle the various offenses that will come against us. If we do not deal with our wounds, there is a good chance that the offenses we have held against our fellowman, will begin to become offenses that we hold against God Himself.

> *LET NO ONE SAY WHEN HE IS TEMPTED, "I AM BEING TEMPTED BY*

GOD"; FOR GOD CANNOT BE TEMPTED BY EVIL.

JAMES 1:13

TRUST IN THE LORD WITH ALL YOUR HEART AND DO NOT LEAN ON YOUR OWN UNDERSTANDING. IN ALL YOUR WAYS ACKNOWLEDGE HIM, AND HE WILL MAKE YOUR PATHS STRAIGHT.

PROVERBS 3:5-6

While in our minds we may know that God never sins. Yet, when we are still holding onto our lives, we lean heavily on our own understanding. The Word of God makes it clear that God's ways are not our ways, and His thoughts are not our thoughts (Isaiah 55:9). Therefore, we will consistently be offended by God's ways if we have not surrendered our understanding completely over to Him. Over time, even many sincere followers of Jesus Christ have experienced a hardening in their hearts against God because they believe that He has offended them in what He has allowed to happen. The truth is our offense against God must be dealt with.

"FATHER, IF YOU ARE WILLING, REMOVE THIS CUP FROM ME; YET NOT MY WILL, BUT YOURS BE DONE."

LUKE 22:42

I've included this scripture of Jesus' sincere interaction with the Father as an example of how to approach God in all honesty. You may know in your mind that it is not true that God has sinned against you, but if your heart feels as though He has offended you, then you need to talk this through with Him. He is able to handle your honest talk with Him. He already knows what you believe about Him anyway.

Tell God about your offense. Tell Him how you feel that He has wronged you. If you need to cry out and weep over how you feel that He did not come through for you then do it. After you have expressed your heart to Him, then give Him an opportunity to share His heart for you, and His perspective. I promise you, that if you will go to Him with this level of honesty you will not be disappointed. Deep wounds that you may have thought could never be overcome can be healed today.

Personal Testimony

One time when I realized that my heart was not merely offended with a person in my life, but I had actually allowed my heart to become offended with God, I shared honestly with Him about how I hated what had happened to me. I was in tears over this situation and I could see how my faith in God had diminished as a result of what took place.

Do you know what He did for me? Instead of reprimanding me for allowing offense in my heart against Him, He revealed to me that He was actually crying with me over what had happened. Then He brought to my mind the scripture, "By His wounds we are healed..." And He spoke to me, "I was wounded so that you could be set free, I have allowed you to be wounded so that you can help set others free. Can you trust Me?" The combination of His crying with me over what took place, and His sharing with me that there was an eternal purpose in why He allowed me to be wounded, had such a healing effect in my heart that words cannot explain the peace that swept over me. I was healed, and our relationship was restored!

If you realize that there is an offense in your heart against God due to some of the sins that He has allowed to be committed against you, please take this to Him in all honesty and allow Him to speak to your heart. This is such a critical issue that we need to hear from God ourselves in regards to this. Only He knows how to speak to our hearts in such a way that we are healed and able to move forward.

Conclusion

As you forgive, release, and bless those who have hurt you, God's Spirit is loosed to give you the same blessing you gave to them. No matter how devastating the wounds may have been, God is more than able to heal them. Even if you were consistently wounded for years or decades, He is capable of healing the hurts that are in your heart.

Moving Forward in Forgiveness, Repentance & Healing

1. **Repentance of our unforgiveness / Chose to forgive and pray blessing for the offender**

- Begin to ask the Holy Spirit to reveal to you the areas of your heart where you have lived in unforgiveness.

- Choose to forgive those who have offended you. Choose to pray for and bless the person or persons who have offended you. As you release and bless them in this way you will simultaneously be released and blessed.

It is always helpful to remember that forgiveness is not a feeling but a choice that we can make at any time no matter how we feel. Forgiveness is a choice of our will in which we release the offense that took place against us. We can do this when we feel peaceful and when we feel angry and upset. At all times, we can make the choice to forgive.

2. **Repentance for responding to the offense with any of our own sin (pride/unbelief)**

- Begin to ask the Holy Spirit to reveal to you any areas of pride and unbelief you have allowed as a result of the offenses against you. (Typically speaking, even though wounds often begin with the other party who has sinned against us, it is our own sin of pride, and unforgiveness that has allowed the wound to remain.)

- As we repent of our own sin (pride and unforgiveness), God's Spirit will be loosed to bring healing, restoration and freedom to every wound that we have been unable to overcome.

3. **Ask the Holy Spirit to heal our hearts of any residue of the wound.** Give God's Spirit time to reveal to you His perspective regarding the offense that you have faced. Allow God to show you what He believes about you. Trust Him to bring you through to the place of full restoration.

- After you have had time to thoroughly repent of any way in which you have reacted wrongly to being sinned against, take time to be before the Holy Spirit and allow Him to speak to your heart. Allow Him to reveal to you why this wound was allowed to remain in your heart. Ask Him to heal you.

- Especially if this wound was in the area of being diminished in the eyes of others, allow God to speak to you about how He sees you. Ask God to bring you to a place of faith in what He believes to be true of you. Allow His Spirit to change your heart so that you begin to believe what He believes about you.

BRETHREN, I DO NOT REGARD MYSELF AS HAVING LAID HOLD OF IT YET; BUT ONE THING I DO: FORGETTING WHAT LIES BEHIND AND REACHING FORWARD TO WHAT LIES AHEAD, I PRESS ON TOWARD THE GOAL FOR THE PRIZE OF THE UPWARD CALL OF GOD IN CHRIST JESUS.

PHILIPPIANS 3:13-14

In order to remain free in the area of woundedness, this is not a one-time exercise but a lifestyle that we must allow God's Spirit to teach us. We may get freed up today but what about the offense that will take place next week or next month. There is a way that God's Spirit can teach us to forget what is behind and press on toward what is ahead so that we are healed in the present, and prepared to handle future offenses. We never need to dwell on past offenses, but always ask the Holy Spirit to keep our hearts pure from any unforgiveness.

If we will allow Him to teach us how to live in this way, we like Jesus, can love our enemies and bless those who curse us. We will be free, and we will be used by God to set many other captives free!

Discussion Questions:

1. Have you ever been offended by someone to such a degree that you felt that you could never forgive them?
2. How have you seen God heal your heart as you have prayed through offenses that have taken place?

3. Have you ever been mad at God due to an offense that you felt that He was responsible for? If so, how have you sought to deal with your offense against God in light of what was shared in this chapter?

4. Have you chosen to forgive those who have sinned against you? (If not please review Matthew 18:21-35. If you did choose to forgive your offender, how has it been going walking out this ongoing forgiveness?)

Action Point:

Take time this week to pray through any offenses that you know you have not fully dealt with at the heart level. Allow the Spirit of God to set you free so that you can be forgiven, and restored back into right relationship with God. If you are having a particularly difficult time forgiving and releasing someone, please consider asking one or two other mature believers to pray with you until you are able to break free into a place of forgiveness and restoration.

Prayer Focus:

Father I acknowledge to You that I have allowed more unforgiveness and pride in my heart than I realized due to the sins that have been committed against me. I choose to repent of the way that I have allowed my heart to hold onto unforgiveness and pride. Today I choose to totally forgive those who have sinned against me. I release them to You and I pray Your blessing to be upon their lives from this point forward. I ask You to heal my heart of every way I was hurt by what took place against me. I choose to trust You to heal me and to bring about a full restoration in my life. I thank You for this healing in faith. (Continue to pray as God leads you.)

Chapter 6: Our Ultimate Hope

STORE UP FOR YOURSELVES TREASURES IN HEAVEN, WHERE NEITHER MOTH NOR RUST DESTROYS, AND WHERE THIEVES DO NOT BREAK IN OR STEAL; FOR WHERE YOUR TREASURE IS, THERE YOUR HEART WILL BE ALSO.

MATTHEW 6:20-21

AND WHAT MORE SHALL I SAY? FOR TIME WILL FAIL ME IF I TELL OF GIDEON, BARAK, SAMSON, JEPHTHAH, OF DAVID AND SAMUEL AND THE PROPHETS, WHO BY FAITH CONQUERED KINGDOMS, PERFORMED ACTS OF RIGHTEOUSNESS, OBTAINED PROMISES, SHUT THE MOUTHS OF LIONS, QUENCHED THE POWER OF FIRE, ESCAPED THE EDGE OF THE SWORD, FROM WEAKNESS WERE MADE STRONG, BECAME MIGHTY IN WAR, PUT FOREIGN ARMIES TO FLIGHT. WOMEN RECEIVED BACK THEIR DEAD BY RESURRECTION; AND OTHERS WERE TORTURED, NOT ACCEPTING THEIR RELEASE, SO THAT THEY MIGHT OBTAIN A BETTER RESURRECTION; AND OTHERS EXPERIENCED MOCKINGS AND SCOURGINGS, YES, ALSO CHAINS AND IMPRISONMENT. THEY WERE STONED, THEY WERE SAWN IN TWO, THEY WERE TEMPTED, THEY WERE PUT TO DEATH WITH THE SWORD; THEY WENT ABOUT IN SHEEPSKINS, IN GOATSKINS, BEING DESTITUTE, AFFLICTED, ILL-TREATED (MEN OF WHOM THE WORLD WAS NOT WORTHY), WANDERING IN DESERTS AND MOUNTAINS AND CAVES AND HOLES IN THE GROUND. AND ALL THESE, HAVING GAINED APPROVAL THROUGH THEIR FAITH, DID NOT RECEIVE WHAT WAS PROMISED, BECAUSE GOD HAD PROVIDED SOMETHING BETTER FOR US, SO THAT APART FROM US THEY WOULD NOT BE MADE PERFECT.

HEBREWS 11:32-40

Our Ultimate Hope is Not of This World

Hebrews 11 gives us an interesting contrast of heroes of the faith. In verses 32-35 we hear of those who saw God work great exploits through them like Gideon and David and Samuel. Then in verses 36-40 we hear of others who experienced what appeared to be defeat in the natural realm, but this resulted in eternal reward. These verses should cause us to realize that we should not place our human picture on what it means for God's Kingdom to advance through our lives. We should instead seek first His Kingdom and His righteousness and leave the physical realm results up to Him.

IF WE HAVE HOPED IN CHRIST IN THIS LIFE ONLY, WE ARE OF ALL MEN MOST TO BE PITIED.

1 COR. 15:19

ARE THEY SERVANTS OF CHRIST?—I SPEAK AS IF INSANE—I MORE SO; IN FAR MORE LABORS, IN FAR MORE IMPRISONMENTS, BEATEN TIMES WITHOUT NUMBER, OFTEN IN DANGER OF DEATH. FIVE TIMES I RECEIVED FROM THE JEWS THIRTY-NINE LASHES. THREE TIMES I WAS BEATEN WITH RODS, ONCE I WAS STONED, THREE TIMES I WAS SHIPWRECKED, A NIGHT AND A DAY I HAVE SPENT IN THE DEEP. I HAVE BEEN ON FREQUENT JOURNEYS, IN DANGERS FROM RIVERS, DANGERS FROM ROBBERS, DANGERS FROM MY COUNTRYMEN, DANGERS FROM THE GENTILES, DANGERS IN THE CITY, DANGERS IN THE WILDERNESS, DANGERS ON THE SEA, DANGERS AMONG FALSE BRETHREN; I HAVE BEEN IN LABOR AND HARDSHIP, THROUGH MANY SLEEPLESS NIGHTS, IN HUNGER AND THIRST, OFTEN WITHOUT FOOD, IN COLD AND EXPOSURE.

2 COR. 11:23-27

Though God has placed us in such a time as this in order to see His will established on the earth as it is in heaven, this earthly life is not our ultimate hope. We have an eternal hope that transcends any earthly security we may seek to find. It is this heavenly hope that gives us the courage to take the Gospel of Christ's Kingdom out to our Jerusalem, Judea, Samaria and to the ends of the earth. We know that even if we are killed in the process of taking forth the Kingdom of God, we do not die but we will live on with God forever. There is a seamless transition from this life to the next, therefore, just as Paul declared, he would rather leave his earthly body and be with Christ, but for God's purpose he remained alive.

I AM HARD-PRESSED FROM BOTH DIRECTIONS, HAVING THE DESIRE TO DEPART AND BE WITH CHRIST, FOR THAT IS VERY MUCH BETTER; YET TO REMAIN ON IN THE FLESH IS MORE NECESSARY FOR YOUR SAKE.

PHILIPPIANS 1:23-24

We ought to take a similar attitude, recognizing that it is better for us if we die but for the sake of others we are here to further the glory of Jesus Christ on the earth. In this mindset, we are freed to have our every remaining breath be expended towards Christ's eternal purposes no matter the earthly cost.

JESUS SAID TO HER, "I AM THE RESURRECTION AND THE LIFE; HE WHO BELIEVES IN ME WILL LIVE EVEN IF HE DIES, AND EVERYONE WHO LIVES AND BELIEVES IN ME WILL NEVER DIE. DO YOU BELIEVE THIS?"

JOHN 11:25-26

TRULY I SAY TO YOU, AMONG THOSE BORN OF WOMEN THERE HAS NOT ARISEN ANYONE GREATER THAN JOHN THE BAPTIST!

YET THE ONE WHO IS LEAST IN THE KINGDOM OF HEAVEN IS GREATER THAN HE. MATTHEW 11:11

Our hope is not whether or not we think we have been successful in the eyes of man. Jesus told us that up to that point none had been greater than John the Baptist, yet he only appeared to have a relatively short ministry that decreased as Jesus' ministry expanded. Ultimately he was beheaded for his faithfulness to the ways of God.

Similarly, by today's standards, Jesus' ministry would seem a colossal failure. The Son of God Himself came to the earth. How would we picture His ministry unfolding? Certainly it would involve crowds of hundreds of thousands, to millions, the breaking and bowing down of the religious system, then the world's system, and eventually worldwide domination, right?

We see in the ministry of Jesus Christ that God's ways are truly not our ways. During the earthly life of Jesus most of those in the large crowds did not continue with Him. Even among the core group one betrayed Him to the death. Rather than ending His life on an earthly throne with a crown of diamonds and gold, He ended His earthly life suffocating on a tree with a crown of thorns dug into His skull. Rather than being properly worshipped by the masses, He was mocked and beaten by the very people He was seeking to save. Even after He was raised from the dead, and revealed to the disciples, He only had 120 people following Him on the Day of Pentecost. Later, church history indicates that nearly every one of the apostles was killed in the proclamation of the Messiah.

The Value of the Blood of the Martyrs

Though we looked at Stephen briefly in the last chapter we want to learn from him once again.

AND STEPHEN, FULL OF GRACE AND POWER, WAS PERFORMING GREAT WONDERS AND SIGNS AMONG THE PEOPLE. BUT SOME MEN FROM WHAT WAS CALLED THE SYNAGOGUE OF THE FREEDMEN, INCLUDING BOTH CYRENIANS AND ALEXANDRIANS, AND SOME FROM CILICIA AND ASIA, ROSE UP AND ARGUED WITH STEPHEN...WHEN THEY HAD DRIVEN HIM OUT OF THE CITY, THEY BEGAN STONING HIM; AND THE WITNESSES LAID ASIDE THEIR ROBES AT THE FEET OF A YOUNG MAN NAMED SAUL. THEY WENT ON STONING STEPHEN AS HE CALLED ON THE LORD AND SAID, "LORD JESUS, RECEIVE MY SPIRIT!" THEN FALLING ON HIS KNEES, HE CRIED OUT WITH A LOUD VOICE, "LORD, DO NOT HOLD THIS SIN AGAINST THEM!" HAVING SAID THIS, HE FELL ASLEEP.

ACTS 6:8-9, 7:58-60

There will be times in this earthly life where our stance on behalf of the Kingdom of Jesus Christ will not look like it is victorious against our enemies. There may be times when we see great victories as Stephen did, in watching God use him to perform great wonders and signs and then within a very short period of time he was killed for his faith in Christ. At times like these, when the discipleship of the nations seems far off and the daily pressures of the enemy are shouting at us, it is vital to remember that our God sees all and will work all these things together for His good and glorious purposes (Romans 8:28).

WHEN THE LAMB BROKE THE FIFTH SEAL, I SAW UNDERNEATH THE ALTAR THE SOULS OF THOSE WHO HAD BEEN SLAIN BECAUSE OF THE

WORD OF GOD, AND BECAUSE OF THE TESTIMONY WHICH THEY HAD MAINTAINED; AND THEY CRIED OUT WITH A LOUD VOICE, SAYING, "HOW LONG, O LORD, HOLY AND TRUE, WILL YOU REFRAIN FROM JUDGING AND AVENGING OUR BLOOD ON THOSE WHO DWELL ON THE EARTH?" AND THERE WAS GIVEN TO EACH OF THEM A WHITE ROBE; AND THEY WERE TOLD THAT THEY SHOULD REST FOR A LITTLE WHILE LONGER, UNTIL THE NUMBER OF THEIR FELLOW SERVANTS AND THEIR BRETHREN WHO WERE TO BE KILLED EVEN AS THEY HAD BEEN, WOULD BE COMPLETED ALSO. REVELATION 6:9-11

It has been stated that we are now seeing more martyrs every year than at any point in the history of the church. The blood of the martyrs has often been the seed of the advancement of Christ's heavenly kingdom. The Old Testament saints and the early church understood this fact and willingly laid their lives down to advance God's Kingdom, whether they saw the fruit of it in their earthly lifetime or not.

As the eternal victory of Jesus Christ is worked in and through our lives, we must choose to stand our ground in faith and trust God to go before us, if and when persecution comes against us. As Paul wrote, whether in life or in death may we be faithful and fruitful to the end.

FOR TO ME, TO LIVE IS CHRIST AND TO DIE IS GAIN. BUT IF I AM TO LIVE ON IN THE FLESH, THIS WILL MEAN FRUITFUL LABOR FOR ME.

PHILIPPIANS 1:21-22

Worldly Success or Heavenly Success

Here is the great dilemma. Will we live for earthly success? Will we live for success in "ministry" that the religious

115

world counts as success? Or will we begin to pursue God so wholeheartedly, and with such reckless abandonment, that whether the world around us, and even the religious system, may view our labors as useless, we know in our heart of hearts that we are fulfilling the very reason why God created us.

Some of us today have not labored at all for God and therefore we need to make a decision as to whether we are going to discard the temporary in order to pursue those things that are of eternal value. Others of us have spent years and even decades laboring for God, yet we must ask ourselves the question, "How much of what I'm doing in ministry is fulfilling the deepest desire of God's heart? How much of what I'm doing in ministry is being dictated by the religious system around me? What needs to change about the way that I'm presently serving God so that He will receive greater glory through my life?"

If we will ask ourselves these hard, penetrating questions, and wait for the Holy Spirit of God to speak to our hearts with clarity, we will find that the answer that He brings to us will bring great liberty to our lives. He is our Redeemer. He is our Savior. He is the only One who is capable of maximizing the short life we have here on planet earth. May we allow His Spirit to cause us to re-examine every way we are currently spending our lives. If anything does not measure up to His eternal purpose for our lives, no matter how religious or "good" it may appear, may we not hesitate to cast it aside to lay hold of the purpose for which He laid hold of us (Phil. 3:12). We have but one life on this earth, may we not allow anything to keep us from spending it exactly the way that our Creator God desires.

We Do Not Lose Hope

FOR CONSIDER HIM WHO HAS ENDURED SUCH HOSTILITY BY SINNERS AGAINST HIMSELF, SO THAT YOU WILL NOT GROW WEARY AND LOSE HEART.

HEBREWS 12:3

The world's hope is tied to results that are here and now. In our labors for the eternal Kingdom of God, we never need to lose hope. As long as we are seeking to be obedient to what God has called us to do, we can be assured that He will bear eternal fruit through our labors. We are blessed to have the testimonies of men and women who labored in parts of the world that seemed very hard and spiritually dry. Some of them waited five, ten, twenty or more years before they saw even one soul surrender their lives to Jesus. Today, several hundred years later, these same nations of the world are some of the greatest fields of harvest with tens of thousands coming to Christ every day.

It took some who were willing to be pioneers for today's great harvests to take place. What if those pioneers were unwilling to pay the price? What if they had measured their success by the religious system that is so focused on numbers and finances? May we have the same courage in our day to pursue whatever God may be asking of us. We are never too old or too young to pursue God's calling on our lives.

NOW FOR THIS VERY REASON ALSO, APPLYING ALL DILIGENCE, IN YOUR FAITH SUPPLY MORAL EXCELLENCE, AND IN YOUR MORAL EXCELLENCE, KNOWLEDGE, AND IN YOUR KNOWLEDGE, SELF-

CONTROL, AND IN YOUR SELF-CONTROL, PERSEVERANCE, AND IN YOUR PERSEVERANCE, GODLINESS, AND IN YOUR GODLINESS, BROTHERLY KINDNESS, AND IN YOUR BROTHERLY KINDNESS, LOVE. FOR IF THESE QUALITIES ARE YOURS AND ARE INCREASING, THEY RENDER YOU NEITHER USELESS NOR UNFRUITFUL IN THE TRUE KNOWLEDGE OF OUR LORD JESUS CHRIST. FOR HE WHO LACKS THESE QUALITIES IS BLIND OR SHORT-SIGHTED, HAVING FORGOTTEN HIS PURIFICATION FROM HIS FORMER SINS. THEREFORE, BRETHREN, BE ALL THE MORE DILIGENT TO MAKE CERTAIN ABOUT HIS CALLING AND CHOOSING YOU; FOR AS LONG AS YOU PRACTICE THESE THINGS, YOU WILL NEVER STUMBLE; FOR IN THIS WAY THE ENTRANCE INTO THE ETERNAL KINGDOM OF OUR LORD AND SAVIOR JESUS CHRIST WILL BE ABUNDANTLY SUPPLIED TO YOU. 2 PETER 1:5-11

We have a strong encouragement from the scriptures and from Church history to recognize the multi-generational Kingdom that we serve. If we are truly serving faithfully in the area to which God has called us, then we can rest assured that in His perfect timing our labors will bear much fruit. Others of us may need to re-examine how we have been spending our time in order to ensure that we are truly serving God in the way that He has asked. We can be certain that as we follow God's plan for our lives we have a hope laid up for us in heaven that transcends even physical death.

Discussion Questions:

1. Is our ultimate hope in heaven or on earth? (Explain/discuss)

2. After reading this chapter, in what way do you believe you have a faulty understanding of what true success is?

118

3. How does God want you to change the way you view success? (In life, marriage/family, work, ministry etc.)

4. How should having a hope that goes behind this life cause you to live differently than those who do not have this hope? (Explain/discuss)

Action Step:

- Write down anything that God speaks to your heart as you reflect on this question, "What needs to change about the way I am presently serving God so that He will receive greater glory through my life?" Seek to put into practice anything that He asks of you.

_____

_____

_____

_____

Prayer Focus:

We want to pray for a greater revelation in our hearts regarding our ultimate hope – Jesus Christ:

Father I thank You that You have provided a hope for me that is not tied to anything in this earth. The hope you have provided for me is eternal and it is stored away in heaven and cannot be stolen. Help me to live a totally abandoned life to You. Help me to not care about any earthly standard of success, but to instead care solely and only about Your opinion of me. I trust You and I believe You to take my life and use it for Your Glory on the earth. (Continue to pray as God leads you.)

119

Section 3: Spirit-Empowered Lifestyle & Fruit

Chapter 7: The Heart of a Spirit-Empowered Life – Part 1

Two Sides to Abiding

In the last section of the book we heard of wonderful testimonies from around the nations (for example, China, Uganda, and Indonesia.) We liken these testimonies to a farming illustration in which a farmer comes to tell other farmers of the glorious harvest he has just had. But if that farmer only tells us about his great harvest, yet fails to tell us how he plowed the soil, what type of seed he used, where he bought the seed, how he cared for the plants, how he managed to keep the soil watered, how he harvested the large crop, and how he handled the distribution process, all of his stories about a large harvest do us little to no good. We are likely to remain with a similar harvest that we had before we heard his encouraging testimony.

It is very helpful to hear of these great harvests, and to learn of some of the battle that we will face, but at this point we would like to begin sharing some of the spiritual principals that God led the Body of Christ in these nations to implement which produced such a large harvest.

I first began to understand these two foundations to a lifestyle of abiding in Christ many years ago when God graciously allowed me to read Andrew Murray's classic book *Absolute Surrender*. This book explained that the victorious Christian life is not a matter of trying harder, but of surrendering further and allowing God to live all on our behalf. I was later introduced to similar teaching through various parts of the Body of Christ around the world. Under the guidance of the Holy Spirit, we believe that by learning and applying these two sides to abiding, and the corresponding spiritual keys, that you too will see similar fruit in your life, in your family and in those around you.

THE MOST IMPORTANT PURPOSE IN LIFE IS AN INTIMATE LOVE RELATIONSHIP WITH GOD

"TEACHER, WHICH IS THE GREAT COMMANDMENT IN THE LAW?" AND HE SAID TO HIM, "'YOU SHALL LOVE THE LORD YOUR GOD WITH ALL YOUR HEART, AND WITH ALL YOUR SOUL, AND WITH ALL YOUR MIND.' THIS IS THE GREAT AND FOREMOST COMMANDMENT.

MATTHEW 22:36-38

Jesus said that the most important thing of all is a wholehearted love for God. Before we discuss the level of lifestyle change that will be required to remain in a depth of relationship with Jesus, it would be helpful to have a fresh reminder that intimacy with God is the primary reason why we were created. If we have a revelation of this truth then we will become willing to make whatever lifestyle adjustments may be necessary so that we do not miss the reason we have breath in our bodies.

THIS IS ETERNAL LIFE, THAT THEY MAY KNOW YOU, THE ONLY TRUE GOD, AND JESUS CHRIST WHOM YOU HAVE SENT.

JOHN 17:3

Sometimes we can get so caught up in living our lives that we can forget the real reason why we are here on planet earth. One of the primary reasons that Jesus lived in a human body, died, and was resurrected was to restore us back into deep and real intimacy with God. Adam and Eve in the Garden before the fall is a perfect visual of God's heart for this intimacy.

GOD CREATED MAN IN HIS OWN IMAGE, IN THE IMAGE OF GOD HE CREATED HIM; MALE AND FEMALE HE CREATED THEM. GOD BLESSED THEM; AND GOD SAID TO THEM, "BE FRUITFUL AND MULTIPLY, AND FILL THE EARTH, AND SUBDUE IT; AND RULE OVER THE FISH OF THE SEA AND OVER THE BIRDS OF THE SKY AND OVER EVERY LIVING THING THAT MOVES ON THE EARTH."

GENESIS 1:27-28

THEY HEARD THE SOUND OF THE LORD GOD WALKING IN THE GARDEN IN THE COOL OF THE DAY, AND THE MAN AND HIS WIFE HID THEMSELVES FROM THE PRESENCE OF THE LORD GOD AMONG THE TREES OF THE GARDEN. THEN THE LORD GOD CALLED TO THE MAN, AND SAID TO HIM, "WHERE ARE YOU?"

GENESIS 3:8-9

The Fall destroyed our intimate relationship with God. It separated us from Him and the wisdom that we so desperately needed in order to govern the earth properly. Ever since that time, we see mankind attempting to re-establish our lost connection with our Creator.

Mankind's Quest for Restored Relationship with God

Throughout the Bible we see various means used by man in order to restore our intimacy with God. Early on in the book of Genesis we see Noah, Abram, Isaac and Jacob erecting altars (Genesis 8:20, 12:7, 26:25, 35:1). Later God gave Moses very detailed instructions on how to build the Tabernacle which would house the ark of the covenant and be a meeting place between God and man (Exodus 25:9, 39:32, 40:34). The entire nation stationed themselves in such a way that the tabernacle was at their center. Then in the time of Solomon the Temple was erected to serve as the place for restored communion between God and man (1 Kings 6:1). The Temple represented the earthly place of residence for the God of the universe.

A common element of each of these physical meeting places with God was that a blood sacrifice was required. The altars were erected to place a sacrifice on them (Gen 8:20). The Tabernacle had a place of sacrifice (Exodus 38:1), as did the Temple (2 Chronicles 4:1). In the New Covenant, the sacrifice that gives us access to restored relationship with God is the blood of Jesus Christ.

WHEN CHRIST APPEARED AS A HIGH PRIEST OF THE GOOD THINGS TO COME, HE ENTERED THROUGH THE GREATER AND MORE PERFECT TABERNACLE, NOT MADE WITH HANDS, THAT IS TO SAY, NOT OF THIS CREATION; AND NOT THROUGH THE BLOOD OF GOATS AND CALVES, BUT THROUGH HIS OWN BLOOD, HE ENTERED THE HOLY PLACE ONCE FOR ALL, HAVING OBTAINED ETERNAL REDEMPTION.

HEBREWS 9:11-12

As we surrender our lives to Jesus, the way has been paved for a full restoration of fellowship between us and God just like Adam and Eve experienced in the Garden before the fall.

BEHOLD, THE VEIL OF THE TEMPLE WAS TORN IN TWO FROM TOP TO BOTTOM; AND THE EARTH SHOOK AND THE ROCKS WERE SPLIT.

MATTHEW 27:51

Through the blood of Jesus mankind can once again commune with God. A way has been opened for us to enter the Most Holy Place. Not only can we have communion with Him, but God offers to live inside us.

DO YOU NOT KNOW THAT YOUR BODY IS A TEMPLE OF THE HOLY SPIRIT WHO IS IN YOU, WHOM YOU HAVE FROM GOD, AND THAT YOU ARE NOT YOUR OWN? FOR YOU HAVE BEEN BOUGHT WITH A PRICE: THEREFORE GLORIFY GOD IN YOUR BODY.

1 COR. 6:19-20

In the New Covenant we are told that each person who has been born again has become a Temple of the Living God. The people of God are now the physical Body of Jesus Christ because He indwells every one us. This should produce a level of awe in us that is indescribable. We ought to have a much greater sense of reverence about how we live our lives than is common among most of God's people in our day.

OUR FATHERS WORSHIPED IN THIS MOUNTAIN, AND YOU PEOPLE SAY THAT IN JERUSALEM IS THE PLACE WHERE MEN OUGHT TO WORSHIP." JESUS SAID TO HER, "WOMAN, BELIEVE ME, AN HOUR IS COMING WHEN NEITHER IN THIS MOUNTAIN NOR IN JERUSALEM WILL YOU WORSHIP THE FATHER. YOU WORSHIP WHAT YOU DO NOT KNOW; WE WORSHIP WHAT WE KNOW, FOR SALVATION IS FROM THE JEWS. BUT AN HOUR IS COMING, AND NOW IS, WHEN THE TRUE WORSHIPERS WILL WORSHIP THE FATHER IN SPIRIT AND TRUTH; FOR SUCH PEOPLE

THE FATHER SEEKS TO BE HIS WORSHIPERS.

JOHN 4:20-23

Rather than needing a physical location to meet with God, God has now come to indwell us. The Church, the Body of Christ, is now the temple of the Holy Spirit. We are the living altar, tabernacle, temple, Body – moving at the direction of His Spirit.

This truth should shake us to our core. It should change everything about the way we currently live. When we recognize that the same GOD who created the heavens and the earth, has decided to take up residence within us, nothing should be the same again. His Presence living inside us should so transform us that the person we were before coming to know Him is unrecognizable in comparison to the person we are now. This is a journey. It is a process of learning to allow Him to live His Life through us.

Be encouraged. The God who knew you before you were even in your mother's womb has an eternal plan for you that is far greater than anything you could have come up with on your own. Surrender your life more fully to Him and watch what He does in and through you. You will never be the same again.

Two Sides to Abiding in God's Spirit

Now that we have seen the vital importance of intimacy with God, we can see that we must be set free from our sin nature if we are to live in that place. The heart-beat of our sinful nature is the twin root of pride and unbelief. In order to break free from our old nature we must allow God's Spirit to lead us into a lifestyle of full surrender and complete trust in

Him. Living in relationship with God in this way breaks the power of sin in our lives and sets us free to live in real communion with Him. These two sides of a lifestyle of abiding are true no matter what nation, language, or culture we may be coming from.

#1 – A Heart of Full Surrender

Helpful prayer to remember in order to remain in this position:

"Father, all that I am and all that I have is Yours."

FOR WHOEVER WISHES TO SAVE HIS LIFE WILL LOSE IT; BUT WHOEVER LOSES HIS LIFE FOR MY SAKE WILL FIND IT.

MATTHEW 16:25

NOW BEN-HADAD KING OF ARAM GATHERED ALL HIS ARMY, AND THERE WERE THIRTY-TWO KINGS WITH HIM, AND HORSES AND CHARIOTS. AND HE WENT UP AND BESIEGED SAMARIA AND FOUGHT AGAINST IT. THEN HE SENT MESSENGERS TO THE CITY TO AHAB KING OF ISRAEL AND SAID TO HIM, "THUS SAYS BEN-HADAD, 'YOUR SILVER AND YOUR GOLD ARE MINE; YOUR MOST BEAUTIFUL WIVES AND CHILDREN ARE ALSO MINE.'" THE KING OF ISRAEL REPLIED, "IT IS ACCORDING TO YOUR WORD, MY LORD, O KING; I AM YOURS, AND ALL THAT I HAVE."

1 KINGS 20:1-4

This scripture is an illustration of a King coming in to possess a territory, and what Ben-hadad asked for was a full surrender. And King Ahab responded to his request stating, "O King; I am yours, and all that I have." In a very similar way, Jesus, the King of Kings is offering to come into our lives and take over, but what He is asking of us is a full surrender of every area of our lives.

This full surrender is a position of the heart, in which we completely abandon everything to the Lord Jesus Christ. "King Jesus, I am yours, and all that I have." In this place, every single element of our lives is given completely over to Him. We are not holding onto our past, our present, or our future. We have given up on our self-led life in every respect and we are no longer attempting to live the Christian life in our own efforts. We have surrendered our family, our friends, our social or ministry status, our means of income, our material possessions, even the state of our physical bodies is entirely given over to Him. Everything that we could possibly withhold from God is given over into His care.

This heart level position of full surrender to God is absolutely essential if we are to be used as a vessel for His glory. Any area of our lives that is not fully given over to Him is an area in which we lack authority, and is an area where we are still in bondage. If we desire to enter more fully into the Christ-Life then we must begin here.

I HAVE BEEN CRUCIFIED WITH CHRIST; AND IT IS NO LONGER I WHO LIVE, BUT CHRIST LIVES IN ME; AND THE LIFE WHICH I NOW LIVE IN THE FLESH I LIVE BY FAITH IN THE SON OF GOD, WHO LOVED ME AND GAVE HIMSELF UP FOR ME.

GALATIANS 2:20

Paul wrote that after coming to know Jesus, we are not to live our own lives anymore. He stated that the life that is lived through us is to be a life of faith in God's Spirit. This speaks of a radical, supernatural Life that would look completely different than the Christianity that is so commonly practiced and accepted in many parts of the world.

There is a way that we can give mental assent to the fact that our lives are not our own and that Jesus is the Lord of our lives. Then there is a completely different level of understanding a full surrender to God in which we begin to seek the Holy Spirit on what it means to live in this place of being dead to ourselves as a literal reality. God wants us living in the reality of truth and not merely the head knowledge of it.

FOR THE LOVE OF CHRIST CONTROLS US, HAVING CONCLUDED THIS, THAT ONE DIED FOR ALL, THEREFORE ALL DIED; AND HE DIED FOR ALL, SO THAT THEY WHO LIVE MIGHT NO LONGER LIVE FOR THEMSELVES, BUT FOR HIM WHO DIED AND ROSE AGAIN ON THEIR BEHALF.

2 COR. 5:14-15

This is a real crucifixion to every desire we ever had prior to coming under the Lordship of Jesus. This is a true giving up of our ways of handling life and a full surrender to Jesus Christ as the New Master of our lives. As we enter more deeply into the reality of being a bond-servant of Christ, we begin to experience a greater and greater manifestation of what Paul talked about in Galatians. We start to experience in reality what it means to have the literal God of the Universe living His Life in us and through us.

Not a One-Time Decision but a Lifetime Journey

WHY ARE WE ALSO IN DANGER EVERY HOUR? I AFFIRM, BRETHREN, BY THE BOASTING IN YOU WHICH I HAVE IN CHRIST JESUS OUR LORD, I

DIE DAILY. *1 COR. 15:30-31*

A common misconception that many sincere believers fall into is that this decision to surrender the entirety of our lives to God is merely a one-time decision that we are to make at the beginning of our journey with Him. Yes, there is a definitive moment when we make this decision for the first time, but this surrender is also to be the daily and moment by moment reality of our lives.

A physical realm example of this is when a man makes a very clear and public decision to enter into a lifelong covenant relationship with his wife. While this decision means he is now married, there is much more to surrendering himself to his wife than simply having a wedding ceremony. Throughout their marriage he should be deepening in his understanding of what it means to love and care for his wife from that point forward until the day that they depart from the earth. In a similar way, just as a marriage is much more than the wedding ceremony, so too is our covenant relationship with Jesus Christ. We have the daily opportunity to learn what it means to live in deepening communion and surrender to Almighty God.

As finite human beings, seeking to learn how to walk with an infinite God, it is inevitable that we will make some mistakes in this journey. One of the keys for us will be to constantly check the position of our hearts in order to see if we have strayed from the position of living in full surrender to the Lordship of Jesus Christ. If we are lacking victory in any area of our relationship with God, then we should begin to examine ourselves to where we may be holding onto our lives.

Personal Testimony:

Before each day begins, I seek to pray through the full surrender of my will, my mind, my speech, my sight and what I will hear that day. I give my body over to Him to use however He sees fit. I also seek to surrender the human relationships that He has allowed me to have. I seek to give everything that I am and will be that day to God. I ask for Him to fill me completely and to live His Life in and through me for His glory. Though this is a relatively simple interaction with God, this daily practice has proven to result in a very real empowerment of His Spirit.

Due to the fact that both sides of abiding are so important, we are going to pause half-way through this chapter to reflect on what we just read about God's request for our full surrender.

Discussion Questions:

- Are there any areas of your life that are not fully surrendered to God in this moment? Allow His Spirit to reveal to you any area of your heart that you are still holding onto:
- Your Past
- Your Present
- Your Future
- Marriage / family relationships
- Friends
- Job / ministry
- Status / position in the eyes of man
- Hurt/unforgiveness
- Finances/provision/material possessions

- Physical body/health
- Sin habits (Anger, pride, lust, greed, jealousy, appetite/gluttony, laziness)

- How would God have you deal with the areas of your life that are unsurrendered to Him?

Action Point:

Ask the Holy Spirit for His wisdom on how He desires to establish a new way of life in which you will regularly/daily allow Him to search your heart for any way in which you are not living in total and complete surrender to Him.

(Write down anything that He reveals to you as an area that you are still holding onto.)

_____

_____

_____

_____

Until this becomes the pattern of your everyday life, you may consider taking what you wrote down above and put it somewhere that you will see it on a daily basis so that you can continue to pray for this. In time, God can teach you how to live in such a way that you are constantly checking your heart for any way in which you have stepped away from the real position of a full surrender of your life to Jesus Christ.

Prayer Focus:

Pray into the need to surrender yourself completely to God. Allow Him to show you any way that you have held onto your life and lived for temporary pleasures rather than for His eternal purposes.

Father, I thank You for showing me the necessity of living in a position of total surrender to Your Holy Spirit. I acknowledge that apart from You I can do nothing, but in You nothing is impossible. I ask You to reveal to me any way in which I have not truly surrendered the fullness of my heart and life to You. I ask for your mercy on me to reveal any way in which I am presently holding onto my life and living for anything other than Your eternal purposes. Teach me to make this a moment by moment practice of allowing my life to remain completely surrendered to You. (Pray as long as you need to in order to enter into a place of full surrender to God.)

#2 – A Heart of Complete Trust

Helpful prayer to remember in order to remain in this position:

"Father, I will trust You with everything."

NOW FAITH IS THE ASSURANCE OF THINGS HOPED FOR, THE CONVICTION OF THINGS NOT SEEN.

HEBREWS 11:1

We are called to not merely surrender everything to God, but to then trust in His character, His will and His ways. A lifestyle of faith lives with a deep assurance that the things God has promised, both present and future will take place. Hebrews chapter 11 also lets us know that many of these things that we are trusting God for are "not seen" in the physical realm at the time we are exercising our faith. A life of complete trust is a life lived in total confidence in a Being who is greater than the physical realities that are in front of our eyes.

If we surrender everything to God, but fail to trust His faithfulness, our surrender will not last very long as we will quickly take things back into our own hands as soon as things do not go the way that we had hoped. We see that surrender and trust are two sides of a lifestyle that remains deeply connected to God. We won't surrender to God if we don't trust Him. If we trust Him, we will come to surrender more and more of our lives to Him.

This trust is the opposite of our sinful nature which lives in unbelief regarding God's faithfulness. We see that Satan targeted Eve by subtly convincing her that God's character was not trustworthy. At first Eve sought to fight his lies with the truth, but eventually she doubted God's character and disobeyed His explicit instructions.

THE WOMAN SAID TO THE SERPENT, "FROM THE FRUIT OF THE TREES OF THE GARDEN WE MAY EAT; BUT FROM THE FRUIT OF THE TREE WHICH IS IN THE MIDDLE OF THE GARDEN, GOD HAS SAID, 'YOU SHALL NOT EAT FROM IT OR TOUCH IT, OR YOU WILL DIE.'" THE SERPENT SAID TO THE WOMAN, "YOU SURELY WILL NOT DIE! FOR GOD KNOWS THAT IN THE DAY YOU EAT FROM IT YOUR EYES WILL BE OPENED, AND YOU WILL BE LIKE GOD, KNOWING GOOD AND EVIL." WHEN THE WOMAN SAW THAT THE TREE WAS GOOD FOR FOOD, AND THAT IT WAS A DELIGHT TO THE EYES, AND THAT THE TREE WAS DESIRABLE TO MAKE ONE WISE, SHE TOOK FROM ITS FRUIT AND ATE; AND SHE GAVE ALSO

TO HER HUSBAND WITH HER, AND HE ATE.

GENESIS 3:2-6

Satan's deception had worked, and from that point forward, mankind has had to fight the very nature within us which naturally doubts God and trusts in ourselves.

Faith Is Based on God's Truth and Not Our Emotions

If we think of faith as something that must come from our emotions then our "faith" will fluctuate daily because our emotions are not stable but can change from moment to moment. Within the same day we can have emotions of excitement and emotions of great fear and anxiety. If we are relying on our emotions to be our guide then we are in for a difficult and unnecessary roller coaster ride.

God does not want us to base our faith on our emotions. We do not need to "feel" like trusting God in order to trust Him. Faith is a choice that is based on God's character and the unchanging truth of His Word. The faithfulness of God is our certainty. Regardless of how we feel, we can always choose to trust God. He is perfectly loving, all powerful and He cares about every detail of our lives more than we can even understand.

God has given us the freedom to choose to trust Him or to not trust Him. This choice is up to us and the ramification of our decision is immense. By choosing to trust God, we rise above the storms of life like an eagle. Our choice to trust God lifts us above our circumstances. When we distrust Him, our circumstances begin to dictate our peace, hope and joy. We can begin to lose sight of reality, and open ourselves to fears, hopelessness, discouragement, confusion and all forms of darkness.

The Corrupt Fruit of Unbelief

There is a reason that the vast majority of the world lives in a constant state of negativity, pessimism and depression. This negativity stems from a sin nature that cannot trust God, because all it trusts is itself. Negativity is inevitable if we have placed our hope in fallen man. If we allow ourselves to go with our unbelief, everything can slide into becoming a worst case scenario in which we just know something bad is going to happen to us or to those we love. Many resign themselves to live a life of unfulfilled expectations.

While this may seem to be an extreme example, this type of negativity must be broken in the lives of all of those who desire to walk in the Life of God's Spirit. The Life offered to us in the Spirit of God is a life of hope, faith and joy no matter what the circumstances of life may look like around us.

We Can Choose to Trust God Regardless of Our Circumstances

WHEN THEY HAD STRUCK THEM WITH MANY BLOWS, THEY THREW THEM INTO PRISON, COMMANDING THE JAILER TO GUARD THEM SECURELY; AND HE, HAVING RECEIVED SUCH A COMMAND, THREW THEM INTO THE INNER PRISON AND FASTENED THEIR FEET IN THE STOCKS. BUT ABOUT MIDNIGHT PAUL AND SILAS WERE PRAYING AND SINGING HYMNS OF PRAISE TO GOD, AND THE PRISONERS WERE LISTENING TO THEM; AND SUDDENLY THERE CAME A GREAT EARTHQUAKE, SO THAT THE FOUNDATIONS OF THE PRISON HOUSE WERE SHAKEN; AND IMMEDIATELY ALL THE DOORS WERE OPENED

AND EVERYONE'S CHAINS WERE UNFASTENED. ACTS 16:23-26

Look at Paul and Silas in a prison cell. Here they were beaten and arrested for their faith, and yet they praised God right in the midst of what could have felt like a hopeless situation. Look at God's response to their faith in Him. He shook the foundations of the prison, and then used them to share the message of Jesus Christ with the jailer and his entire family. This is the often quoted passage where the man asks them, "Sirs, what must I do to be saved?" (Acts 16:30) Their difficult circumstances, combined with their faith, turned out to be God's opportunity to show Himself strong and receive great glory for His Name.

As God's people, we are called to remain in a place of total assurance in the character and ways of God no matter what our circumstances may look like. Even when things may not make sense to our minds, Jesus Christ has liberated us to choose to "give thanks in all circumstances" for "this is God's will for you in Christ Jesus" (1 Thess. 5:18). If we will simply begin to put the Word of God into practice in this one area of giving thanks in every circumstance, it will begin to break the grip of negativity off of our lives, and set us free to trust God in everything.

NO ONE CAN COME TO ME UNLESS THE FATHER WHO SENT ME DRAWS HIM; AND I WILL RAISE HIM UP ON THE LAST DAY. JOHN 6:44

FOR BY GRACE YOU HAVE BEEN SAVED THROUGH FAITH; AND THAT NOT OF YOURSELVES, IT IS THE GIFT OF GOD. EPHESIANS 2:8

We see through Jesus' words, and in Paul's writing in Ephesians, that we cannot take credit for our faith, but even our faith is a gift from God. Every time we have the awareness in our hearts to choose to trust God this is His grace. Therefore we should never become self-righteous in thinking our own goodness caused us to have faith in God.

If we desire to remain in the reality of Christ's Life flowing through us, then we must combine a full surrender of our lives to Him, with an ongoing decision to trust in Him completely. This faith is not of our own efforts but it must come from the Spirit of God. We must learn to lean on God's Spirit for everything. Since our faith is a gift from God, we must learn to rely on God's Spirit to grant us the necessary faith to stand firm. Perhaps one reason so many have had their faith damaged is that they were attempting to manufacture the necessary faith to stand, instead of relying on God's Spirit to provide the faith that was needed.

Example from Daily Life:

A man has come through to the place of truly surrendering all of his life to God. He surrenders his marriage, his children, his finances, his labors for God etc. Yet in his heart of hearts, he still has little to no real faith that God is trustworthy and will take care of these things. How long will he remain surrendered? How long will he live in the place of total abandonment to God?

It is clear that this man, with little to no real faith in God's character, will quickly resort to picking his life back up the moment things begin to go in a direction that is not what he had desired. In the same way, many sincere souls seek to surrender their lives to God, but in a short time find that they have picked them back up again. The problem is that they have failed to put into practice God's solution for victory. God calls us to not merely surrender the entirety of our lives to Him, but to then choose to consistently trust His unchanging character, will and ways. If we will put both of these into practice, surrendering to God, and trusting God, we will begin to experience the Spirit of God living through us a life that is humanly impossible.

Why Does God Say That This Is a Humanly Impossible Life?

WITHOUT FAITH IT IS IMPOSSIBLE TO PLEASE HIM, FOR HE WHO COMES TO GOD MUST BELIEVE THAT HE IS AND THAT HE IS A REWARDER OF THOSE WHO SEEK HIM. HEBREWS 11:6

Our human nature cannot please God because it does not trust Him and therefore will not remain surrendered to Him. When the Spirit of God comes to indwell us, He has all the faith that we need. He trusts the Father with total abandonment and rests in His goodness. He has absolutely no doubt in the Father's character and knows that He will always take everything that unfolds and use it for His glory. Therefore, if we realize that even our faith is a gift from God, then the key to greater lasting faith is to ask the Holy Spirit to reveal His faith to us.

Discussion Questions:

1. In what way have you found it difficult to trust God in the past?
2. Have you ever thought of faith as an emotion rather than a choice? If so, how do you believe that this understanding of faith affected your ability to consistently trust God?

3. Have you ever had the experience of surrendering something to God and then taking it back from Him? If so, why do you think you took it back?

4. Are you holding any bitterness in your heart towards God due to difficult or painful circumstances from the past?
   - If so, do you believe that this bitterness is keeping you from trusting Him today?
   - Are you willing to take this bitterness and share it honestly with God? (God can handle when we share our pain, our disillusionment, and our unbelief with Him. He is willing to listen and desires to help bring us through to a place where we can truly trust Him again.)

5. What is the number one thing that you think keeps you from a life of complete trust in God? Are you willing to allow God's Spirit to begin to remove this barrier from your heart so that you will be able to live a life of faith?

Action Point:

Take time to meditate on the reasons why you have had difficulty trusting God in the past. Allow His Spirit to bring reasons for your unbelief to your mind and write them down below. Use these areas of difficulty as prayer targets in the days ahead. Believe God to take every circumstance, every relationship, every reason for your unbelief, no matter how awful it may have been, and to use it for His Glory in the days ahead.

Prayer Point:

Holy Spirit, I thank You for coming to live inside of me. I thank You that You have all the faith that I need. You never doubt the character, the will, or the ways of the Father. Help me to understand Your faith so that I may walk in it all the days of my life. I choose as an act of my will to trust You to lead me into all Truth. You are Truth, and I believe You to impart into my life the same faith that You have. Teach me to choose to give thanks in every circumstance and to reject all forms of negativity so that I will not grieve You. I desire to walk in Your faith, and I believe this is more Your will than it is mine, therefore right now I receive Your unwavering faith in God the Father and God the Son. (Continue to pray as God's Spirit leads you.)

Conclusion

If you can remember the two prayers that we mentioned this will help you to check your heart to see if you are remaining in a place of abiding.

*"**Father, all that I am and all that I have is Yours.**"*

And

*"**I will trust You with everything.**"*

This heart-level position of surrender and faith is essential to our relationship with God. These two elements go hand in hand to keep us in a place of great usefulness to God's Spirit. They are both a position of the heart, and they are both humanly impossible apart from the Spirit of God. We should allow God's Spirit to teach us to do a daily heart check to see where we are in regards to our surrender and faith.

- *Is there anything in my life that I have not fully surrendered to God?*
- *Is there any way that I am not fully trusting God?*

In time, as God's Spirit teaches you to remain in a place of constant communion with Him, you will learn to keep watch over your heart position. If you ever sense that there is even the slightest break in communion, allow the two questions mentioned here to be the first place you go in order to check to see what is wrong. Chances are that your break in communion has something to do with an area of your will that is no longer choosing to surrender and trust God. As you choose to return to a place of full surrender and full trust, you can be assured that God's Spirit will fill and use you for His Glory.

A Lifestyle That Can Transform Nations

Can you begin to see how raising this standard of life over every member in the Body of Christ in any nation will begin to produce a tremendous revival in the Church that begins to affect the whole of society? This is not just another program, but a call to return to the heart of what God's Word tells us it means to follow Jesus Christ.

While this lifestyle is amazingly powerful, and while it is the Biblical standard for all true followers of Jesus Christ, how do we learn to live in this place of full surrender and complete trust? It is one thing to know these truths in our minds but how do we remain in them in reality? All too often we can find ourselves living like Paul described in Romans 7:

"FOR THE GOOD THAT I WANT, I DO NOT DO, BUT I PRACTICE THE VERY EVIL THAT I DO NOT WANT. BUT IF I AM DOING THE VERY THING I DO NOT WANT, I AM NO LONGER THE ONE DOING IT, BUT SIN WHICH DWELLS IN ME...WRETCHED MAN THAT I AM! WHO WILL SET ME FREE FROM THE BODY OF THIS DEATH?

ROMANS 7:19-20, 24

Happily Paul goes on to state that there is a place in the Spirit of God where we no longer walk according to our flesh, but the Spirit of God fulfills His purposes through us (Romans 8:1-4). In the next chapter, we will learn about several spiritual keys that God has given us to help us to remain positioned in a place of victory. These keys will help us to remain in a place of surrender and trust in Jesus Christ, and therefore bear much fruit for His Glory.

Chapter 8: The Heart of a Spirit-Empowered Life – Part 2

Keys to Abiding in Christ

I AM THE VINE, YOU ARE THE BRANCHES; HE WHO ABIDES IN ME AND I IN HIM, HE BEARS MUCH FRUIT, FOR APART FROM ME YOU CAN DO NOTHING.

JOHN 15:5

When we seek to spend time with God, our goal should be nothing more and nothing less than to connect with Him in a very real way. We cannot afford to miss connecting with Him. He is everything! All spiritual life comes from him. If we desire to have true spiritual life then we must connect with Him. He is what the world around us truly needs. They don't need more religious rhetoric. What they need is the Person of Jesus Christ. Therefore, the deeper we can tap into Him ourselves, the more of His Life we will have to give to others.

It is our intimacy with God that models what it means for the Kingdom of God to dwell among men. Whenever an individual, a family, a local congregation, or even the Body of Christ in a city is living in deep intimacy with God, His Kingdom will be manifested on the earth as it is in heaven. If we find ourselves running dry, don't blame The Vine. The Vine is right there where He has always been. He is just waiting for us to tap into His sap. It is we who have, for whatever reason, taken steps away from a lifestyle that depends exclusively on Jesus for all of life.

Personal Testimony

By God's grace, before entering formal ministry work, I had the privilege of reading a book about the life of Rees Howells, entitled "The Intercessor". It tells the story of how Rees Howells and a small group of Christ-followers, who through their lifestyle of deep and extended intercessory prayer, saw God move in miraculous ways. Eventually God built them up in their faith so that this small company of prayer warriors was affecting the course of nations. Specifically during World War II their prayers were used mightily by God to avert disaster and help to establish the Kingdom of God on the earth. This book made such an impression on me that I began to assume that everyone understood that one of our most important functions in "ministry work" was the work of intercessory prayer.

I was soon rudely awakened to the reality that in many sectors of the western world, a lifestyle of prayer and intercession is too little preached and practiced. I began to see that the pattern of ministry in most sectors of the Body of Christ was far from a lifestyle of abiding in Christ. Eventually this religious culture of planning and strategizing without really praying and waiting on God, began to get the better of me.

In time I had almost completely forgotten what God had revealed to me about the importance of prayer and intimacy with Him. I found myself running head long into a lifestyle of unfruitfulness in life and ministry. Trying this and that strategy which all resulted in such little fruit that even I myself was

146

struggling with personal compromise, let alone helping to bring others into a state of revival and transformation.

In retrospect, I look back on this season as God's means of:

A. Showing me the danger of the religious system.

B. Giving me His compassion and grace for those who are still bound by the dictates of the religious system as I myself have personally experienced it.

In a recent conversation with a missionary working in the Middle East among Muslims, without batting an eye he stated that each of the missionaries at their mission base spends at least 6 hours a day before the Lord ministering to Him before even going out into the marketplace to win souls. We may consider that extreme in the western world, but could our lack of fruitfulness personally, in our families, and sphere of influence be tied to a lack of depth in our connection with God? What if we too began to allow the Holy Spirit to so order our lives that we daily started to spend hours with Him in extended worship, prayer, and meditation in His Word? Would we not see a tremendous increase in the eternal fruitfulness of our lives?

Overcoming Sin through Intimacy with God

THEREFORE DO NOT LET SIN REIGN IN YOUR MORTAL BODY SO THAT YOU OBEY ITS LUSTS, AND DO NOT GO ON PRESENTING THE MEMBERS OF YOUR BODY TO SIN AS INSTRUMENTS OF UNRIGHTEOUSNESS; BUT PRESENT YOURSELVES TO GOD AS THOSE ALIVE FROM THE DEAD, AND YOUR MEMBERS AS INSTRUMENTS OF RIGHTEOUSNESS TO GOD. FOR SIN SHALL NOT BE MASTER OVER YOU, FOR YOU ARE NOT UNDER LAW

BUT UNDER GRACE. ROMANS 6:12-14

The grace of God is the supernatural empowerment to live in victory over sin. Far too many of us in the Body of Christ are still attempting to live the Christian life in our own strength because we have failed to understand the need to abide in Christ. As a result, when difficulties arise, or besetting sin seeks to keep us in bondage, the only thing that we know how to do is to seek to overcome in our own power. We can be sure that we are attempting to overcome in our own power whenever we fail to have victory over sin. The Holy Spirit of God has never sinned once. Therefore, if we are failing to overcome sin, we can be sure that it is still us trying instead of us trusting God's Spirit to live His Life through us.

What if instead of focusing on our weaknesses and our inability to overcome sin, we simply sought to fill our lives with the things of God. Is it possible that this dramatically different approach to overcoming sin would cause us to be set free? Is it possible that if we sought to draw into a deeper intimacy with God, that we could watch His Life overcome sin on our behalf?

Personal Testimony

I used to have a little piece of paper on the side of my bed when I was growing up. On the paper was a code that only I understood. It stated "SW10TJDJD". This code was my attempt to overcome sin. The meaning of these words was, "Stop, wait 10 seconds, think about what Jesus would do, then do what Jesus would do." It seemed so good and godly to have this means of seeking to do what God wanted me to do. The only problem was that it did not work!

I tried this method for years always failing to overcome sin on many levels of my life. I had not been equipped in what it meant to die to myself and trust God's Spirit to live all through me. Instead, with all my human resolve, I was focusing on the besetting sins around me, gathering as much strength as I could, and attempting to overcome sin on my own. This pattern led to years of bondage because it was me, in all my human power, attempting to live the Life that only God can live.

Are you like me? Have you ever found yourself attempting to be a "good Christian" through your own efforts? It is not that we are to excuse sin because it is humanly impossible to overcome it. Instead, God expects us to overcome sin, but not through our own efforts. As we discussed in the last chapter, He expects us to overcome sin through our trust in Him. He will live a victorious life through us if we will learn how to abide in Him.

HE WHO HAS AN EAR, LET HIM HEAR WHAT THE SPIRIT SAYS TO THE CHURCHES. TO HIM WHO OVERCOMES, I WILL GRANT TO EAT OF THE TREE OF LIFE WHICH IS IN THE PARADISE OF GOD.'

REVELATION 2:7

HE WHO HAS AN EAR, LET HIM HEAR WHAT THE SPIRIT SAYS TO THE CHURCHES. HE WHO OVERCOMES WILL NOT BE HURT BY THE SECOND DEATH.'

REVELATION 2:11

Based on the Word of God, overcoming sin is not optional attire. We must overcome the three battlefields that seek to hinder the expansion of Christ's Kingdom. We must trust God to move us beyond our past wounds. The main issue is to learn how God expects us to overcome.

As we discussed in the last chapter, the key to overcoming is keeping our hearts in a place of full surrender and complete trust in God. But the question arises, "How do I remain there?" It is nice to know that we should live in that place in our minds, but what are some practical components of a Godly lifestyle that can be applied in order to keep us in the reality of being dead to ourselves and alive in Christ?

Personal Testimony

When I first came to really know the Person of Jesus Christ after decades of just learning about Him, it completely changed the course of my life. I wanted to spend every waking minute with Him. His Word was living and active in my life and I drank it in like water. The words of the Bible seemed to jump off the page and straight into my heart. I felt that God was speaking directly to me when I read the Bible. I would spend hours in prayer, just talking to God, loving on Him, and worshipping Him with songs that I came up with right then and there. As a single missionary, I would take some days to just be before the Lord, interceding for His purposes in the nations, and crying out for lost souls to come to faith in Christ. It was a vibrant and active relationship with the Living God!

At that time I assumed that this relationship would go on like this forever. No one had taught me about the "Spiritual

Keys to intimacy with God". It was just that the Spirit of God had so transformed my heart's desires that all I wanted was Him. What I didn't see coming was several areas of darkness that began to slowly snuff out the life and intimacy I had with God.

Enemy number one that snuck in without any warning was the religious system. I began to be elevated in my ministry position, moving from a beginning missionary, to a youth pastor, to an assistant pastor, to a regional overseer, to a national coordinator, to functioning globally. Wow, I must be important and successful right?

Yet somehow I began to buy into a lie. The lie that busyness and ministry activity translate into a life that is somehow pleasing to God. More and more of my time was spent in ministry activities, and those times of living fellowship in the Word of God, deep intercessory prayer, and spontaneous worship started to seem like a distant memory. I would still be in the Word on an almost daily basis but it was dry and like I was out in a desert somewhere, picking up a few drops of water so that I could carry on another day. At times I found myself preaching more out of my past experience than my present reality. During this same time period, I began to realize that I did not know how to fulfill my role as a husband, as a father to our four children, as a full time minister and simultaneously remain in a place of deep abiding in Jesus.

Where had the intimacy with God gone? Where did my first love go?

"I KNOW YOUR DEEDS AND YOUR TOIL AND PERSEVERANCE, AND THAT YOU CANNOT TOLERATE EVIL MEN, AND YOU PUT TO THE TEST THOSE

*WHO CALL THEMSELVES APOSTLES, AND THEY ARE NOT, AND YOU
FOUND THEM TO BE FALSE; AND YOU HAVE PERSEVERANCE AND HAVE
ENDURED FOR MY NAME'S SAKE, AND HAVE NOT GROWN WEARY. BUT
I HAVE THIS AGAINST YOU, THAT YOU HAVE LEFT YOUR FIRST LOVE.
THEREFORE REMEMBER FROM WHERE YOU HAVE FALLEN, AND
REPENT AND DO THE DEEDS YOU DID AT FIRST."*

REV. 2:2-5

It is humbling to admit, but God had to take me back to square one before He could use me again for the purposes that were in His heart. He began to show me every way in which the religious system demanded my time in such a way that it nearly forced me out of a place of deep and real intimacy with God. Can you see the madness in this? A soul that is living in real intimacy with God's Spirit is the only means of ministering God's Life to others. Yet the way the religious system is set up in far too many places of the earth causes those who are "in ministry" to be in activities to such a degree that they have little to no time for intimacy with God. It is a trap that has taken out some of the most sincere brothers and sisters in the Lord. It has caused countless numbers of souls to leave ministry altogether because they see the madness of it all.

For those who can relate to this testimony, and especially for those in some form of ministry service, I implore you, as your fellow brother in Christ, do not under any circumstances allow the work of ministry to rob you of your first love for God. If you see this has taken place, stop what you are doing, and no matter what the reaction of those around you, pull back into Him and allow Him to restore your intimacy with Him. There is no sense of going on in ministry when we *ourselves are in need of ministry. Stop, repent and return wholeheartedly to Jesus. Allow Him to restore you and rebuild your intimacy with Him.*

If you will do this, the work that He does in and through you will exceed anything you were doing previously! Intimacy first, then fruitfulness, this is true in human relationships and it is true in our relationship with God (John 15). In the natural, a husband and wife do not have a child without first having intimacy. Neither can we be spiritually fruitful and multiply without first having intimacy with God.

God's Spirit Gives Us the Desire to Seek Him

As we transition into our discussion on the Spiritual Keys it should be noted that these are not listed here to cause us to go into any form of human striving to attempt to put them into practice. Just as this testimony illustrates, these keys were being put into practice in my life without much formal teaching. The reason I was utilizing these spiritual keys was because they were the desire of my heart and not something I felt like I was forced to do. There is something of great importance in this statement. Only as we desire something will we pursue it. A lack of seeking God often reveals our lack of desire for Him.

As long as these Spiritual Keys are a "have to" and not a "want to", then something is wrong. There is some form of darkness (pride/unbelief, the world's system, satanic attack) that is keeping us from allowing God's Spirit to stir a deeper desire in our hearts for Him. As this darkness is repented of, and God's Spirit is loosed to kindle a desire in our hearts for Him, no one and nothing will be able to keep us from pursuing Him. Therefore, as we prepare our hearts to lay hold of these

153

spiritual keys, let's begin with a time of prayer for our hearts to be cleansed and a desire for God to be kindled.

Prayer Focus

Father, I thank You that You have provided spiritual means for me to have an intimate relationship with You. I ask that You would reveal any darkness that I have allowed in my heart that has been keeping me from desiring to seek You. Reveal to me any pride and unbelief in my heart. Reveal any way that the world's system or the religious system has stifled my hunger for You. Show me any way that demonic forces have sought to keep me from pursuing You.

I choose to turn away from this darkness right now and I trust You to restore our relationship to a place of intimacy. Right now, I receive from You the desire to seek Your face. I thank You in advance for rekindling this desire in my heart for You and I look forward to pursuing You in the days ahead.

Having the desire for an intimate relationship with God is critical. When we have a hunger for God, then each of these aspects of seeking Him becomes like gasoline to the fire. As we begin to put these into practice our desire for God will grow and grow until we are consumed by Him!

Jesus is The Way to intimacy with God. If we will allow His Spirit to begin to lead our times of extended fellowship, He will grow us more in one month than we would have grown in a year or a decade through our own efforts. A year of training by the Spirit of God is equal to decades elsewhere. In fact the Word of God says one day in His Presence is greater than a thousand days elsewhere (Psalm 84:10). Think of the multiplication of your time if you spend it in God's Presence. Based on the Word of God, every day in God's Spirit is equal to three years elsewhere. Therefore you can accomplish more in one week in the empowerment of God's Spirit than others will accomplish in 20 years!

Spiritual Keys to a Lifestyle of Intimacy with God

While there are many things that are critical to an intimate relationship with God, we are just going to focus on 5 Spiritual Keys that will help to ensure that we continue to progress in our journey of Christ-likeness. Some devotional books might title these aspects of our relationship with God "disciplines". The word discipline often implies a sense of having to do something even though we really do not want to do it. Therefore, we are calling them "spiritual keys" to indicate that they are a blessed gift from God. Each one of them can be pictured as a key that opens a door to journey into a closer relationship with Jesus Christ. These keys help us to position our lives in such a way that God's Spirit is released to live more and more of His Divine life through us. The reality is that only God's Spirit can lead us deeper into Himself, but He has given us spiritual resources to position our lives for His Spirit to work.

These spiritual keys help us to remain grounded in our faith. Without using these keys the spiritual battle that takes place in life is far too great. In time, if they are not established in our lifestyle, we will often find ourselves knocked off the foundation of our faith. For some, this may not result in obvious outward rebellion, but our hearts may subtly drift to a place where we are holding onto our lives and failing to trust God.

I have deliberately not numbered these keys to abiding so as not to create a specific form or singular way of approaching God. From moment to moment, only the Spirit of the Living God has the right and ability to direct us into the Person of Truth. The moment we begin to set a form that God Himself has not asked of us, we begin to step away from the source of Life and create our own means of seeking to remain near to God. We will notice the lack of freshness in our times with God whenever we allow a form that does not cause us to truly depend on Him to fill us with His Life.

If we desire to walk in a greater measure of the Life of God's Spirit, then we must become increasingly sensitive to His guidance. Only He knows all the specifics of that particular moment in time, and only He knows the specific aspects of Jesus, the Person of Truth, that we need right then and there. Therefore, when you are seeking to engage with God, begin by simply going to Him as a child. Share your heart with Him and begin to open yourself to the leading of His Spirit. He cannot fail to lead you into His Life and liberty.

Spiritual Key: A Lifestyle of Praise and Worship

YOU WORSHIP WHAT YOU DO NOT KNOW; WE WORSHIP WHAT WE KNOW, FOR SALVATION IS FROM THE JEWS. BUT AN HOUR IS COMING, AND NOW IS, WHEN THE TRUE WORSHIPERS WILL WORSHIP THE FATHER IN SPIRIT AND TRUTH; FOR SUCH PEOPLE THE FATHER SEEKS TO BE HIS WORSHIPERS. GOD IS SPIRIT, AND THOSE WHO WORSHIP HIM MUST WORSHIP IN SPIRIT AND TRUTH."

JOHN 4:22-24

REJOICE ALWAYS; PRAY WITHOUT CEASING; IN EVERYTHING GIVE THANKS; FOR THIS IS GOD'S WILL FOR YOU IN CHRIST JESUS.

1 THES. 5:16-18

We don't want to stop at the point of just singing a few songs with our lips, but we want to enter into a deep place of true heart-level worship of our King. We want to learn what it means to lose ourselves in His Presence and give ourselves unashamedly over to Him. It is out of these deep encounters with God's Spirit in worship that we are molded and shaped more and more into the image of Jesus Christ.

I heard something in Uganda related to praise and worship that continues to stick out to me. They have a phase in which they say, "Never miss an opportunity to praise the Lord!" When we realize that worship will be a part of our lives forever and ever, we would be wise to allow God's Spirit to take us deeper in worship than we have ever known. We will never regret allowing the Spirit of God to take us past where we've been into the depths of His Life.

Practical Instructions for a Lifestyle of Praise and Worship:

- The best practical tip is to begin asking the Holy Spirit how He would have you change your lifestyle, and specifically your way of speaking, to become one of praise and worship.

- Practice choosing to give thanks in every circumstance. Continue to choose to do this whether or not you understand the value in it at first. Ask the Holy Spirit to build this into you as part of your lifestyle.

- Practice looking at people and situations around you not as you see them, but ask God how He sees them. Give Him thanks for what He is desiring to do in the people and circumstances around you.

- Consider playing worship music to keep your mind focused on praising God.

Spiritual Key: A Lifestyle of Waiting and Listening to God's Spirit

MY SHEEP HEAR MY VOICE, AND I KNOW THEM, AND THEY FOLLOW ME. JOHN 10:27

I HAVE MANY MORE THINGS TO SAY TO YOU, BUT YOU CANNOT BEAR THEM NOW. BUT WHEN HE, THE SPIRIT OF TRUTH, COMES, HE WILL GUIDE YOU INTO ALL THE TRUTH; FOR HE WILL NOT SPEAK ON HIS OWN INITIATIVE, BUT WHATEVER HE HEARS, HE WILL SPEAK; AND HE WILL DISCLOSE TO YOU WHAT IS TO COME.

HE WILL GLORIFY ME, FOR HE WILL TAKE OF MINE AND WILL DISCLOSE IT TO YOU. JOHN 16:12-14

As we enter into a place of heart-level worship, we begin to empty ourselves of our human understandings. As our human desires and ways are laid down, we can begin to hear the wisdom and ways of God. As we wait before the Lord with a surrendered will, we are prepared to hear clearly what the Spirit of God is speaking to His Church. In this place we receive clear direction from God regarding His character, His purposes, and His ways.

"I HAVE MANY THINGS TO SPEAK AND TO JUDGE CONCERNING YOU,

BUT HE WHO SENT ME IS TRUE; AND THE THINGS WHICH I HEARD FROM HIM, THESE I SPEAK TO THE WORLD."

JOHN 8:26

Jesus stated that He only spoke as He first heard from His Father. Likewise, hearing clearly from the Spirit of God is absolutely essential for every Christ-follower. This is not relegated to the responsibility of a pastor. All of God's children must learn to be attuned to the voice of God so that they can walk in the confidence that comes from knowing that their thoughts, words, and actions are led by God's Spirit.

CEASE STRIVING AND KNOW THAT I AM GOD; I WILL BE EXALTED AMONG THE NATIONS, I WILL BE EXALTED IN THE EARTH.

PSALM 46:10

YET THOSE WHO WAIT FOR THE LORD WILL GAIN NEW STRENGTH; THEY WILL MOUNT UP WITH WINGS LIKE EAGLES, THEY WILL RUN AND NOT GET TIRED, THEY WILL WALK AND NOT BECOME WEARY.

ISAIAH 40:31

Taking the time to wait on God and hear His will is very critical both in our personal relationship with Him, as well as in our partnership in His work. Knowing His will is what gives us the strength to stand. Knowing the will of God causes us to be able to keep going and not get weary even when those around us may be falling down and failing to persevere.

Only as we know that we have heard from God will we have the supernatural faith that we need in order to step out and continue to trust God's instructions. As we persist in

159

obedience to the specific direction God has given us, victory will result. Many testify that it was only as they heard clearly from God's Spirit, and persevered in His instructions, that they saw breakthroughs take place that had not come in any other way.

Learn to rest in God. Get comfortable in His Presence. Take the time to just be before Him and learn to allow His Spirit to set the agenda for your time together. When we begin to allow God's Spirit to lead our time spent together, we will come to realize just how good a leader He is.

Practical Instructions for a Lifestyle of Waiting and Listening to God's Spirit:

- Take the time necessary to quiet yourself before the Lord.

- Actively trust Him to lead your time together.

- Take time to surrender your own will in regards to anything that you may be seeking God's wisdom on. (Until our will is truly surrendered, hearing from God will be difficult as we are prone to insert our own desires into the process of seeking to hear from Him.)

- Once you have come into a surrendered state of heart, ask God to speak to you and wait long enough to hear from Him with clarity. Don't pull away too soon as the revelation of God often takes time to unfold. The longer we wait, the fuller the picture He will be able to give to us.

- Write down anything that you believe that you have heard from Him. This will help to solidify what God has spoken to you. Use this written record of what He has spoken as a means to pray into what God has said.

- Allow the Holy Spirit the liberty to expand on any revelation that He has already given to you, through the Word, prayer, circumstances, and the rest of the Body of Christ, recognizing that each of us only sees in part (1 Cor. 13:12).

- On critical decisions it is important to involve at least 2-3 other spiritually sensitive believers who do not have a vested interest in the outcome to join you in seeking God's will.

Spiritual Key: A Lifestyle of Being Filled with the Word of God

HOW BLESSED IS THE MAN WHO DOES NOT WALK IN THE COUNSEL OF THE WICKED, NOR STAND IN THE PATH OF SINNERS, NOR SIT IN THE SEAT OF SCOFFERS! BUT HIS DELIGHT IS IN THE LAW OF THE LORD, AND IN HIS LAW HE MEDITATES DAY AND NIGHT. HE WILL BE LIKE A TREE FIRMLY PLANTED BY STREAMS OF WATER, WHICH YIELDS ITS FRUIT IN ITS SEASON AND ITS LEAF DOES NOT WITHER; AND IN WHATEVER HE DOES, HE PROSPERS.

PSALM 1:1-3

HOW CAN A YOUNG MAN KEEP HIS WAY PURE? BY KEEPING IT ACCORDING TO YOUR WORD. WITH ALL MY HEART I HAVE SOUGHT YOU; DO NOT LET ME WANDER FROM YOUR COMMANDMENTS. YOUR WORD I HAVE TREASURED IN MY HEART, THAT I MAY NOT SIN AGAINST YOU. PSALM 119:9-11

Clearly a life that is filled with the Word of God is a key to keeping our hearts on fire for God. While many have a discipline of regularly reading God's Word, this spiritual key is encouraging us to go much deeper than the normal routine. May we make it a daily priority to spend extended time in the Word of God. May we make it our goal to allow God's Spirit to teach us how He desires the Word of God to fill us.

At times the Person of the Holy Spirit may lead us to specific passages in which He wants to speak an urgent message that is essential in that moment. At other times He may lead us to study a particular aspect of His character so that our faith is built up for what He knows we will face next. At other times He may lead us to meditate deeply on a single verse, or take time to read large sections of the Bible in order to get a fuller picture of His character throughout history. At other times God may lead us to memorize a particular scripture. In all of this, we should never forget that we have the Author of the book right there with us as we are reading. If we need clarity on a particular passage, why not ask Him for His insight? If we are confused, or we need Him to refresh us so that His Word comes alive again why not ask Him to do this?

In all the various ways that the Holy Spirit may lead us to interact with the Word of God, He is using this to fill our minds with the mind of Christ (1 Cor. 2:16).

Filling Our Minds with the Promises of God's Word

The Word of God contains important promises that are available to everyone who has exchanged their life for the life of Christ. It is helpful to learn what God believes about us so that our faith will be stirred to believe as He believes. There are whole books written on this topic but in this section we just want to look at a few key promises that God has given to those who have entered the New Covenant by surrendering to His Lordship and trusting Jesus Christ for the forgiveness of their sins. Let us begin to fill ourselves with what God Himself has declared about us.

Based on the Word's of God, as His child you are:

- **Loved** (John 3:16, 13:34, 15:9, 15:12, 16:27, 17:26, Romans 5:5, 5:8, 8:35-39, 1 Cor. 13:1-13, Eph. 2:4, Col 3:12, Thes. 1:4, 1 John 4:11, 4:16, 4:19, Rev. 1:5)
- **Forgiven** (Acts 2:38, 10:43, Eph. 1:7, Col. 1:14)
- **Justified and qualified** (Romans 3:24, 3:28, 5:1, 5:9, 10:10, 1 Cor. 6:11, Gal 2:16, 3:24, Col. 1:12, Titus 3:7)
- **Called to be holy/sanctified/set apart/blameless** (Acts 26:18, Romans 1:7, 5:16, 1 Cor. 1:2, 6:11, Eph. 1:4, 3:18, 5:3, Phil. 1:1, Col. 1:2, 1:22, 3:12, 1 Thes. 4:7, 2 Tim. 1:9, Hebrews 10:10, 10:14, 12:14, 1 Peter 1:16, 2 Peter 3:11)
- **Protected/Provided for** (John 17:11, 15, Romans 5:17, 2 Thes. 3:3)
- **Appreciated/celebrated/honored by God/respected** (John 12:26, 17:22, 1 Cor. 12:24, Hebrews 2:7)
- **Glorified** (John 17:22, Romans 8:30)
- **Called and chosen** (John 15:19, Romans 8:30, 8:33, 11:5, Eph. 1:11, Col. 3:12, 1 Thes. 1:4, 1 Peter 2:9, Rev. 17:14)
- **Indwelt with the Holy Spirit** (Luke 11:13, John 14:16-20, Acts 2:38, Eph. 4:30, 2 Tim. 1:14)
- **A new creation** (2 Cor. 5:17, Gal. 6:15)
- **Heirs of God and co-heirs with Christ/awaiting a glorious inheritance** (Romans 8:17, Eph. 1:18)

- **Taken out of the kingdom of darkness and brought into the kingdom of Light** (Eph. 5:8, Col. 1:13, 1 Thes. 5:5, 1 Peter 2:9)
- **A part of Christ's Body** (1 Cor. 12:27)
- **The Messiah's official representative/ambassador/and a royal priest** (2 Cor. 5:18-20, 1 Peter 2:4-5, 9, Rev. 5:9-10)
- **Blessed with every spiritual blessing** (Eph. 1:3)
- **Seated with Christ in the heavenly places** (Eph. 2:6)
- **More than a conqueror** (Romans 8:37)
- **The light of the world** (Matthew 5:14)

Just one of these great promises is enough to transform our entire lives. If you will consistently take time to mediate on what God has spoken about you in His Word, you will find yourself beginning to live out of a place of being filled and empowered by His Spirit. Consider taking time to mediate on these great promises on a regular basis, and lay claim to them before God in prayer as this is His provision for you in the New Covenant.

Personal Testimony

For many years I sought to mentally claim these promises regarding the New Covenant yet I found myself still struggling with sin. Though these promises brought encouragement I was failing because I did not know that these promises are only made an experiential reality as we are abiding in Christ. It was only after several years of failure that I came to the realization that without fully surrendering my life to God, I could not live in the reality of what God has promised me.

Though I was verbally claiming these promises, I failed to experience their reality because my life was still my own.

For instance, I could claim that I am justified and set apart for holiness, but if by my choices I opened a door for lust or anger, then I effectively stepped back into my sin nature which is just as corrupt as it ever was prior to Christ. I was to blame for not experiencing what God had promised me. As I began to surrender myself more fully to God's Spirit, these promises began to become the reality of my life.

These promises are available to anyone who will abide in the Life of Jesus Christ, because they are true "in Christ." In this way, we see how vital it is to remain deeply connected to God's Spirit because all of our lives are dependent upon Him. It is only as we surrender to God and then trust Him that each of His promises become like spiritual diamonds and gold.

ALL SCRIPTURE IS INSPIRED BY GOD AND PROFITABLE FOR TEACHING, FOR REPROOF, FOR CORRECTION, FOR TRAINING IN RIGHTEOUSNESS.

2 TIM. 3:16

FOR THE WORD OF GOD IS LIVING AND ACTIVE AND SHARPER THAN ANY TWO-EDGED SWORD, AND PIERCING AS FAR AS THE DIVISION OF SOUL AND SPIRIT, OF BOTH JOINTS AND MARROW, AND ABLE TO JUDGE THE THOUGHTS AND INTENTIONS OF THE HEART.

HEBREWS 4:12

The Word of God can rightly be compared to an endless warehouse filled with spiritual treasures. These spiritual treasures reveal various facets about the character of God, His will for Creation, and His ways of fulfilling His plans. The Word of God gives clear guidance for virtually every aspect of life on earth. It contains endless treasures about the knowledge of God because the Author is living inside of us as we go through the Word. Just when we may have thought we have exhausted the treasures of the Bible, God's Spirit leads us to understand a new facet of Him that we had never seen before. In short, He is able to keep our times in His Word living and active (Hebrews 4:12).

As this element of a Spirit-Empowered lifestyle was implemented in Uganda the Lord spoke to them that a time would come when they would be so saturated in the Word of God, that whenever they spoke, all that would come out would be His Word. May we allow the Holy Spirit to lead us into a lifestyle that interacts with the Word of God in a vibrant way so that we can be filled with God's perspective. As God's Word comes in it will expose what needs to be uprooted and removed, as well as raise up what needs to be built and strengthened.

Practical Instructions for a Lifestyle of Being Filled with the Word of God:

- **Begin by asking God to place a hunger in your heart for His Word.** As He answers your prayer, He will give you the desire to read His Word so that this shifts from being something you are supposed to do, to being something you look forward to.

- Ask God's Spirit how He would have you fill your life with the Word of God.

There are many ways that the Holy Spirit may choose to take the Word of God and help us to receive it into our hearts.

WHILE THEY STOOD IN THEIR PLACE, THEY READ FROM THE BOOK OF

THE LAW OF THE LORD THEIR GOD FOR A FOURTH OF THE DAY; AND
FOR ANOTHER FOURTH THEY CONFESSED AND WORSHIPED THE LORD
THEIR GOD.   NEHEMIAH 9:3

A. Read large amounts of scripture

(For example, reading 5-10 chapters at a time)

If reading that much on your own is difficult, another way to consume large amounts of scripture is to listen to a live person reading from the Word or through an audio/video resource.

THIS BOOK OF THE LAW SHALL NOT DEPART FROM YOUR MOUTH, BUT
YOU SHALL MEDITATE ON IT DAY AND NIGHT, SO THAT YOU MAY BE
CAREFUL TO DO ACCORDING TO ALL THAT IS WRITTEN IN IT; FOR THEN
YOU WILL MAKE YOUR WAY PROSPEROUS, AND THEN YOU WILL HAVE
SUCCESS. JOSHUA 1:8

B. Meditation

When reflecting on the scriptures you have read ask yourself some simple questions, "How did I see God in what I just read? Based on what I just read, what did I learn about God's character? Based on what I just read what lifestyle adjustments do I need to make in order for my life to be in alignment with the will and ways of God? Based on what I just read, what does God believe to be true about me?"

FOR EZRA HAD SET HIS HEART TO STUDY THE LAW OF THE LORD AND
TO PRACTICE IT, AND TO TEACH HIS STATUTES AND ORDINANCES IN
ISRAEL.

EZRA 7:10

C. Study

Allow the Holy Spirit to direct you as to how He wants you to study His Word. There may be times in which He has you study certain themes that will take weeks or months, such as studying the lifestyle of Jesus Christ. As His Spirit leads you in the study of His Word, He will build a deep understanding of this theme in your heart.

AND THE TEMPTER CAME AND SAID TO HIM, "IF YOU ARE THE SON OF GOD, COMMAND THAT THESE STONES BECOME BREAD." BUT HE ANSWERED AND SAID, "IT IS WRITTEN, 'MAN SHALL NOT LIVE ON BREAD ALONE, BUT ON EVERY WORD THAT PROCEEDS OUT OF THE MOUTH OF GOD.'"

MATTHEW 4:3-4

D. Memorization

Consider taking time to memorize the Word of God and allow it to fill your heart and mind. If you will fill yourself with God's Word, just as Jesus experienced, it will come to your mind in your hour of need.

Each of these ways of receiving the Word of God has a unique quality and importance therefore we would encourage you to regularly ask the Holy Spirit to help you remain in a place where you are being filled with His Word.

IF YOU ABIDE IN ME, AND MY WORDS ABIDE IN YOU, ASK WHATEVER YOU WISH, AND IT WILL BE DONE FOR YOU.

JOHN 15:7

Jesus said that if His words remained in us, that we would have power in prayer. There are areas of the world where people do not have access to a Bible and some believers even risk their lives to hold onto portions of the scriptures. For those of us who have the written Word available to us, we ought to take advantage of this tremendous privilege. We have the freedom to fill our lives with the teachings of Jesus, as well as to personally read the record of God's dealing with man from the beginning of creation through the birth of the Church. This is a resource we should view as a key to our relationship with God.

Spiritual Key: Lifestyle of Prayer and Intercession

Too often people come to God in a very religious way. They may be speaking in their normal manner to those around them, but when someone suggests that they pray there is a tendency to launch into a very formal and solemn means of speaking. In some instances, they may even include dramatic intonations in their voice that they would never use in ordinary conversation with their fellow human beings. This religious way of approaching God is completely unnecessary and can hinder us and our hearers from entering into an intimate relationship with God. Instead, begin prayer by coming to God like a child. Give yourself the liberty to just be yourself with God. He already knows everything about you any way.

I know from experience that in certain settings, especially public ministry, that there can be a strong pressure to say a prayer that impresses others. Instead, may we make up our minds today that we are no longer going to perform for a human audience. Some of us have gotten in this habit to such a degree that we pray this way even when we are all by ourselves with God.

WOE TO YOU, SCRIBES AND PHARISEES, HYPOCRITES, BECAUSE YOU DEVOUR WIDOWS' HOUSES, AND FOR A PRETENSE YOU MAKE LONG

PRAYERS; THEREFORE YOU WILL RECEIVE GREATER CONDEMNATION.

MATTHEW 23:14

Jesus spoke against prayers done out of pretense. Instead, may we make a choice today that we are simply going to go to God as our Abba Daddy. We are going to talk with Him intimately as a Father who loves us and cares for us and knows us even better than we know ourselves. Away with pretense. Away with performance.

Yes to being yourself with God. Yes to talking with Him as your friend. Yes to bearing the depths of your soul to Him and allowing Him to speak to you in your innermost parts. Yes to asking Him to fill you with His heart for those around you. Yes to receiving His heart for the nations.

"MY SHEEP HEAR MY VOICE, AND I KNOW THEM, AND THEY FOLLOW ME." JOHN 10:27

As was previously mentioned, a critical element in our prayer lives is taking time to listen to God. Due to the fact that God knows all things, it would be unwise of us to spend the majority of our prayer time talking to Him about what we think should happen. Why not take the time to listen to what He wants to share with us? Only He knows the way forward. Why not ask Him what He believes we need to pray for?

BE ANXIOUS FOR NOTHING, BUT IN EVERYTHING BY PRAYER AND SUPPLICATION WITH THANKSGIVING LET YOUR REQUESTS BE MADE KNOWN TO GOD. AND THE PEACE OF GOD, WHICH SURPASSES ALL COMPREHENSION, WILL GUARD YOUR HEARTS AND YOUR MINDS IN CHRIST JESUS. PHILIPPIANS 4:6-7

As the Word of God and worship begin to become more and more a part of our lives, we will begin to tap more deeply into God's heart for us, our families and the world around us. As His heart begins to fill us, we will begin to long to see what is in His heart become manifested on the earth.

This is where prayer begins to flow supernaturally in our hearts as we long for His will to be done on earth as it is in heaven. As we see the contrast between what is currently being experienced, and what God actually desires to see happen, we are led to petition God for an answer. It is this type of prayer that is born out of the heart and will of God which begins to give birth to the Kingdom of God on the earth.

AND HE WITHDREW FROM THEM ABOUT A STONE'S THROW, AND HE KNELT DOWN AND BEGAN TO PRAY, SAYING, "FATHER, IF YOU ARE WILLING, REMOVE THIS CUP FROM ME; YET NOT MY WILL, BUT YOURS BE DONE." NOW AN ANGEL FROM HEAVEN APPEARED TO HIM, STRENGTHENING HIM. AND BEING IN AGONY HE WAS PRAYING VERY FERVENTLY; AND HIS SWEAT BECAME LIKE DROPS OF BLOOD, FALLING DOWN UPON THE GROUND.

LUKE 22:41-44

ONE OF THOSE DAYS JESUS WENT OUT TO A MOUNTAINSIDE TO PRAY, AND SPENT THE NIGHT PRAYING TO GOD.

LUKE 6:12 (NIV)

Jesus knew deep prayer. There were times that He prayed through the night. It was following one of these all night prayer times that He selected the 12 disciples (Luke 6:13). We should ask ourselves a question, "If the Son of God Himself needed to pray this much in order to abide in the Father, how much more do you and I need to learn how to remain in a constant state of prayer?"

Many of the heroes of the faith lived a life of intercessory prayer. Abraham interceded for Sodom and Gomorrah, Moses stood in the gap for the Israelites on Mt. Sinai, David prayed throughout his life from a shepherd boy to his kingship, Daniel fasted and prayed for the fulfillment of the Word of God given to Jeremiah. Men and women of God throughout the history of the Church have modeled the necessity of a lifestyle given over to deep seeking of God in intercessory prayer.

I SEARCHED FOR A MAN AMONG THEM WHO WOULD BUILD UP THE WALL AND STAND IN THE GAP BEFORE ME FOR THE LAND, SO THAT I WOULD NOT DESTROY IT; BUT I FOUND NO ONE.

EZEKIEL 22:30

To enter into the heart of God and feel His agony for the state of His Church, to experience His desperate longing for the salvation of lost souls, is a privilege and responsibility of every child of God. According to the Word of God this is not reserved for a select few who are believed to be intercessors. Every member of Christ's Body has been given the privilege and responsibility of allowing God's Spirit to use them as an instrument of prevailing prayer that ushers in the Kingdom of God from heaven to earth.

IN THE SAME WAY THE SPIRIT ALSO HELPS OUR WEAKNESS; FOR WE DO NOT KNOW HOW TO PRAY AS WE SHOULD, BUT THE SPIRIT HIMSELF INTERCEDES FOR US WITH GROANINGS TOO DEEP FOR WORDS; AND HE WHO SEARCHES THE HEARTS KNOWS WHAT THE MIND OF THE SPIRIT IS, BECAUSE HE INTERCEDES FOR THE SAINTS ACCORDING TO THE WILL OF GOD. ROMANS 8:26-27

As our love for God grows in intensity, the level of prayer in and through us ought to always be increasing. There should be a deeper hunger for lost souls which causes us to groan for them to enter the Kingdom of Jesus Christ. We should believe God to give us a deeper longing for His purposes to take place in our community, which causes us to cry out to Him in prayer. As this prayer life deepens, and as we begin to see more and more answers to prayer, intercessory prayer will begin to become a treasured part of our lifestyle.

Practical Instructions for a Lifestyle of Prayer and Intercession:

- Just as one of the disciples asked Jesus, you too can regularly ask God's Spirit, "Teach me how to pray." (Luke 11:1)

- Take time to wait before the Lord and ask Him, "What is Your will for this person/circumstance?" As you have heard from Him what His will is then you can pray with the utmost confidence that what you are asking for will come to pass because you know that it is God's will (1 John 5:14-15).

- Ask God's Spirit to help you to see that person/circumstance as He sees them. In this way you will begin to have a greater understanding of God's heart. As His heart becomes our heart, prayer will begin to flow towards that person/circumstance.

- You may consider recording specific prayer requests, as well as specific answers to prayer. This will allow you to regularly bring these targeted requests before the Lord.

As you remember the victories that God has already brought to pass your faith will remain strong and immovable.

One of the ways that Satan seeks to deceive us into prayerlessness is to get us to believe that the character of our God is not really good and that our prayers will not make a real difference. When you have pages of answered prayer in front of you it is virtually impossible for this lie to stand for very long. Hold up these answers to prayer from the past, and then march forward in faith as you pray for current situations. Know that these prayers will make a difference!

Spiritual Key: A Lifestyle of Accountability and Mutual Submission

LET US CONSIDER HOW WE MAY SPUR ONE ANOTHER ON TOWARD LOVE AND GOOD DEEDS, NOT GIVING UP MEETING TOGETHER, AS SOME ARE IN THE HABIT OF DOING, BUT ENCOURAGING ONE ANOTHER—AND ALL THE MORE AS YOU SEE THE DAY APPROACHING.

HEBREWS 10:24-25 (NIV)

No matter how mature we are in our faith in Christ, we need regular fellowship with other believers. Specifically, even within a larger Body of believers we should have at least one or two other close relationships with whom we are open and honest and who we allow to hold us accountable. While we should seek to be in fellowship with all believers in a general way, it is vitally important to have several other Christ-followers that we are deeply real with and who are aware of our faults, and who can support us in prayer and admonishment. These close companions in the faith should be those who challenge us

174

to go even deeper in our walk with Jesus. When we spend time with them, this should stir a greater hunger in our hearts to surrender and trust Jesus even more.

AS IRON SHARPENS IRON, SO ONE PERSON SHARPENS ANOTHER.

PROVERBS 27:17 (NIV)

SUBMIT TO ONE ANOTHER OUT OF REVERENCE FOR CHRIST.

EPHESIANS 5:21 (NIV)

Having a support group of this nature is a key to our spiritual growth. Jesus modeled this type of relationship with the twelve, and He even had three within the twelve in which He revealed more of Himself (Matthew 17:1). There is no substitute for having this type of deep relationship with others who are seeking to walk closely with God.

Practical Instructions for a Lifestyle of Accountability and Mutual Submission:

- Ask God's Spirit to reveal to you at least one or two people within your sphere of influence that you can begin to view as accountability partners.

- As God reveals to you who you should entrust yourself to in this way, take the step of faith to ask them about establishing a relationship of this type.

- Make a decision to be the one who gets vulnerable first, even if they have not yet gotten vulnerable with the difficulties that they are facing. In this way, you are modeling the depth of relationship that will be critical for you to have in the days ahead. In time, God can cause

175

them to share struggles and prayer requests with you too.

- If you have a spouse who is a believer in Jesus, he or she should be one of the people that you view as an accountability partner. If you do not yet have this level of relationship with your spouse, begin asking God's Spirit to go before you and establish this level of love and trust in your marriage.

- Persevere in these relationships until a depth of trust is built between you, where you can share anything that you may be facing, and receive encouragement from those who are following Jesus alongside you.

Real Intimacy with God Is the Goal

WHEN ALL THE PEOPLE SAW THE PILLAR OF CLOUD STANDING AT THE ENTRANCE OF THE TENT, ALL THE PEOPLE WOULD ARISE AND WORSHIP, EACH AT THE ENTRANCE OF HIS TENT. THUS THE LORD USED TO SPEAK TO MOSES FACE TO FACE, JUST AS A MAN SPEAKS TO HIS FRIEND.

EXODUS 33:10-11

We read that God spoke with Moses "face to face" as with a friend. Has this been your regular experience with God? Do you regularly come away from your time spent with Him aware of who He is in such a real way that you are transformed?

Our goal in pursuing God is to really know Him as our friend. We are seeking a deep and real encounter with the Living God. One encounter with God is more valuable than years of simply going through religious disciplines. Therefore, do not allow yourself to fall into a routine of utilizing the spiritual keys yet failing to actually meet with God. Push past this by asking God to revive you once again.

FOR THUS SAYS THE HIGH AND EXALTED ONE WHO LIVES FOREVER, WHOSE NAME IS HOLY, "I DWELL ON A HIGH AND HOLY PLACE, AND ALSO WITH THE CONTRITE AND LOWLY OF SPIRIT IN ORDER TO REVIVE THE SPIRIT OF THE LOWLY AND TO REVIVE THE HEART OF THE CONTRITE."

ISAIAH 57:15

ONLY THE HOLY SPIRIT CAN GUIDE US INTO JESUS

BUT WHEN HE, THE SPIRIT OF TRUTH, COMES, HE WILL GUIDE YOU INTO ALL THE TRUTH; FOR HE WILL NOT SPEAK ON HIS OWN INITIATIVE, BUT WHATEVER HE HEARS, HE WILL SPEAK; AND HE WILL DISCLOSE TO YOU WHAT IS TO COME.

JOHN 16:13

We all desire to walk in freedom. The Word of God tells us that the Truth sets us free and that God's Spirit is the Living Truth. Truth is a Person. Therefore, if we want freedom in our lives and freedom flowing through our lives to others, then we must seek the Person of Truth.

BUT IF ANY OF YOU LACKS WISDOM, LET HIM ASK OF GOD, WHO GIVES TO ALL GENEROUSLY AND WITHOUT REPROACH, AND IT WILL BE GIVEN TO HIM. BUT HE MUST ASK IN FAITH WITHOUT ANY DOUBTING, FOR THE ONE WHO DOUBTS IS LIKE THE SURF OF THE SEA, DRIVEN AND TOSSED BY THE WIND. FOR THAT MAN OUGHT NOT TO EXPECT THAT HE WILL RECEIVE ANYTHING FROM THE LORD, BEING A DOUBLE-MINDED MAN, UNSTABLE IN ALL HIS WAYS. JAMES 1:5-8

There is a reason we have endeavored to lay a foundation of the Holy Spirit being our Guide into deeper intimacy with God. All too often, especially in the Western culture of human effort, individualism, and self-sufficiency, we can be deceived into attempting to get closer to God through religious striving, rather than coming to Him as a child and allowing Him to lead us. We must be broken of human striving if we desire to enter into the life that is truly led by God's Spirit. When you come to God, come in faith, believing that He will give you wisdom and direct your time of fellowship. Then proceed however His Spirit leads you.

We serve a creative God. The God we are seeking intimacy with is more than able to keep our times with Him fresh, vibrant and alive each and every moment of every day! If we ever find our time with Him lacking life, there is a good chance that we have allowed unconfessed sin, or we have begun to lean on a form of godliness, that is limiting His Spirit from truly guiding us into His Life.

Final Practical Encouragement Related to the Spiritual Keys

At this point we have moved beyond just sharing about the wonderful harvests that were seen in China, Taiwan and in other parts of the world. We have taken the time to get down into the soil and discuss the types of seeds that were used, where to purchase the seeds, how the soil was plowed, how to keep the soil irrigated, how to take care of the plants, how to harvest and distribute the crops when they come in. We hope that you will continue to pour over these Spiritual Keys until they become a part of your lifestyle with the Lord. You may even consider re-reading the two sections on the Heart of a Spirit-Empowered Life multiple times to give God's Spirit the opportunity to bring deeper revelation. We hope that this lifestyle will remain at the heart of your life for as long as you live. May your attitude be, "Lord, whatever it takes for this to become a reality in my life, I am willing."

In this process of establishing a Spirit-Empowered Life, we are not looking for a quick fix but we are seeking to learn what it means to dwell in Jesus in such a way that this lifestyle remains. Rather than thinking of this like a race in which we are trying to get all the spiritual keys figured out and into practice as quickly as possible, think of this as a journey with God's Spirit in which He is teaching you how to put this lifestyle into practice. Be thinking in terms of taking weeks, months, and even years to allow the Holy Spirit to grow and mature each aspect of this lifestyle to such a degree that you are consumed with the Life of God Himself. First start in your individual life, and then out to your family, and then to your sphere of influence.

Throughout Church history, as this lifestyle has been held up as the normal way to walk with Christ, it has been used of the Lord to bear much fruit. The fruit of this type of lifestyle in Uganda has resulted in a national level impact, as the Gospel of Jesus Christ has affected virtually every sector of life. As Taiwan took up a similar challenge to raise this standard of walking with Jesus across their nation, they have begun to reap similar national level fruit. In just four years, they have seen the number of Christ-followers nearly double with hundreds of thousands coming to Christ in a nation that had been resistant to prayer and the Gospel of Jesus Christ.

Could something similar take place in your nation if this same standard was put in place across the Body of Christ in every sector of life? We believe it is not only possible, but that it is in fact the desire of God to see this take place. If He is for us, who can be against us? If we will pay the price to establish a Spirit-Empowered lifestyle across our nation, we can believe God to respond in power just as He is doing elsewhere.

OPENING HIS MOUTH, PETER SAID:

"I MOST CERTAINLY UNDERSTAND NOW THAT GOD IS NOT ONE TO SHOW PARTIALITY, BUT IN EVERY NATION THE MAN WHO FEARS HIM AND DOES WHAT IS RIGHT IS WELCOME TO HIM."

ACTS 10:34-35

Practical Instructions

- Ask the Holy Spirit for His Guidance in this process. He is your leader and He will guide you into all Truth (John 16:13). If you don't rely on Him you will be prone to go into your own human efforts to try to quickly get all the spiritual keys up and going immediately, or you may be so overwhelmed by the thought of doing this that you don't even begin with one. Instead, rest yourself in God's Spirit and allow Him to lead you in this process. He is a Faithful Guide. He has never failed even once to produce the fruit of perfection.

- Some of us have various elements of this lifestyle already in place in our lives. Others of us have few if any of these keys in place. For those who have already begun this journey, rather than assuming that we are already fulfilling everything that God would ask of us, let us bring every one of these Spiritual Keys to the Holy Spirit and allow Him to take us deeper. For each Spiritual Key there is always a deeper place that God can take us, no matter how long we have walked with Him.

- Consider taking just 1 Spiritual Key at a time and allow the Holy Spirit to take you deeper in it until He has really unlocked a door and you have entered in nearer to the heart of God. Once that Spiritual Key is in place begin to move on to the next one, and then the next. In this way, you are allowing the Holy Spirit to take you on a journey deeper into Him that will last the rest of your life. That is the goal. The goal is not to quickly set about trying to pick up every key in such a haphazard way that they will be lost in a matter of days, or weeks. Our hope is that we will allow the Holy Spirit to build a pattern of walking with Him that will cause these spiritual keys to continue to deepen for the rest of our lives.

Discussion Questions:

1. Out of the 5 Spiritual Keys mentioned in this chapter, which one do you feel you are actively putting into practice the most? What does this look like for you and how has this spiritual key impacted your life as you have put it into practice?

2. Out of the 5 Spiritual Keys, which one do you feel you are walking in the least right now? What impact do you believe that this has had on your life by not walking in this spiritual key?

Action Step:

Take time to ask God how He would have you begin to put into practice one of the spiritual keys. You may consider choosing the one you are weakest in, or simply allow His Spirit to lead you to where He wants you to begin. Write down any immediate steps that He asks you to take and begin to put them into practice.

_____

_____

_____

Prayer Focus:

Only God can establish these Spiritual Keys in our lives so that they remain vibrant and alive. Take time to pray into this, asking God's Spirit to teach you how to use these keys to position yourself for greater fruitfulness.

Father, I thank you that you have given me spiritual means of drawing near to You. I desire to learn what it means to put these spiritual keys into practice in every area of my life. I confess that I have not been practicing_____. (Make a decision to repent and agree to put these spiritual keys into practice).

I ask that You would teach Me how to order my life in such a way that I make more time for us to be together. Thank You for hearing my prayer and teaching me ways that I can draw near to You. I love You! (Share your heart with God regarding any way in which He spoke to you through this chapter.)

Chapter 9: Fruit of a Spirit-Empowered Lifestyle – Part 1

Overcoming Darkness

If we are truly empowered by the Spirit of the Living God, what type of fruit should we expect to see in our lives? Though we are all a work in progress, it is helpful to look at the level of fruitfulness that God desires for us. As we look at this expected fruit, and compare it to the fruit that we are currently experiencing, this can be used of God to bring conviction, repentance, and a new lifestyle.

We previously discussed that the fruit of the kingdom of darkness is to bring us into bondage to our flesh, the world's system, the religious system, and demonic forces. Therefore, when the Spirit of God is given greater freedom to live His Life in and through us, we should begin to be set free from each of these traps of the enemy.

Let's take a look at the fruit that should come when God's Spirit takes over our lives.

1. Spiritual Fruit: A Lifestyle of Overcoming the Flesh

BUT I SAY, WALK BY THE SPIRIT, AND YOU WILL NOT CARRY OUT THE DESIRE OF THE FLESH. FOR THE FLESH SETS ITS DESIRE AGAINST THE SPIRIT, AND THE SPIRIT AGAINST THE FLESH; FOR THESE ARE IN OPPOSITION TO ONE ANOTHER, SO THAT YOU MAY NOT DO THE THINGS THAT YOU PLEASE. GALATIANS 5:16-17

For obvious reasons, if we are to truly walk in the Christ-Life, then we must learn to allow the Spirit of God to overcome our flesh. The flesh and the Spirit of God "are in opposition to one another". A fruit that we should expect to see when we surrender more fully to God is that His Spirit overcomes our flesh. In time this victory should become so consistent that it is the regular pattern of our lives.

FOR IF YOU ARE LIVING ACCORDING TO THE FLESH, YOU MUST DIE; BUT IF BY THE SPIRIT YOU ARE PUTTING TO DEATH THE DEEDS OF THE BODY, YOU WILL LIVE.

ROMANS 8:13

We see that the Word of God gives us no other option. We either learn what it means for the Spirit to put our flesh to death or we will die. Happily for us God has given us the perfect solution to our sin nature. Every born again believer in Jesus Christ has now received the Holy Spirit of God who has an entirely new nature that longs to please Him. The nature of the Holy Spirit is one of humility which uproots and removes the pride of our sinful nature. And the Holy Spirit has a childlike faith in the Father which removes the unbelief we had in our hearts toward God. In this way, the Christ-Life overcomes the sinful nature.

There is a beautiful place in God's Spirit where we have so discarded our corrupted human understanding, that all we want is the will and the ways of God. As we consistently reject our own wisdom in favor of the wisdom of God, we begin to experience the Holy Spirit pouring through us in greater and greater measure. Rather than striving to live in victory over sin,

God's Spirit gains the victory for us. This place of victorious rest is available to every child of God.

Practical Instructions for a Lifestyle of Overcoming the Flesh:

If we do not allow God's Spirit to overcome both our "worldly" flesh and our "religious" flesh, then they will be a constant stumbling block to us, even when we desire to serve the Lord.

- Ask God how He wants your human appetites to be brought into submission to His Spirit in such a way that they are not ruling your life in any way. If we find any of our human appetites attempting to rule us, then we should consider fasting.

Fasting food is one way to see all of our fleshly desires brought back into submission to the Spirit of God. As we fast from food (whether it be a half a day, a full day, or many days) the power of our flesh is broken and put into subjection. You may even ask the Lord for a regular pattern of fasting that He would have you undertake which will keep your flesh in subjection to the Spirit as a lifestyle. (Note: Due to medical reasons, some people should not go on a liquid only fast. If you think that may be the case with you consult a medical doctor before starting a fast.) Though it may not be comfortable at first, most people's bodies are capable of fasting. In fact, Jesus taught us, "When you fast..." not "if you fast" and included it in the same passage where He instructed us on giving and praying. (Matthew 6:1-18)

- Prayerfully examine the entertainment that you have been watching and listening to. Reject meaningless television or movies that have no eternal value. Choose to reject anything that you would not watch or listen to were God Himself with you in the room, because the fact of the matter is, He is with you. Take the time you used to spend on this and use it to fill yourself with the things of God. You are not overcoming your flesh in your power, but seemingly subtle decisions like this can make a big difference in allowing God's Spirit to fill you and overcome the flesh through you.

- Take time and allow God's Spirit to show you any way that you are still seeking to live the Christ-Life in your own efforts or ability.

- When God reveals something, or gives you specific steps to take, write these down and turn them into prayer targets. As you take time to pray through God's revelation, He will give you the victory every time. God's Spirit will show you how to overcome your human desires and human ways of living. As He leads you in this you will find that more and more of the Christ-Life is flowing in and through you.

2. Spiritual Fruit: A Lifestyle of Overcoming the World's System and the Religious System

DO NOT LOVE THE WORLD OR ANYTHING IN THE WORLD. IF ANYONE LOVES THE WORLD, LOVE FOR THE FATHER IS NOT IN THEM.

1 JOHN 2:15

Here John refers to the necessity of forsaking temporary pursuits if we are to truly possess the love of God. The world's system seeks to push us to make our lives about ourselves and our pleasures. The religious system tries to push us to be seen as significant in the eyes of our fellowman and to do things for God in our own strength. When God's Spirit begins to lead every aspect of our lives, we die to our desire for temporary pleasure, we lose our desire to be approved of by our fellowman, we die to our attempts to live a godly life apart from Christ and we begin to live solely and only by the empowerment of the Spirit of God. God's Spirit does nothing without having an eternal purpose in mind. Therefore, if He is truly living His life in and through us, we will find that our desires will become more and more focused on that which is eternal.

Spirit-Led Time Management

TEACH US TO NUMBER OUR DAYS, THAT WE MAY GAIN A HEART OF WISDOM. PSALM 90:12 (NIV)

One way that we should see God's Spirit setting us free is in the area of our time management. One of the primary ways that both the world's system and the religious system seek to place us in bondage is in the use of our time. How we spend time is how we live our lives. If the enemy can get us disconnected from God's Spirit in how we spend time he can render us ineffective. When the Spirit of God begins to take control of our lives, we should see Him beginning to teach us how to more effectively utilize the time that He has given us.

When our hearts are truly given over to God, then we desire to be pleasing to Him. We desire to honor Him with the

187

way we use time. We desire for our lives to be redeemed. The ultimate way to redeem time is to seek to allow the Holy Spirit to lead and guide every minute of our day.

Since our lives are now completely surrendered to Jesus, our time is not ours but God's. Therefore, we do not want to waste even one minute of His time on that which will burn up on the last day. In seeking God's Spirit about time management, we are purposefully looking at the allocation of our time. This is not just time management principals that are applied in much of the western world, where people are on time to appointments and their calendars are filled every minute of the day with activities. This goes beyond just avoiding being late to an appointment. This refers to looking at everything through an eternal lens and asking the Holy Spirit to teach us what it means to number our days.

I CONSIDER MY LIFE WORTH NOTHING TO ME; MY ONLY AIM IS TO FINISH THE RACE AND COMPLETE THE TASK THE LORD JESUS HAS GIVEN ME—THE TASK OF TESTIFYING TO THE GOOD NEWS OF GOD'S GRACE. ACTS 20:24 (NIV)

Everything we do should begin to be run through a filter of whether or not our activities are part of what God has called us to do. This can take place in an individual, in a family, in a business and in a local congregation. This is less of a discipline than it is a shift in the priorities of our heart that comes when we fully surrender every aspect of our lives to Jesus Christ.

If we have truly given our lives to Him and we realize that He only lives for those things that will last forever, then we should expect the desires of our heart to come more and more in line with His heart. In this way, we will desire to make major

188

adjustments in the way our time is allocated. Instead of desiring to spend the majority of our time on ourselves, our comforts and hobbies, or even on religious activities, we will now begin to ask God's Spirit how He wants to spend His time. There will be a corresponding adjustment that takes place which causes us to expend more and more of the time we've been given to help and bless those around us.

As we allow the Holy Spirit to remove activities from our lives that are not eternally valuable, we will find that our time is filled with the things of God. More and more of the time God has given us will be redeemed for that which is of eternal value rather than that which is temporary. On the final Day of Judgment we will be so grateful that we made the lifestyle adjustments to ensure that we did not waste even one second of the time that God had entrusted to us.

EACH MAN'S WORK WILL BECOME EVIDENT; FOR THE DAY WILL SHOW IT BECAUSE IT IS TO BE REVEALED WITH FIRE, AND THE FIRE ITSELF WILL TEST THE QUALITY OF EACH MAN'S WORK.

1 COR. 3:13

Personal Testimony

Early on in my relationship with Jesus He placed the prayer in my heart, "Use my day for the maximization of Your glory." My desire was for every second of my life to be maximized for His Glory. May we each begin to desire this and put it into practice.

Practical Instructions for a Lifestyle of Spirit-Led Time Management:

- Take time to allow God's Spirit to set your daily schedule. Allow Him to show you how much time you are to spend alone with Him on a daily basis, how you are to allocate your time with family, friends, work etc. The truth is that from the moment we gave our lives to Jesus, our time is no longer our own, it is His. We should regularly stop and ask Him if we are using His time wisely and if there are any time adjustments He would like for us to make.

- Record any specific direction that God gives you regarding the proper use of time. This will allow you to re-evaluate and put into practice the things that He shares with you.

- Regularly reassess where you are with the utilization of time. Are you living in the reality of the fact that only the time that was spent under the empowerment of the Spirit of God will stand on the Judgment Day? Or are there still areas where you waste time or do activities, even ministry work, in your own strength and understanding?

Impacting Every Sphere of Society with the Gospel

Only as we have been set free from the world's system do we then have real authority to go back in and call others to come out and be free. As we allow God's Spirit to set us free we will be positioned in such a way to impact the spheres of influence that God has allowed us to be a part of:

- Marriage/Family

190

- Marketplace/Business
- Government
- Belief System (Education, media, arts)
- Priesthood/worship system

Being on God's Mission

But He said to them, "I have food to eat that you do not know about." So the disciples were saying to one another, "No one brought Him anything to eat, did he?" Jesus said to them, "My food is to do the will of Him who sent Me and to accomplish His work. John 4:32-34

"Do not work for the food which perishes, but for the food which endures to eternal life, which the Son of Man will give to you, for on Him the Father, God, has set His seal."

John 6:27

As God's servants what type of life have we been called to live?

Now that we have died to everything that was of our selfish nature we have only one reason to live, and that is for the glory of God. God has called us to make disciples of all nations (Matthew 28:18-20). If we are going to be a part of disicpling the nations, then the fruit we should begin to see is that the will and ways of Jesus Christ begin to fill every sphere of influence that God has entrusted to us. As we are set free from the world's system we now have authority to tell others to no longer live for temporary pleasures but to pursue eternal riches. The reason the Church, in some parts of the world has had so little power to impact their culture is that they are too much a part of their culture to have any authority to call others out.

I WILL NOT SPEAK MUCH MORE WITH YOU, FOR THE RULER OF THE WORLD IS COMING, AND HE HAS NOTHING IN ME.

JOHN 14:30

Jesus was making the statement that though Satan was coming for Him, Satan had nothing in Him. There was no area of compromise in His life. There was no legal ground for Satan to come against Him. How about you and me? Is this the case in our lives? Have we so died to the ways of the world and the temporary pleasures of this life that we can say, "Satan has nothing in me."?

This is the key to impacting marriage and family relationships. This is the key to transforming our workplaces, government offices, schools, and media. As long as our lives are still lived under the same dictates of the system, we will fail to have the impact that God intends. If instead, we allow His Spirit to overcome the dictates of the world's system, in time He will be able to send us to influence others in a way that we never could have if we were still living in compromise.

THE PEOPLE WERE AMAZED AT HIS TEACHING, BECAUSE HE TAUGHT THEM AS ONE WHO HAD AUTHORITY, NOT AS THE TEACHERS OF THE LAW.

MARK 1:22 (NIV)

The people were amazed at the "authority" by which Jesus spoke. Why do you think Jesus had authority? We see that the teachers of the law also were instructing the people but they lacked authority. Why?

Authority lies in a life that is truly walking out what we are sharing with others. If we want to share anything with authority, then we must first be living it ourselves or we have no authority. In that case, we are a hypocrite, telling others to do something that we are not willing to do ourselves (Matthew 23:13).

If we desire to share the Gospel of Jesus Christ with those within our sphere of influence, this will only be effective when we are walking in the authority that comes from a life completely given over to God. In that place of full surrender and complete trust, there is authority to break the strongholds of Satan and set captives free. There is authority to share the Word of God with others and see blind eyes opened and deaf ears unstopped to receive the King of Glory.

SO JESUS SAID TO THEM AGAIN, "PEACE BE WITH YOU; AS THE FATHER HAS SENT ME, I ALSO SEND YOU." JOHN 20:21

Through our full surrender we join God's Spirit in His earthly mission. In the place of real abandonment we are no longer debating with God, "I don't want to do this. I want to do that." We have given Him our lives, and He in turn has given us responsibility to be on the mission of Jesus Christ. As the Father has sent Him, He now sends us. We have been called to be a part of His work on the earth. Can you believe that the same mission that God the Father gave to Jesus Christ, He has now entrusted to you?

THEREFORE IF ANYONE IS IN CHRIST, HE IS A NEW CREATURE; THE OLD THINGS PASSED AWAY; BEHOLD, NEW THINGS HAVE COME. NOW ALL THESE THINGS ARE FROM GOD, WHO RECONCILED US TO HIMSELF THROUGH CHRIST AND GAVE US THE MINISTRY OF RECONCILIATION, NAMELY, THAT GOD WAS IN CHRIST RECONCILING

THE WORLD TO HIMSELF, NOT COUNTING THEIR TRESPASSES AGAINST THEM, AND HE HAS COMMITTED TO US THE WORD OF RECONCILIATION. THEREFORE, WE ARE AMBASSADORS FOR CHRIST, AS THOUGH GOD WERE MAKING AN APPEAL THROUGH US.

2 COR. 5:17-20

Imagine the power of even one life that has truly died to itself, and instead of living for the temporary worldly pleasures, or the applause of the religious system, now lives every moment of the day solely for the eternal purposes of God. As we picture the impact of such a life, we are beginning to see that as the Church in an entire region is equipped in a Spirit-Empowered Lifestyle that this could begin to transform all of society.

3. Spiritual Fruit: A Lifestyle of Discerning and Overcoming Satanic Opposition

THEN GOD SAID, "LET US MAKE MAN IN OUR IMAGE, ACCORDING TO OUR LIKENESS; AND LET THEM RULE OVER THE FISH OF THE SEA AND OVER THE BIRDS OF THE SKY AND OVER THE CATTLE AND OVER ALL THE EARTH, AND OVER EVERY CREEPING THING THAT CREEPS ON THE EARTH."

GENESIS 1:26

Responsibility Given to Mankind

At creation God gave mankind a tremendous responsibility when He made us in His image. A key way that we were made in the image of God is that He gave us the God-like qualities of having a mind, will, and emotions.

He then delegated authority to us, so that we could exercise our will in order to rule over creation. God effectively entrusted the care of creation to us. If mankind chose to remain dependent on God, then we would have His wisdom to bring forth His Kingdom rule on the earth. If mankind chose independence and rebellion from God, we then surrender our authority to rule creation over to Satan. This is exactly what happened in the fall of mankind in the Garden (Genesis 3:1-7).

Today, even if someone who is a follower of Jesus Christ chooses to exercise their will to agree with darkness, they effectively surrender over to Satan the legal authority that God has given them to rule. At that point, Satan has legal authority to rule over the area they surrendered to him. It's "legal" authority, because God gave this authority to us, and we chose to give it to Satan. This is true in our personal lives, families and sphere of influence. In this way, by our own choices we give Satan legal ground to torment us and those around us. This is how the kingdom of darkness rules on the earth, and effectively holds ground in many parts of the world. As the inhabitants of the land continue to surrender their authority over to demons, they in turn enslave the people. This cycle of death and darkness can be broken.

When we surrender our will over to Jesus Christ's will, we come back within the protection of God. When God is given His rightful authority in our lives, in our families, in our sphere of influence, darkness is pushed back and the Kingdom of God is manifested on earth as it is in heaven. This process of surrendering legal authority over to God can take place all the way up to the national level as the Body of Christ unites in prayer, and takes back the ground Satan has stolen.

The secret here is tied to the tremendous responsibility God gave humanity at creation. He did not have to delegate His authority to us, but He chose to. In this way, mankind has a tremendous responsibility. God has given us a critical role to play in seeing His will manifested on the earth. The Word of God even states that by our surrender and faith in God's Spirit that we can be a part of speeding the Second coming of Jesus Christ (2 Peter 3:12).

Our decisions matter. Our decisions can have an eternal impact on ourselves and on those around us. Jesus taught us that our prayers are significant to bringing forth God's will on the earth (Matthew 6:9-10). As we, the people of the land, the people given delegated authority over the land, surrender our will to Jesus Christ, and as we repent on behalf of our land, we welcome God to come and rule and reign in our midst.

Do you see how the surrender of your will to God is essential to see a manifestation of His Kingdom? It is the difference between life and death. It is the difference between the kingdom of light and the kingdom of darkness. This realization has the power to affect not only ourselves but many other souls who are bound in darkness.

BE OF SOBER SPIRIT, BE ON THE ALERT. YOUR ADVERSARY, THE DEVIL, PROWLS AROUND LIKE A ROARING LION, SEEKING SOMEONE TO DEVOUR. BUT RESIST HIM, FIRM IN YOUR FAITH, KNOWING THAT THE SAME EXPERIENCES OF SUFFERING ARE BEING ACCOMPLISHED BY YOUR BRETHREN WHO ARE IN THE WORLD.

1 PETER 5:8-9

Aware of Satan's Schemes

As we give ourselves over to a lifestyle of abiding in God's Spirit, we will become increasingly sensitive to the calculated ways that Satan is seeking to come against us. We must be aware of the tactics that the enemy is using against us if we are going to effectively resist him and experience the victory that Jesus Christ has purchased for us. Many in the Western world have been lulled into a false sense of complacency regarding spiritual warfare, but the Bible clearly illustrates the reality of the unseen spiritual war that rages around us (Daniel 10:5-14, Eph 6:12). Just as in a physical war, if a military unit is unaware of the strategy that the enemy forces are planning against them then they are very vulnerable to being attacked and defeated. Like a blind man in a fight they are an easy target because they do not know which way their enemy will strike.

In order to be aware of what Satan is seeking to bring against us we must ask God's Spirit to reveal this to us. In Biblical times, when the Israelites were about to move into the promised land the Lord spoke to Moses to have them send out spies to view where the enemy encampments were located.

THEN THE LORD SPOKE TO MOSES SAYING, "SEND OUT FOR YOURSELF MEN SO THAT THEY MAY SPY OUT THE LAND OF CANAAN, WHICH I AM GOING TO GIVE TO THE SONS OF ISRAEL; YOU SHALL SEND A MAN FROM EACH OF THEIR FATHERS TRIBES, EVERY ONE A LEADER AMONG THEM."

NUMBERS 13:1-2

WHEN MOSES SENT THEM TO SPY OUT THE LAND OF CANAAN, HE

SAID TO THEM, "GO UP THERE INTO THE NEGEV; THEN GO UP INTO THE HILL COUNTRY. SEE WHAT THE LAND IS LIKE, AND WHETHER THE PEOPLE WHO LIVE IN IT ARE STRONG OR WEAK, WHETHER THEY ARE FEW OR MANY. HOW IS THE LAND IN WHICH THEY LIVE, IS IT GOOD OR BAD? AND HOW ARE THE CITIES IN WHICH THEY LIVE, ARE THEY LIKE OPEN CAMPS OR WITH FORTIFICATIONS? HOW IS THE LAND FAT OR LEAN? ARE THERE TREES IN IT OR NOT? MAKE AN EFFORT THEN TO GET SOME OF THE FRUIT OF THE LAND."

NUMBERS 13:17-20

These scriptures reveal a detailed analysis of the territory that God had instructed them to go to war against. They identified strongholds in the land, areas of vulnerability where the enemy could be easily overtaken, and examined the fruit of the land which was intended to strengthen their faith to believe God for this good land flowing with milk and honey.

In the same way, in our personal lives, families, congregations, sphere of influence, as well as in our cities and region, we should have a detailed understanding of the schemes that Satan has set against us and the people of the land so that we will be able to see more clearly how God desires to defeat him. As God's Spirit reveals each area that Satan is seeking to come against us, we should write these down and begin to take them to the Lord in prayer. We can believe God to give us clear wisdom and understanding as to how He would have us overcome.

"HE WHO OVERCOMES AND HE WHO KEEPS MY DEEDS UNTIL THE END, TO HIM I WILL GIVE AUTHORITY OVER THE NATIONS."

REVELATION 2:26

Can the Holy Priesthood Truly Overcome the Unholy Priesthood

In order to answer this question we need to look no further than the prophet Elijah. One holy priest against 850 unholy priests (1 Kings 18:19). They did everything they knew how to do in order to call upon their gods and invite the demons to come in power. But the power of one righteous man, in agreement with God was greater than them all. Elijah erected an altar to the Lord, and God responded by sending His fire.

ELIJAH CAME NEAR TO ALL THE PEOPLE AND SAID, "HOW LONG WILL YOU HESITATE BETWEEN TWO OPINIONS? IF THE LORD IS GOD, FOLLOW HIM; BUT IF BAAL, FOLLOW HIM." BUT THE PEOPLE DID NOT ANSWER HIM A WORD. 1 KINGS 18:21

THEN ELIJAH SAID TO ALL THE PEOPLE, "COME NEAR TO ME." SO ALL THE PEOPLE CAME NEAR TO HIM. AND HE REPAIRED THE ALTAR OF THE LORD WHICH HAD BEEN TORN DOWN. ELIJAH TOOK TWELVE STONES ACCORDING TO THE NUMBER OF THE TRIBES OF THE SONS OF JACOB, TO WHOM THE WORD OF THE LORD HAD COME, SAYING, "ISRAEL SHALL BE YOUR NAME." SO WITH THE STONES HE BUILT AN ALTAR IN THE NAME OF THE LORD. 1 KINGS 18:30-32

"ANSWER ME, O LORD, ANSWER ME, THAT THIS PEOPLE MAY KNOW THAT YOU, O LORD, ARE GOD, AND THAT YOU HAVE TURNED THEIR HEART BACK AGAIN." THEN THE FIRE OF THE LORD FELL AND CONSUMED THE BURNT OFFERING AND THE WOOD AND THE STONES AND THE DUST, AND LICKED UP THE WATER THAT WAS IN THE TRENCH. WHEN ALL THE PEOPLE SAW IT, THEY FELL ON THEIR FACES; AND THEY SAID, "THE LORD, HE IS GOD; THE LORD, HE IS GOD." THEN ELIJAH SAID TO THEM, "SEIZE THE PROPHETS OF BAAL; DO NOT LET ONE OF

THEM ESCAPE." SO THEY SEIZED THEM; AND ELIJAH BROUGHT THEM DOWN TO THE BROOK KISHON, AND SLEW THEM THERE.
1 KINGS 18:37-40

God is the same yesterday, today, and forever. If one holy priest could conquer a nation of unholy priests, then the same can take place today. In the New Covenant ushered in through the blood of Christ, our battle is not against other human beings but against the spiritual forces of wickedness in the heavenly realm. If one man, filled with the Life of God, could stand against the spiritual powers of a nation, we can to. All over the world there are testimonies of the kingdom of darkness being pushed back and overthrown by the kingdom of Jesus Christ. Why not here? Why not now?

THE EFFECTIVE PRAYER OF A RIGHTEOUS MAN CAN ACCOMPLISH MUCH. JAMES 5:16

WHAT, THEN, SHALL WE SAY IN RESPONSE TO THESE THINGS? IF GOD IS FOR US, WHO CAN BE AGAINST US? ROMANS 8:31

Practical Instructions for a Lifestyle of Discerning and Overcoming Satanic Opposition:

- Since the spiritual battlefield is largely unseen, we must rely upon the Holy Spirit to reveal the tactics that the enemy is using against us. Take the time to allow God's Spirit to reveal Satan's tactics.

- As God exposes Satan's plans, write them down and then begin to focus regular targeted prayer against his schemes. Jesus stated that He has been given all authority. As we surrender our lives completely to Him, we are in position to exercise the delegated authority of Jesus Christ over every power and scheme of the enemy.

- Have faith that the Holy Spirit is more than able to uproot and remove anything that the enemy has been planning against you. We are more than conquerors through Jesus Christ (Romans 8:37)!

Fruit of Overcomers

As we allow the Spirit of God to bring us through to a place of victory in these three battlefields, we are now in position to be used of God to affect the lives of those around us. We can ask the Holy Spirit how He desires us to impact our families, our local congregation and our sphere of influence. We can pray about how God would have us share our faith with those who do not know Jesus, and to disciple those who have come to know Christ. In the next chapter we will discuss how this lifestyle of evangelism, discipleship and unconditional love is a powerful weapon in the hands of our God.

Discussion Questions:

1. In what way have you experienced God's Spirit overcome your flesh/sin nature?
2. How do you find yourself still struggling with your flesh?
3. In what way have you experienced God's Spirit overcome the world system?
4. How do you find yourself still fighting to overcome the world?
5. In what way have you experienced God's Spirit discern and overcome spiritual opposition?
6. How do you find yourself still fighting to overcome spiritual opposition?

Action Step:

Take time to ask God how He would have you begin to overcome in a deeper way.   Write down anything that He is asking of you and put this into practice.

Overcoming the Flesh_____

_____

Overcoming the world's system/religious system_____

_____

Overcoming spiritual opposition_____

_____

Prayer Focus:

Only God can overcome and cause us to live in consistent victory over these hindrances to His Kingdom. Take time to pray into this, asking God's Spirit to show you how He desires to live a life of victory in and through you.

Father, I thank you that through Your Son's life, death, and resurrection that you have purchased a full victory for me. I thank You that You have already made a way for me to overcome.   I ask You to show me any way that I have compromised and failed to do what You have asked of me. I abandon myself to You in a fresh way and I now trust You to teach me Your way of living in victory. (Continue to pray as God's Spirit leads you.)

Chapter 10: Fruit of a Spirit-Empowered Lifestyle – Part 2

Evangelism, Discipleship & Love

When we are still bound by our flesh, the world, and the enemy it is difficult to even begin to help others. We lack real authority to call them to be free when we are still living in bondage. As God's Spirit sets us free we are simultaneously released to be used of God to assist others. As we look at the sphere of influence that God has entrusted to us it is helpful to be equipped in three key areas: Evangelism, Discipleship & Love.

A Spirit-Empowered Lifestyle Prepares Us for Effective Evangelism

PREACH THE WORD; BE READY IN SEASON AND OUT OF SEASON; REPROVE, REBUKE, EXHORT, WITH GREAT PATIENCE AND INSTRUCTION.

2 TIMOTHY 4:2

BUT IN YOUR HEARTS REVERE CHRIST AS LORD. ALWAYS BE PREPARED TO GIVE AN ANSWER TO EVERYONE WHO ASKS YOU TO GIVE THE REASON FOR THE HOPE THAT YOU HAVE. BUT DO THIS WITH GENTLENESS AND RESPECT, KEEPING A CLEAR CONSCIENCE, SO THAT THOSE WHO SPEAK MALICIOUSLY AGAINST YOUR GOOD BEHAVIOR IN CHRIST MAY BE ASHAMED OF THEIR SLANDER.

1 PETER 3:15-16 (NIV)

While not everyone is called to be an evangelist, as Peter mentions here, we are all called to "be prepared to give an answer" to those who ask us about the hope that we have. Paul speaks of a fearless readiness, to proclaim the Good News of Jesus Christ in every situation at any time (Eph 6:19-20). This lifestyle of evangelism is more than simply going on a specific outreach to declare Christ to those who do not know Him, but it speaks of a faith that flourishes in every situation from morning until night. We may share Jesus through our words, as well as through our service. When we are living in victory in our personal lives, we are positioned to be effective witnesses for the Kingdom of God. We should experience a desire to seek opportunities to share the reason for the hope that we have in Jesus.

Living in this way, keeps us from becoming apathetic in our faith, and encourages us to walk in a vibrant intimacy with God that is attractive to those He brings into our lives. We should always look to make the most of every opportunity. Whether that be in the area where we live, a business, a school, while we walk along the way, or whether we are among family and friends at home.

PRAY ALSO FOR ME, THAT WHENEVER I SPEAK, WORDS MAY BE GIVEN ME SO THAT I WILL FEARLESSLY MAKE KNOWN THE MYSTERY OF THE GOSPEL, FOR WHICH I AM AN AMBASSADOR IN CHAINS. PRAY THAT I MAY DECLARE IT FEARLESSLY, AS I SHOULD.

EPHESIANS 6:19-20 (NIV)

HE WHO IS WISE WINS SOULS. PROVERBS 11:30

Are we regularly winning souls into the Kingdom of God? Do we live in the awareness that if the souls of those around us do not come to know Jesus Christ that they will spend an eternity in hell? What level of urgency do we have towards the lost? When was the last time we tapped deeply into the heart of God which "desires all men to be saved and to come to the knowledge of the truth."?

Practical Instructions for a Lifestyle of Effective Evangelism:

- Consider asking God's Spirit to give you at least 5-10 names of unsaved family, friends and acquaintances that you can be regularly praying for their salvation. Write these names down and keep them in your Bible or in a place where you will regularly see them. Pray for them as regularly as God's Spirit leads you to.

- Daily make yourself available to be used of the Holy Spirit by letting Him know each day that you are willing to be used of Him to share the Good News of Jesus Christ with others. As you make yourself available to Him, He will make the opportunity for you to share His message. If you pray this way regularly, you will find amazing doors begin to open to share your faith.

- Consider recording answers to prayer. These big and small victories will serve as an encouragement to keep believing God to use your life as a vessel of His Good News.

A Spirit-Empowered Lifestyle Prepares Us for Effective Discipleship

AND JESUS CAME UP AND SPOKE TO THEM, SAYING, "ALL AUTHORITY HAS BEEN GIVEN TO ME IN HEAVEN AND ON EARTH. GO THEREFORE AND MAKE DISCIPLES OF ALL THE NATIONS, BAPTIZING THEM IN THE NAME OF THE FATHER AND THE SON AND THE HOLY SPIRIT, TEACHING THEM TO OBSERVE ALL THAT I COMMANDED YOU; AND LO, I AM WITH YOU ALWAYS, EVEN TO THE END OF THE AGE." MATTHEW 28:18-20

Jesus did not simply ask us to make converts but to make disciples. Jesus told us that the way we are to disciple an individual, our family, and our sphere of influence is a process of teaching them "to observe all that I commanded you". It is difficult to teach others to observe all that Jesus has commanded us when we ourselves are not yet surrendered to this lifestyle.

When the Holy Spirit begins to bring us through to the reality of a full surrender to His will and ways, we are being prepared to become an instructor of others. As we seek to encourage those around us in a lifestyle of radical abandonment to Jesus, we can take courage from His final statement in Matthew 28 where He promised to be with us "always, even to the end of the age".

Do not be surprised if your discipleship of others does not look glamorous in the eyes of the world or even the religious system. The religious system of our day often displays a hyped up image of what successful ministry looks like. Sadly, this image of being a success in the eyes of other people is often in direct contradiction to the ways of God.

206

Jesus modeled for us what a life of discipleship looked like. With a massive vision to disciple every nation; He made a very interesting decision to invest the majority of His earthy life by pouring into just 12 men. He lived in close relationship with them and taught them His commandments, both through His Words, but most importantly through His Life. In this lifestyle of discipleship, Jesus laid the foundation for His Church.

THE THINGS YOU HAVE LEARNED AND RECEIVED AND HEARD AND SEEN IN ME, PRACTICE THESE THINGS, AND THE GOD OF PEACE WILL BE WITH YOU. PHILIPPIANS 4:9

Paul shared about the need for mentoring and modeling a Spirit-Empowered lifestyle in close relationship with others. This same pattern of discipleship is just as essential today, if we are going to see Christ's Kingdom established on earth as it is in heaven. The discipleship of our families ought to be our first priority (1 Tim. 3:1-2, 12, Titus 1:6-7). Then we are in a position to disciple every other facet of the sphere of influence that God has entrusted to us.

Practical Instructions for a Lifestyle of Effective Discipleship:

- Ask God's Spirit for His wisdom and timing as to whether He believes you are equipped to begin to step out and disciple others. If our own lives are still in a position of compromise, we would be wise to wait and allow God to disciple us first before we launch out and start seeking to lead others.

- As your life is consecrated and living a Spirit-Empowered lifestyle, begin to ask God how He would have you pour your life into others.

- Trust God to reveal those He wants you to connect with in this way. Learn to allow His Spirit to disciple others through you. This is not a matter of attempting to disciple others in your own strength. It is learning to trust Him to disciple others through you.

The Ultimate Goal – A Lifestyle of Unconditional Love

THE ONE WHO DOES NOT LOVE DOES NOT KNOW GOD, FOR GOD IS LOVE. 1 JOHN 4:8

While there are many fruits of the Spirit, the scriptures are clear that none compare to love. Unconditional or "agape" love has no parallel. This type of love is the greatest measure of our depth of connection with God. God has revealed His loving character to us, and if we desire to properly represent Him to the world, we must tap deeply into His love for us and for others.

BUT NOW FAITH, HOPE, LOVE, ABIDE THESE THREE; BUT THE GREATEST OF THESE IS LOVE.

1 CORINTHIANS 13:13

"TEACHER, WHICH IS THE GREAT COMMANDMENT IN THE LAW?" AND HE SAID TO HIM, "'YOU SHALL LOVE THE LORD YOUR GOD WITH ALL YOUR HEART, AND WITH ALL YOUR SOUL, AND WITH ALL YOUR MIND.' THIS IS THE GREAT AND FOREMOST COMMANDMENT. THE SECOND IS LIKE IT, 'YOU SHALL LOVE YOUR NEIGHBOR AS

YOURSELF.' ON THESE TWO COMMANDMENTS DEPEND THE WHOLE LAW AND THE PROPHETS." MATTHEW 22:36-40

The Spirit-Empowered Life is a life of faith, of hope, and of love, but the greatest indication of being indwelt with the Holy Spirit is our level of love. It is clear that Jesus intended for love to be the primary distinctive that caused the people of God to stand out above every other people on the earth. It was by our love for God and our love for others that Kingdoms would be conquered and nations discipled. Our love for God was to be far superior to our love for any other earthly thing.

The Gospel calls us to die to ourselves, and live for Christ's purposes. In order to live for His purposes and properly represent Him as His ambassadors we must allow His standard of Love to become our standard of love. We must allow the Spirit of God to remove any root of bitterness that may be there from our past. We must forgive as Christ has forgiven us, and daily ask the Holy Spirit to take us deeper in our understanding of His love for us, and of His love for all men.

(JESUS SPEAKING) "A NEW COMMANDMENT I GIVE TO YOU, THAT YOU LOVE ONE ANOTHER, EVEN AS I HAVE LOVED YOU, THAT YOU ALSO LOVE ONE ANOTHER. BY THIS ALL MEN WILL KNOW THAT YOU ARE MY DISCIPLES, IF YOU HAVE LOVE FOR ONE ANOTHER."

JOHN 13:34-35

We do not need to look any further than the lack of love in the church in order to see our grievous disconnection from The Vine. God is Love. Whenever an individual lacks love, this points to their lack of relationship with the source of all Love.

We love because He first loved us (1 John 4:19). But what if we have not allowed God to love us? What if we have rejected His love? Then it should be no surprise that many non-believers lack love. They have not received God's love for them therefore they have no sacrificial love to give to others.

But what about those who claim to follow Christ and yet lack love? What about the many believers who are easily irritated, frustrated, and lack love on a daily basis? Could it be that we too have failed to receive God's Love for us?

DO EVERYTHING IN LOVE.

1 COR. 16:14 (NIV)

THE ONLY THING THAT COUNTS IS FAITH EXPRESSING ITSELF THROUGH LOVE. GAL. 5:6 (NIV)

When was the last time that you allowed God to reveal to you just how much He loves you?

Why don't you take some time right now and stop whatever you are doing and allow the Spirit of God to show you just how much He loves you? Will you let Him do this for you now?

Prayer time:

God I ask that You would reveal the love that You have for me. (Take time to wait on Him.)

I hope that you took the time to allow God to saturate you in His Love for you. This is the most important thing in all of life. God is Love. We can only love others when we have a revelation of His love for us. Love is the most powerful witness

210

to the reality of God. Therefore, allowing God to love us must become top priority in our lives.

From this place of love, we have the Life of God necessary to impact every circumstance no matter how difficult. Love covers over a multitude of sins (1 Peter 4:8). Love breaths new life into places that were dead. A vast throng in heaven can testify that it was the love of another believer that won their heart over to Jesus.

"YOU HAVE HEARD THAT IT WAS SAID, 'YOU SHALL LOVE YOUR NEIGHBOR AND HATE YOUR ENEMY.' BUT I SAY TO YOU, LOVE YOUR ENEMIES AND PRAY FOR THOSE WHO PERSECUTE YOU, SO THAT YOU MAY BE SONS OF YOUR FATHER WHO IS IN HEAVEN; FOR HE CAUSES HIS SUN TO RISE ON THE EVIL AND THE GOOD, AND SENDS RAIN ON THE RIGHTEOUS AND THE UNRIGHTEOUS."

MATTHEW 5:43-45

In this passage, it is not just any type of love that is being asked for, but Jesus says that we are to have agape love for our enemies. We are to have unconditional love for those who hate us and we are to do good for them. Why? Because God Himself passionately loves those who are His enemies and He expects us to have the same love that He has for those around us.

AND THIS IS HIS COMMAND: TO BELIEVE IN THE NAME OF HIS SON, JESUS CHRIST, AND TO LOVE ONE ANOTHER AS HE COMMANDED US.

1 JOHN 3:23

In the Middle East it is love that triumphs and causes hearts to turn to Christ. In Communist countries, it is love that shines like a bright beacon testifying to the reality of Jesus. In a cold and hardened individualistic culture in the western nations it is love that cuts through the ice and rescues souls from eternal darkness to eternal light. Don't underestimate the power of love. It is love that compelled God the Father to willingly allow His Son to be killed in our place (John 3:16). It is love that motivated Jesus to willingly lay down His life for humanity. It is love that will bring about the exaltation of Jesus Christ in the nations of the earth.

If we realize that love is the most powerful spiritual weapon, the most effective means of evangelism and discipleship, the most needed and rare resource on the earth, then we would ask ourselves the question: "How do I increase the level of love that I am living in?"

The answer to this question is quite simple. Enter more deeply into the One and Only Person who is Love. Unlike our desire for other spiritual gifts, such as the desire for miracle working power, or a deeper understanding of future events, there are sources of darkness and sources of light. But real, genuine, self-sacrificing, and unconditional love has only One Source.

If we wish to lay hold of more of the most precious commodity on earth, then we must abandon ourselves more completely to Jesus. We must allow His Life to so infill us, that it is no longer us living, but Him Living through us. We must allow Him to love us completely, and allow Him to remove the areas of our lives that are lived in contradiction to His Spirit, so that we are clean and pure vessels. As His Love consumes us, and as we find ourselves willingly melting into Him, our lives will appear as a blazing inferno of love to show the nations that Jesus Christ is alive.

Will you begin to allow His Great Love to consume you? Will you allow Him to fill you with a deeper revelation of His Love for you? Start now and don't stop until He takes you home to be with Him forever.

Conclusion

Can you envision this lifestyle of evangelism, discipleship and love, flowing from your personal life into your marriage / parenting? How about your workplace? What about an entire congregation that begins to embrace this lifestyle? What if the Body of Christ in a community or city began to be equipped and sent out to bear this type of good fruit everywhere they went? Could we not see entire cities and nations turned upside down? Let's allow God to work this good fruit in our lives so that we can begin to share this with others.

Discussion Questions:

1. Do you presently live as though the only reason you are here on earth is to give glory to God? If not, what are some of the common ways that you have been pulled away from living for God's purposes?

Evangelism

2. In what way have you experienced God's Spirit winning lost souls to Christ through your life?

3. How do you believe God's Spirit wants to win even more souls to Himself through you in the days ahead?

Discipleship

4. In what way have you experienced God's Spirit discipling others in the will and ways of Jesus Christ through your life?

5. How do you believe God's Spirit wants to disciple others even more effectively through you in the future?

Love

6. In what way have you experienced God's Spirit loving others through you? Do you see yourself consistently living in the level of love that Jesus loves? If not, what makes it difficult for you to love others as Jesus loves them?

7. How do you believe God's Spirit wants to love others at an even deeper level through your life in the future?

Action Step:

Take time to ask God how He would have you begin to be even more fruitful as it relates to evangelism, discipleship, and love. Write down any immediate action steps that He asks you to take and through prayer and obedience put them into practice.

Evangelism_____

_____

Discipleship_____

_____

Love for others_____

_____

Prayer Focus:

Father God, I need You. It is clear that apart from You that I cannot help others to know You more. You have promised me in Your Word that if I would remain in You that I would bear much for fruit for Your glory. I ask that You would show me how to let my light shine more brightly so that those around me will come to know You. I ask that you would teach me Your ways of discipling others so that you can use me to mature other believers. I believe You to continue to reveal Your great love for me so that I will have an abundance of love to give to others. I ask that You would give me a greater understanding of Your love for those around me. (Continue to pray as God's Spirit leads you.)

Section 4: Establishing Christ's Kingdom

Chapter 11:
Establishing Christ's Kingdom in Our Marriages and Families

God is the creator of the institution of marriage and family. Therefore, it should be no surprise that there is a global assault by Satan against the Biblical standards of marriage and family. This battle is raging in nearly every nation on the planet. Satan is using the media as a primary means of seeking to dismantle the family unit. Satan is seeking to bring in adultery, fornication, divorce, homosexuality and the like. He is pushing this in many overt and subtle ways.

Throughout human history the family unit has been the bedrock of any nation, and its stability or instability has been the cause of the rise and fall of many empires. In the last several decades it seems that Satan has leveled a heavy attack on marriage, and on the raising of children in the will and ways of God. The enemy of our souls knows that if our homes are intact then we are spiritually prepared to take authority over the nation in which we live. He also knows that if we fail at home, we are ill-equipped and without real authority to bring the Kingdom of God to anyone else (1 Tim. 3:1-2, 12, Titus 1:6-7).

It is essential to see God's original intention when He established marriage and family, in order for us to see just how far away we are from His hearts desire. Every culture on earth has various standards for what a marriage should look like, but for the follower of Jesus Christ, the only standard for marriage is what God's Word has to say about it. Every one of our cultural ways must bow to His Kingdom standards. As we raise God's standard for marriage and parenting, we should be humbled in such a way that we begin to seek His Holy Spirit for a deeper breakthrough so that our marriages and families begin to fulfill His purposes in our day. Even if we may not yet be married, or if we have not had a good experience with our family relationships, it will be helpful to see God's intention for marriage and family so that we can know what to be praying for in our nation.

What Was God's Intention in Establishing Marriage?

THEN GOD SAID, "LET US MAKE MAN IN OUR IMAGE, ACCORDING TO OUR LIKENESS; AND LET THEM RULE OVER THE FISH OF THE SEA AND OVER THE BIRDS OF THE SKY AND OVER THE CATTLE AND OVER ALL THE EARTH, AND OVER EVERY CREEPING THING THAT CREEPS ON THE EARTH." GOD CREATED MAN IN HIS OWN IMAGE, IN THE IMAGE OF GOD HE CREATED HIM; MALE AND FEMALE HE CREATED THEM. GOD BLESSED THEM; AND GOD SAID TO THEM, "BE FRUITFUL AND MULTIPLY, AND FILL THE EARTH, AND SUBDUE IT; AND RULE OVER THE FISH OF THE SEA AND OVER THE BIRDS OF THE SKY AND OVER EVERY LIVING THING THAT MOVES ON THE EARTH."

GENESIS 1:26-28

God's desire for marriage was that the relationship of husband and wife would be an earthly representation of the same love and unity that exists in the Trinity! Wow! That is a high standard for marriage.

- What kind of love and unity exists in the Trinity?

- Do the members of the Trinity ever care about their own rights?
- Does one member of the Trinity ever care about themselves more than the others?

WIVES, BE SUBJECT TO YOUR OWN HUSBANDS, AS TO THE LORD. FOR THE HUSBAND IS THE HEAD OF THE WIFE, AS CHRIST ALSO IS THE HEAD OF THE CHURCH, HE HIMSELF BEING THE SAVIOR OF THE BODY. BUT AS THE CHURCH IS SUBJECT TO CHRIST, SO ALSO THE WIVES OUGHT TO BE TO THEIR HUSBANDS IN EVERYTHING.

HUSBANDS, LOVE YOUR WIVES, JUST AS CHRIST ALSO LOVED THE CHURCH AND GAVE HIMSELF UP FOR HER, SO THAT HE MIGHT SANCTIFY HER, HAVING CLEANSED HER BY THE WASHING OF WATER WITH THE WORD, THAT HE MIGHT PRESENT TO HIMSELF THE CHURCH IN ALL HER GLORY, HAVING NO SPOT OR WRINKLE OR ANY SUCH THING; BUT THAT SHE WOULD BE HOLY AND BLAMELESS. SO HUSBANDS OUGHT ALSO TO LOVE THEIR OWN WIVES AS THEIR OWN BODIES. HE WHO LOVES HIS OWN WIFE LOVES HIMSELF; FOR NO ONE EVER HATED HIS OWN FLESH, BUT NOURISHES AND CHERISHES IT, JUST AS CHRIST ALSO DOES THE CHURCH, BECAUSE WE ARE MEMBERS OF HIS BODY. FOR THIS REASON A MAN SHALL LEAVE HIS FATHER AND MOTHER AND SHALL BE JOINED TO HIS WIFE, AND THE TWO SHALL BECOME ONE FLESH...

NEVERTHELESS, EACH INDIVIDUAL AMONG YOU ALSO IS TO LOVE HIS OWN WIFE EVEN AS HIMSELF, AND THE WIFE MUST SEE TO IT THAT SHE RESPECTS HER HUSBAND.

EPHESIANS 5:22-31, 33

What does God's Word say about the role of a <u>Husband</u>?

- The husband is to be the head of the wife as Christ is the head of the Church (vs. 23).
- The husband's love for his wife is to be an earthly representation of Christ's Love for the Church (vs. 25).
- Husbands are to love their wives as they love themselves (vs. 33)

- How much does Jesus Christ love His bride the Church?
- How much is Jesus willing to sacrifice Himself on behalf of His Church?
- What would Jesus not do to express His love and devotion to His Church?
- Has this level of love been the reality in your relationship with your wife?
- In what way/s have you not walked in the fullness of God's love towards your wife? (Example: Critical, harsh, lack of service, lack of self-sacrifice etc...)
- What would God have you change so that your love for your wife is at the level He is asking of you?

_____

_____

_____

_____

Husbands, we would encourage you to really take time to pray through these questions, and begin a journey to allow God's Spirit to build His level of love within your heart towards your wife. Repentance in the area of pride is a large step that many husbands need to take in order to enter more deeply into the love that Jesus wants for us to have towards our wives. If we will humble ourselves, He will lift us up (1 Peter 5:6).

What does God's Word say about the role of a <u>Wife</u>?

- Wives are to be subject to their husbands as to Jesus (vs. 22).
- The husband is head of the wife as Christ is the head of the Church (vs. 23).
- Wives are to be subject to their husbands in everything (vs. 24).
- Wives are to respect their husbands (vs. 33)

In the Word of God we see the power of this true heart-level submission to win husbands over to Christ if they are not yet following Him:

FOR YOU HAVE BEEN CALLED FOR THIS PURPOSE, SINCE CHRIST ALSO SUFFERED FOR YOU, LEAVING YOU AN EXAMPLE FOR YOU TO FOLLOW IN HIS STEPS, WHO COMMITTED NO SIN, NOR WAS ANY DECEIT FOUND IN HIS MOUTH; AND WHILE BEING REVILED, HE DID NOT REVILE IN RETURN; WHILE SUFFERING, HE UTTERED NO THREATS, BUT KEPT ENTRUSTING HIMSELF TO HIM WHO JUDGES RIGHTEOUSLY...IN THE SAME WAY, YOU WIVES, BE SUBMISSIVE TO YOUR OWN HUSBANDS SO THAT EVEN IF ANY OF THEM ARE DISOBEDIENT TO THE WORD, THEY MAY BE WON WITHOUT A WORD BY THE BEHAVIOR OF THEIR WIVES, AS THEY OBSERVE YOUR CHASTE AND RESPECTFUL BEHAVIOR.

1 PETER 2:21-23, 3:1-2

- Have you acted as though your husband is the head in your house?

- Have you been subject to your husband in everything as to the Lord Jesus Himself?
- Have you remained submissive to your husband "even if any of them are disobedient to the word"?
- Have you thought, spoken, and acted with true respect for your husband both when he is there and when he is not around?
- Has this level of submission and respect been the reality in your relationship with your husband?
- If not, what would God have you change so that your submission and respect for your husband is at the level He requires of you?

_____

_____

_____

_____

Wives, we would encourage you to really take time to pray through these questions and begin a journey to allow God's Spirit to build His level of submission and respect within your heart towards your husband. If there is any woundedness in your heart due to the way that he has treated you in the past, we encourage you to take this woundedness to the Lord Jesus Christ and trust Him to heal you (Matt. 6:14-15, Phil. 3:13). Make the choice to forgive him of any past wounds and ask God's Spirit to teach you how He can love your husband through you.

Raising God's Standard for Marriage

It is very helpful to raise God's original intention for a husband and a wife. His standard ought to humble us and show us how far we are from His original intention. This should cause us to cry out to God to see His standard established in our marriage.

What Was God's Intention in Establishing Family?

To begin to see God's intention for the creation of the family, it is helpful to look at the life of Abraham. We know Abraham as a man who had a great call from God upon his life. In fact, he is viewed as the father of our faith. It would be helpful to see what God's instructions were to this man's family in order to see how we can fulfill God's purposes for our families.

> THE LORD SAID, "SHALL I HIDE FROM ABRAHAM WHAT I AM ABOUT TO DO, SINCE ABRAHAM WILL SURELY BECOME A GREAT AND MIGHTY NATION, AND IN HIM ALL THE NATIONS OF THE EARTH WILL BE BLESSED? FOR I HAVE CHOSEN HIM, SO THAT HE MAY COMMAND HIS CHILDREN AND HIS HOUSEHOLD AFTER HIM TO KEEP THE WAY OF THE LORD BY DOING RIGHTEOUSNESS AND JUSTICE, SO THAT THE LORD MAY BRING UPON ABRAHAM WHAT HE HAS SPOKEN ABOUT HIM."

> *GENESIS 18:17-19*

Why did God choose Abraham? For someone having such a great call on his life we might assume that God would ask a great deal of him. Yet as we examine the scriptures, God's reason for choosing him is simply so that he would "command his children and his household after him to keep the way of the Lord". It is as though God is saying, "If you will properly instruct your spouse and your children in My ways, I will fulfill every other good thing that I have purposed for you."

Could it be that we have a similar call on our marriages and families today? Could it be that if we would simply treat our spouse and our children as our first mission field, that our children will walk in the ways of God when we have left this earth and be faithful to fulfill the purposes of God in their generation?

Look at God's instructions to Moses and the Israelites regarding discipleship in the family:

THESE COMMANDMENTS THAT I GIVE YOU TODAY ARE TO BE ON YOUR HEARTS. IMPRESS THEM ON YOUR CHILDREN. TALK ABOUT THEM WHEN YOU SIT AT HOME AND WHEN YOU WALK ALONG THE ROAD, WHEN YOU LIE DOWN AND WHEN YOU GET UP. TIE THEM AS SYMBOLS ON YOUR HANDS AND BIND THEM ON YOUR FOREHEADS. WRITE THEM ON THE DOORFRAMES OF YOUR HOUSES AND ON YOUR GATES.

DEUT. 6:6-9 (NIV)

In this passage, Moses is shown the depth of discipleship that God desired within the family. God expects us to be continuously training our children in the will and the ways of God. While we sit at home, when we walk along the road, when we go to bed and when we arise in the morning. Even the doorframes and the gates of our homes are to instruct our families in the will and ways of God. He is to be the centerpiece of everything going on in our family life. His will and His ways are to be impressed upon our children continuously.

225

As we see in the lifestyle of Jesus, our instruction of others is not merely to be with our lips and tongue (Mark 7:6-8) but as our lives model the love and life of God, our children will be drawn to love God as we love Him. This is not a religious exercise of going through the motions but a vibrant love relationship with the Living God that we are to model for our children. Our children should see our passion for God. They should see that we are deeply in love with Him.

They should see their father modeling what it means to be the spiritual head of the home. They should see their father setting the example of what it means to love and pursue Jesus Christ above everything else. They should see their father laying his life down and loving their mother as Christ loves the Church.

They should see their mother submitting and respecting her husband as if she were submitting and respecting Jesus Christ Himself. They should see a deeply pure and consistent faith in God in their mother that causes them to desire to draw near to God. In this way the home is the perfect spiritual environment to ensure that the next generation follows wholeheartedly after God. This was God's intention for marriage and parenting.

Establishing God's Kingdom in Our Marriage and Family

We just want to reiterate the two sides of abiding as they relate to our marriage and family life. We will then look at how we can implement the spiritual keys in our homes so that our marriage/family begins to bear the good fruit of a Spirit-Empowered Life.

Two Sides to Establishing Christ's Kingdom in Our Marriage and Family:

- **A Heart of Full Surrender** – Towards God and towards each other

- **A Heart of Complete Trust** – Towards God and towards each other

Practical Discussion on Establishing a Corporate Marriage/Family Time That Seeks to Encounter God through Worship, Prayer and the Word:

While we have specifically sought to make it clear that these spiritual keys are to be part of our lifestyle and not relegated just to a set time of the day, there is also a very important element of gathering corporately as a husband and wife, as well as gathering our children with the specific intention of seeking God. This can be called a "Family Devotional", it can be called family worship or fellowship, but the point is that our spouse/children are coming together to enter into a place where we truly encounter the Spirit of God together.

In this section we are going to briefly discuss how the "Spiritual Keys" that we mentioned for our individual lives can be put into practice in our marriages and in our families. It is our hope that as you ask the Holy Spirit for His guidance for each of these areas you will have a practical guide to move forward in seeking God together as a family.

If you are just beginning to seek God corporately as a family, it is often better to start small and gradually increase your time together, rather than attempting to force everyone to go for a long time when they have not been used to it. You can believe God to build these corporate times of seeking Him to become one of your greatest joys in your marriage and family.

Begin by simply asking God's Spirit how He would like to direct your family to seek Him corporately. Give Him the freedom to lead you wherever He wants to go. From one corporate time to the next God may have a completely different agenda so we must learn to be sensitive to His leading. It is great to have a mixture of worship, prayer, the Word etc. Unless we learn to follow the Spirit's lead in this, we should not be surprised that we end up with a form of godliness but lack His power.

1. A Marriage/Family Lifestyle of Praise and Worship that Truly Encounters God's Spirit

Times of corporate of worship should not be a rarity in our homes, but a key part of our marriage and family lifestyle. We should seek to not merely have a devotional time, but a true encounter with the Spirit of God in which our hearts and lives are transformed. We should believe God for an enjoyable lifestyle of worshipping the Lord together. The Holy Spirit is very creative, so let Him lead you in how to make this a meaningful aspect of your corporate times of seeking Him. Don't settle for just going through the motions, but seek to enter into a deep place of real worship.

Ask the Holy Spirit how He would have your marriage/family begin to go deeper in praise and worship. Write down anything that He speaks to you:

_____

_____

_____

2. A Marriage/Family Lifestyle of Waiting and Listening to God's Spirit

- Ask the Holy Spirit how He would have your marriage/family begin to wait and listen to His Spirit together. Write down anything that He speaks to you:

_____

_____

_____

3. A Marriage/Family Lifestyle of Being Filled with the Word of God

Ask the Holy Spirit how He would have your marriage/family begin to fill yourselves with God's Word. Write down anything that He speaks to you:

_____

_____

_____

Testimony

By establishing the Word of God as a part of the lifestyle of our family, it has produced a hunger in the hearts of our children to read the Word of God on their own. Our two oldest sons learned to read by reading the Bible, with the first one reading through the entire Bible at the age of seven. He could be found reading 10, 20 or more chapters a day, as God placed it on his heart to be filled with the Word of God. One of the keys to this was that this was not something we told him that he "had to do", but it was something that God's Spirit placed in his heart to do on his own. Now as our third son is learning to read, he is also learning to read by reading the Bible.

4. A Family Lifestyle of Prayer and Intercession

Ask the Holy Spirit how He would have your marriage/family begin to pray for others. Write down anything that He speaks to you:

_____

_____

_____

5. A Family Lifestyle of Accountability and Mutual Submission

Ask the Holy Spirit how He would have your marriage/family begin to go deeper in your accountability and mutual submission to one another. Write down anything that He speaks to you:

_____

_____

_____

The Fruit of Establishing a Spirit-Empowered Lifestyle in Marriage and Family

A. A Lifestyle of Overcoming the Flesh in Our Marriage and Family

As God's Spirit is released to move with greater freedom in your home, He desires to teach you about the necessity of overcoming your flesh.

As a married couple or as a family, He may lead you to make the decision to turn off the television. Depending on if you have children and what their ages are you may even choose to engage in some form of corporate fasting and prayer. If you notice that any of the human appetites are beginning to take control of your family life, be quick to humble yourselves before the Lord and ask Him for wisdom in overcoming this.

Teach your children that following Jesus is not about trying harder in our human effort, but it is about surrendering ourselves more fully to God, and trusting Him to live His life through us.

B. A Lifestyle of Overcoming the World's System and the Religious System in Our Marriage and Family

Allow the Holy Spirit to show you how He desires to use the time that He has given you. Don't waste the time that God has given to your marriage and family.

Practical tips:

- As a family, take time to ask God's Spirit how He wants you to use your time together in the most productive way.

- Write down anything that He speaks to you, so that your entire family has a record of what the Lord showed you.

Example: You have two hours before bedtime. This time could be used to watch a movie or it could be used to read a book that has little to no eternal value. Or it could be used to read through 10 chapters of the Bible, discuss key elements of God's character, and end the night with a missionary story of a man or woman of God who was used mightily to establish God's Kingdom on the earth. As you and your children go to bed, think of the different images that they would have running through their minds. One choice would have them thinking all night of meaningless stories. The other choice would have them consider if they are willing to lay their lives down so that they can know Christ in the way they heard from the Bible or from the missionary testimony. By allowing God's Spirit to lead our time management, it makes a big difference in our family life!

C. A Lifestyle of Discerning and Overcoming Satanic Opposition in Our Marriage and Family

As our marriages and families begin to enter more deeply into a lifestyle of seeking God, we can believe God to reveal to us how to uproot the patterns that have been there in the past. May we trust God to uproot every way that the Kingdom of darkness has sought to rule in our homes. May we believe Him to change the lifestyle in our marriage/family into His lifestyle. In this way, the hold that Satan had over our homes is broken.

Testimony:

In a home where the parents had raised their children in a Christian environment, one of their teenage sons began to close himself off and get involved in Satanism. His activities with darkness were having an effect on the entire family. The parents made a decision to begin to meet for corporate prayer every evening from 5pm-7pm. As a result of this corporate family prayer, within a period of time their son began to become more open again. Eventually he stated that he knew he needed to change his life.

As believers in Jesus Christ, we do not need to sit as victims of Satan's schemes against our families. We can begin to humble ourselves before God, call upon His Name, and watch as He does what was humanly impossible.

Practical Instruction for Those with Children:

Take time to teach your children about the battle that they are in. Help them to understand how the enemy seeks to come against us in order to get us to give into His schemes. Even children can learn to discern the ways in which Satan is seeking to come against them and your family. Believe God to create a sensitive heart in them that is able to know when they are under attack from the enemy.

Evangelism, Discipleship and Love in Marriage and Family

Imagine if our marriages and families were on fire in our relationship with God and sharing about Jesus with everyone we met. What if we began to disciple our community together? What if the dinner table became a place for sharing testimonies of the activity of God's Spirit throughout the day? There are few things more exciting than a family that has been prepared to go on God's mission together.

A Spirit-Empowered Lifestyle Prepares Our Marriage and Family for Effective Evangelism

Ask the Holy Spirit how He would have your marriage/family begin to engage in effective evangelism. Write down anything that He speaks to you:

_____

_____

_____

Testimony

As a result of having been read many missionary stories over the course of the last few years our 3 boys, ages 9, 8 and 6, have started a ministry entitled "Reach the World" in which they have a vision of reaching the lost with the Good News of Jesus Christ. They are looking to raise money to be able to help those who do not know Jesus. They have helped with various outreaches to the community as well as to students at the bus stop. Through conversations with neighborhood friends it is clear that they are hungry to share Christ with others.

A Spirit-Empowered Lifestyle Prepares Our Marriage and Family for Effective Discipleship

WE WILL NOT CONCEAL THEM FROM THEIR CHILDREN, BUT TELL TO THE GENERATION TO COME THE PRAISES OF THE LORD, AND HIS

STRENGTH AND HIS WONDROUS WORKS THAT HE HAS DONE. FOR HE ESTABLISHED A TESTIMONY IN JACOB AND APPOINTED A LAW IN ISRAEL, WHICH HE COMMANDED OUR FATHERS THAT THEY SHOULD TEACH THEM TO THEIR CHILDREN, THAT THE GENERATION TO COME MIGHT KNOW, EVEN THE CHILDREN YET TO BE BORN, THAT THEY MAY ARISE AND TELL THEM TO THEIR CHILDREN, THAT THEY SHOULD PUT THEIR CONFIDENCE IN GOD AND NOT FORGET THE WORKS OF GOD, BUT KEEP HIS COMMANDMENTS.

PSALM 78:4-7

To disciple someone involves a life on life relationship that is deep and real. In order to disciple our family members, we must be willing to take the time to get to know them and share life at their level. We must recognize that our lives speak louder than our words. What our lives are modeling in front of them is the largest part of what we are teaching them about the importance of a relationship with God.

Ask the Holy Spirit how He would have your marriage/family begin to go deeper in effective discipleship. Write down anything that He speaks to you:

_____

_____

_____

The Ultimate Goal of Marriage and Family Life – A Lifestyle of Unconditional Love

WE KNOW THAT WE HAVE PASSED FROM DEATH TO LIFE, BECAUSE WE

LOVE EACH OTHER. ANYONE WHO DOES NOT LOVE REMAINS IN DEATH.

1 JOHN 3:14

Too many of our marriages and families have suffered spiritual death due to a lack of love in the home. As we prepare our lives to be vessels of God's Spirit we can believe Him to fill us with His love and transform every aspect of our family.

Ask the Holy Spirit how He would have your marriage/family begin to go deeper in your unconditional love for one another. Write down anything that He speaks to you:

_____

_____

_____

A Family Story from Taiwan

In Taiwan, there was a man who claimed to be a Christian, but he was in the habit of beating his wife. As a result she had vowed that if this was Christianity, she wanted nothing to do with it. Their daughter became a Christian and heard about the teaching of establishing God's Kingdom in the family. She was instructed that even if one member of the family is born again, they can shift the spiritual atmosphere of the home.

As a result, she began to personally ask God's Spirit to establish His Kingdom in their family. She began to be a Spirit-Empowered vessel of His Life to those around her. As a result of this shift in her lifestyle and the spiritual fruit that was coming from her life, within a short period of time, God had so changed the heart of her mother that she began asking her daughter questions about Jesus. Soon after this, her mother gave her life to Jesus Christ. She then forgave her husband and began to love him unconditionally, in spite of his past sins against her.

The man was so touched by this undeserved love that he surrendered his life to Jesus Christ as well. The whole family then began seeking Jesus together! Praise God!

This is just one of thousands of family testimonies across the nation of Taiwan, as the Body of Christ there has sought to equip husbands and wives to establish God's Kingdom in their families.

A Testimony of a Single Congregation That Sought to Establish Corporate Times of Seeking God in Their Marriages and Families

(Timeframe: Approx. 6 months – 1 year)

Marriages Restored

Many marriages were brought back from the brink of divorce. Couples testify that there is a depth of spiritual union that never existed prior to establishing a Spirit-Empowered lifestyle in their marriages. One couple in England that started this lifestyle in their home, admittedly nominal in their faith at the time, has been so transformed as individuals and in their marriage that doors have opened for them to share their testimony in cities across the nation. Many are hungry to experience what God has accomplished in them.

Children and Youth Encountering God

- Small children passionately worshipping God without being prompted by an adult

- Those who have begun seeking this lifestyle in their families testify that there is now less need for discipline in the home as God's Spirit began to convict and instruct their children. One young boy had a dream in which Jesus was riding on a donkey next to him. Jesus instructed the boy, "I want you to obey your mother and father." When he woke up he remembered what Jesus had told him.

- A young child was physically healed of an illness as she cried out to God in prayer. Prior to this healing she was about to be taken to the hospital.

- Youth spontaneously having times of seeking God's Presence outside of the official "family worship" time. In a home where they were having just one night of seeking God a week, their 18 year old son said, "Can we have two or three times of seeking God every week, because I think we're just scratching the surface of what God can do here."

- Several young children (ages 5-7) have approached their parents asking, at times even begging, to have the Bible read to them

- A large percentage of the youth in the church are now considering or have already begun the process of being equipped for missions work. Seeing their parents model a lifestyle that is lived solely for the purposes of God is having an impact on the long-term dreams of their children. "I want to be a missionary" is increasingly becoming the refrain of many.

Doors Open to the Unchurched

- Example: A 9 year old reading his Bible caused his unchurched 9 year friend to start reading his Bible. The confused family was eventually admonished by their young child, "We need to go to church."

- Where the church previously had no ministry presence doors began to open to establish this lifestyle in workplaces, and in other sectors of society.

Final Practical Encouragement with Regards to Establishing God's Kingdom in Our Marriages & Families

I hope that you can see the tremendous value there is in establishing a Spirit-Empowered lifestyle in your marriage and family. I hope that you are inspired by this chapter to begin this lifestyle in your home. For those who have already begun, I hope and pray that you are encouraged to go deeper than where you are currently. Even if you are the only one in your marriage or family who is interested in establishing this lifestyle, there are countless testimonies of those who began by themselves, but in time God changed the heart of their spouse, or their children, so that the whole family began to desire God's Kingdom to come in their midst.

Please keep in mind that only the Holy Spirit of God can lead us to implement a Spirit-Empowered lifestyle in such a way that the fruit remains. I trust that as you seek Him in regards to this, God will give you wisdom in how to apply each of these keys within the context of your marriage and family. I trust that as you do, it will bring a deepening richness to your lives. I also trust that it will position you to make a difference in the lives of many others around you.

Do not get discouraged if the fruit does not take place immediately. Though it will not likely be easy to see this lifestyle firmly established in your marriage and family, our God is able to do this good work. I encourage you to persevere until this lifestyle is deeply established and flowing in and through your family for the Glory of God!

LET US NOT LOSE HEART IN DOING GOOD, FOR IN DUE TIME WE WILL REAP IF WE DO NOT GROW WEARY. GALATIANS 6:9

Next Steps

If you took the time to pray and ask God's Spirit how He specifically desires your marriage and/or family to begin to seek him, then you should have a good practical starting point to begin seeking God together. I hesitate to say that you have a manual or strategy, but you should have some clear next steps. As you seek Him over time, He will continue to reveal to you even greater depths of how He desires you to seek Him. You may consider regularly coming back to this section of the book just to pray into what God revealed to you, until this is firmly established.

Discussion Questions:

1. Based on the scriptures we looked at, what do you believe God's original intention was in establishing marriage and family? (Genesis 18:16-18, Deut. 6:6-9)
2. How does your real life experience with marriage and family compare with God's original intention?

3. How were you encouraged to implement these Spiritual Keys in your home/place of living?

For Those Married/with a Family

4. How would you describe the present state of your marriage/family relationships?
5. Do you believe that by implementing the Spiritual Keys in your marriage/family that this would improve the Spiritual state of these relationships? In what way?
6. In what ways were you inspired by God's Spirit to begin to implement these Spiritual keys in your home?

Action Step:

Take time to ask God's Spirit for at least one way that He wants you to begin to make an adjustment in your lifestyle as it relates to your marriage/family. Write down anything that He speaks to your heart and begin to pray into this. Only He is able to give you the strength to walk this out, so you will want to bring this regularly to Him in prayer.

_____

_____

_____

Prayer Focus:

We want to pray into our marriage/family relationships:

Father, I thank You that You are the Creator of marriage and family. I thank You that You had a good purpose in Your heart when You caused this type of relationship to be established on the earth. I ask for Your mercy for every way that I have not followed Your ways in my family relationships. Help me to repent and turn wholeheartedly to You. Help me to be a part of Your solution in my family. I want to be a vessel that You can use. Grant me Your grace to put into practice these spiritual keys, so that my marriage / family become everything that You desire for it to be. (Keep praying as God's Spirit leads you.)

More resources on marriage and family are available in the *Spirit Empowered Family* section of our website: www.dninternational/SpiritEmpoweredFamily

Here are some further Scriptures for those interested in studying the subject of marriage and family at a deeper level. You may consider taking time to meditate on the scriptures from each area that applies to you.

Marriage: Genesis 2:18-25, Matthew 19:3-9, Mark 10:6-9, 1 Cor. 13:4-13, Col. 3:18-23, Hebrews 13:4

Husbands: Psalm 128:1-6, Proverbs 5:18-20, 13:22, 1 Cor. 7:2-5, 11:3, Eph. 5:21-33, Col. 3:19, 1 Tim. 3:1-6, 1 Peter 3:7-12

Wives: Genesis 2:18-25, Proverbs 19:14, 31:10-31, 1 Cor. 7:1-5, Eph. 5:21-33, Col. 3:18, 1 Tim. 3:11, Titus 2:3-5, 1 Peter 3:1-6, 8-12

Parenting: Genesis 1:27-28, Exodus 12:23-27, 20:4-6, 34:5-8, Numbers 14:17-19, Deut. 4:9-10, 39-40, 5:8-10, 6:4-9, 31:12-13, Joshua 4:6-7, 4:20-22, 14:9, Judges 13:6-8, 2 Kings 17:41, 2 Chron. 20:13, Ezra 10:1, Job 1:1-5, Psalm 34:11, 78:4-6, 103:13, 17, 127:3-4, Prov. 3:12, 13:22, 24, 17:6, 22:6, 22:15, 23:13, 29:15, Isaiah 49:15, Jer. 31:29-30, 32:17-19, Hosea 4:6, Joel 2:15-17, Mal. 4:6, Matthew 18:1-6, 19:13-14, John 9:1-3, Acts 2:39, Eph. 6:1-4, Col. 3:21, 1 Tim. 3:4, 12, Titus 1:6, Hebrews 12:5-11,

Children: Psalm 127:3, 139:13, 144:12, Proverbs 1:7-10, 4:1, 5:7, 7:24, Matthew 18:1-6, 19:13-14, John 9:1-3, Acts 13:33, Romans 1:30, 9:8, Eph. 6:1-3, Col. 3:20, 1 Tim. 5:4, 2 Tim. 3:2, Titus 1:6, 1 John 2:28

Chapter 12: Is a Regional Move of God Even Possible?

IF I SHUT UP THE HEAVENS SO THAT THERE IS NO RAIN, OR IF I COMMAND THE LOCUST TO DEVOUR THE LAND, OR IF I SEND PESTILENCE AMONG MY PEOPLE, AND MY PEOPLE WHO ARE CALLED BY MY NAME HUMBLE THEMSELVES AND PRAY AND SEEK MY FACE AND TURN FROM THEIR WICKED WAYS, THEN I WILL HEAR FROM HEAVEN, WILL FORGIVE THEIR SIN AND WILL HEAL THEIR LAND.

2 CHRONICLES 7:13-14

Some of us have heard this scripture so often that we have become dull to its meaning. But we cannot afford to become dull to this message. It is truly a message for the people of God for all time. These verses speak of a season when there is difficulty among the people of God. The heavens have been shut and there is a physical or spiritual lack of "rain". How many individuals, marriages, families and local congregations, if brought to the place of sharing honestly about their present state, would have to confess a lack of "rain"? A lack of the greater things that Jesus said would be done through His Spirit-Empowered followers.

Others are experiencing the abundance of God's Spirit working in their personal lives, and even in their marriages and families, but they are looking at a situation in their local congregation, or in their nation, and they feel like there is little that can be done to change the situation. In either case, we must examine the four areas that God highlights in verse 14 and ask God's Spirit to take each of them deeper in us and in those that He would have us share this with. It is these four "Keys to Renewal" that have been present in every true revival in the history of mankind.

Key to Renewal #1: Humility

"GOD IS OPPOSED TO THE PROUD, BUT GIVES GRACE TO THE HUMBLE." SUBMIT THEREFORE TO GOD. RESIST THE DEVIL AND HE WILL FLEE FROM YOU.

JAMES 4:6-7

We will never get to the bottom of humility. We will never figure it out to such a degree that we no longer need to go deeper. In fact, the moment we think we have obtained humility is the moment that we have lost it. Only the Spirit of God can build true humility into our hearts, because it is the exact opposite of our prideful human nature. If we are failing to see a move of God in and through our lives, let us we begin to ask God if we are allowing any pride to remain in our hearts.

Key to Renewal #2: Prayer

NOW WHEN ALL THE PEOPLE WERE BAPTIZED, JESUS WAS ALSO BAPTIZED, AND WHILE HE WAS PRAYING, HEAVEN WAS OPENED, AND THE HOLY SPIRIT DESCENDED UPON HIM IN BODILY FORM LIKE A DOVE, AND A VOICE CAME OUT OF HEAVEN, "YOU ARE MY BELOVED SON, IN YOU I AM WELL-PLEASED."

LUKE 3:21-22

IT WAS AT THIS TIME THAT HE WENT OFF TO THE MOUNTAIN TO PRAY,

AND HE SPENT THE WHOLE NIGHT IN PRAYER TO GOD. AND WHEN DAY CAME, HE CALLED HIS DISCIPLES TO HIM AND CHOSE TWELVE OF THEM, WHOM HE ALSO NAMED AS APOSTLES. LUKE 6:12-13

PRAY WITHOUT CEASING. 1 THESS. 5:17

It was while Jesus prayed that the heavens were opened and the Holy Spirit descended on Him. Jesus Himself modeled a lifestyle of prayer that at times needed to pray through the night. If Jesus, the sinless Son of God was in need of such a prayer life in order to remain deep fellowship with the Father, doesn't it make sense that you and I need to spend even more time in prayer than He did? As those born with a sinful, prideful, unbelieving nature, we should recognize that our prayer life should be like breathing. We need prayer like we need air. If we have not had this type of prayer life, then we should approach Jesus as the disciples did and simply begin to ask Him, "Teach me to pray."

Key to Renewal #3: Seeking God's Face

HOW BLESSED ARE THOSE WHO OBSERVE HIS TESTIMONIES, WHO SEEK HIM WITH ALL THEIR HEART.

PSALM 119:2

I LOVE THOSE WHO LOVE ME; AND THOSE WHO DILIGENTLY SEEK ME WILL FIND ME.

PROVERBS 8:17

"ASK, AND IT WILL BE GIVEN TO YOU; SEEK, AND YOU WILL FIND; KNOCK, AND IT WILL BE OPENED TO YOU. FOR EVERYONE WHO ASKS RECEIVES, AND HE WHO SEEKS FINDS, AND TO HIM WHO KNOCKS IT

WILL BE OPENED." MATTHEW 7:7-8

Seeking implies a focused exertion of effort towards a goal. If we have determined that we are in need of more of the reality of God's Spirit in our lives, then our lifestyle should begin to show that we are seeking Him as often and as fully as possible. This seeking of God will bear much fruit.

Key to Renewal #4: Repentance

THEREFORE REPENT AND RETURN, SO THAT YOUR SINS MAY BE WIPED AWAY, IN ORDER THAT TIMES OF REFRESHING MAY COME FROM THE PRESENCE OF THE LORD.

ACTS 3:19

I NOW REJOICE, NOT THAT YOU WERE MADE SORROWFUL, BUT THAT YOU WERE MADE SORROWFUL TO THE POINT OF REPENTANCE; FOR YOU WERE MADE SORROWFUL ACCORDING TO THE WILL OF GOD, SO THAT YOU MIGHT NOT SUFFER LOSS IN ANYTHING THROUGH US. FOR THE SORROW THAT IS ACCORDING TO THE WILL OF GOD PRODUCES A REPENTANCE WITHOUT REGRET, LEADING TO SALVATION.

2 CORINTHIANS 7:9-10

Confession involves agreeing with God that what we have done is wrong. True repentance goes even further, as we actually choose to turn away from our sin. If we simply agree that our sin is wrong yet continue to live in sin, we are only fooling ourselves. This type of verbal confession that is devoid of true repentance is not beneficial to our relationship with God. God desires a people who will allow His Holy Spirit to convict us moment by moment of every way in which our lives are an

248

offense to Him. Only as we allow true repentance to come into every area of our lives will we be in a position to live as a vessel of God's Holy Spirit.

The Word of God states very plainly that it is only after God's people have come to Him in this humble, prayerful, seeking and repentant way, that He will hear from heaven and heal our land. While the Scriptures are clear that God can heal an entire region, do we have the faith to believe Him for this where we live? The truth is that God desires to do even more than what we think is possible:

NOW TO HIM WHO IS ABLE TO DO FAR MORE ABUNDANTLY BEYOND ALL THAT WE ASK OR THINK, ACCORDING TO THE POWER THAT WORKS WITHIN US, TO HIM BE THE GLORY IN THE CHURCH AND IN CHRIST JESUS TO ALL GENERATIONS FOREVER AND EVER.

EPHESIANS 3:20-21

What would a city or regional revival look like if it took place?

Far too many of us have not witnessed even a congregational revival, let alone an entire city or region entering into the manifestation of God's Kingdom. But just because we have not personally witnessed something does not mean it does not exist or that it is impossible. Scientists with large telescopes tell us about distant planets. We could stand up and say to them, "I don't believe such things are possible. Distant planets do not exist." Why might we react in this manner? If we have not seen these planets for ourselves and we do not trust the scientists, then we may remain in unbelief. Now if the scientists allowed us into their observatory, and we were able to personally look through the telescope and see the planets for ourselves, then we would begin to trust that they exist.

Similarly, due to the fact that many Christ-followers have never seen a regional revival, such a thing may seem difficult to believe. But if we would simply look into the "telescope" of Church history, we will find that not only are regional moves of God's Spirit possible, but they are even greater than what our minds may have thought. Stories are shared about entire villages and regions that have come so heavily into the Presence of God that if you even set foot in that town a sense of awe would so grip your heart that it would be difficult to keep yourself from weeping. The conviction of sin is reported as being so strong that even the most ungodly and skeptical people in the area would be broken underneath it and converted to Jesus Christ.

In some parts of the world, as the regional work of God spread, the Body of Christ would cast aside their previous doctrinal debates and begin to work in unity for their region, resulting in mass conversions of souls into Christ's Kingdom. In other instances, those who stood in opposition to what God was doing would be struck dead for no apparent reason, other than the fact that God would not allow them to stop what He was doing.

It is not uncommon in times of revival that pastors and ministers would be among those whom God convicted and converted. His Spirit revealed to them that though they may be missionaries themselves, they had not yet laid hold of what it means to be truly born again. The Shantung Revival in northern

China in the early 1930's is an example of a time when revival began in the hearts of the missionaries. God's Spirit showed the leadership in the church that they were still unconverted themselves. Here they were laboring in a foreign land for the salvation of others souls, but God had to first show them that they themselves needed the new birth and the empowerment of His Holy Spirit. These missionaries, who had previously been wondering why they lacked power to change the lives of those around them, began to become empowered soul winners for Christ's Kingdom.

These glorious works of God's Spirit beg the question, *"Can anything be done to assist such a revival to take place in our city and region, or are these simply mysterious occurrences that mankind can only receive from God when He chooses to pour out His Spirit in this way?"*

We need only to look at the life of an individual to answer that question. What if an unconverted soul was to tell us, "I'm just waiting on God to change my heart. At present I'm not choosing to humble myself, nor am I seeking Him, but if He comes down to meet with me I suppose I would be open to that."

How would we reply to this apathetic response? Would we not point out that the responsibility of seeing a breakthrough in their lives is not with God but with them? Would we not share that God has already made all the provision necessary for them to come near to Him through the shed blood of His Son Jesus Christ? Would we not labor to show them their need to humble themselves, pray, seek God, and repent of any area of sin that God reveals to them?

The point here being, in an individual life it is abundantly evident that God has already made provision for them to enter into His Kingdom and to live life in communion with Him. The problem is not on God's side of things, and there is no sense of acting as though they are waiting on God to do His part, when God has already done everything that is necessary for them to be birthed into His Kingdom. The responsibility in this situation is not with God to humble Himself, or to seek them, He has already sought us, and expressed that He desires all men to be saved and come to a knowledge of the truth. The burden of responsibility lies entirely with that unconverted soul. Will they choose to humble themselves, pray, seek God and repent or will they not?

Consider King Ahab when it comes to personal revival. The Word of God tells us in 1 Kings that no one else had ever sold themselves to do evil as he did.

SURELY THERE WAS NO ONE LIKE AHAB WHO SOLD HIMSELF TO DO EVIL IN THE SIGHT OF THE LORD, BECAUSE JEZEBEL HIS WIFE INCITED HIM. 1 KINGS 21:25

But a mere two verses later, when Ahab heard of God's judgment against him, and he humbled himself, and look at God's amazing response:

IT CAME ABOUT WHEN AHAB HEARD THESE WORDS, THAT HE TORE HIS CLOTHES AND PUT ON SACKCLOTH AND FASTED, AND HE LAY IN SACKCLOTH AND WENT ABOUT DESPONDENTLY. THEN THE WORD OF THE LORD CAME TO ELIJAH THE TISHBITE, SAYING, "DO YOU SEE HOW AHAB HAS HUMBLED HIMSELF BEFORE ME? BECAUSE HE HAS HUMBLED HIMSELF BEFORE ME, I WILL NOT BRING THE EVIL IN HIS DAYS." 1 KINGS 21:27-29

We serve an extraordinarily merciful God! If anyone chooses to do these four simple things in their individual life, do we have any doubt that He will respond with forgiveness and restoration? How long would it take for that individual to begin to enter into an encounter with God? Surely it would not take more than a few minutes, hours, days, or weeks. If a month went by without a real breakthrough, then we would have to question the sincerity of their humility and repentance.

While this is abundantly clear in the life of an individual, it should be equally clear at every level of society. If any marriage or family will seek God in this way can there be any doubt that God will respond? Are we not aware that God desires to move even more powerfully and in a greater measure than we could even ask or imagine? (Ephesians 3:20)

What if a local congregation set itself to seek God with an aim to humble themselves, pray, and repent of every area of sin that they may be living in, would God respond? Would He make them wait months or years or decades before any movement began to take place? Could it be that our unbelief regarding God's ability to move has much more to do with our own lack of true heart level repentance than it does with His lack of desire and power to change things? We can choose to seek God, we can even fast and pray, but if we fail to truly repent of our sin, then we will find a barrier remains.

FOR THE EYES OF THE LORD MOVE TO AND FRO THROUGHOUT THE EARTH THAT HE MAY STRONGLY SUPPORT THOSE WHOSE HEART IS COMPLETELY HIS.

2 CHRONICLES 16:9

What if the Body of Christ in a city, region or nation collectively decided to humble themselves, pray, seek His face, and repent of every one of their wicked ways, would God not respond? Would He not answer them and begin to heal their region? Would He not willingly pour out His Spirit to establish His Kingdom on earth as it is in heaven? We must understand the heart of God in these matters. He longs to answer our prayers for regional revival even more than we desire to ask for it. He comes running to those who are seeking to invite Him into their situation. Therefore, the real hindrance lies in our lack of humility, prayer, seeking, and repentance. If we have diligently dealt with each of these areas and it is still not happening immediately, then we can trust God's timing and help be a part of His corporate solution.

Firsthand Testimony of Congregational Revival

I have personally had the privilege of witnessing a congregational level revival that eventually began to impact other cities around the country. This revival was much like one you would read about in a book from the past. It was not showy or loud and did not call attention to a human personality. It began small, in the hearts of a few of the leaders. God was showing us just how self-reliant we had been in seeking to do His work in the congregation as well as in our city. We had been so earnest to unite the Body of Christ and to labor together for a city-wide revival that we had failed to see just how much of what we were doing was in human effort and in human ways.

I personally watched as God's Spirit began to corporately deal with the sin patterns which were present within our group.

254

We would come into times of corporate prayer and worship during the week and God's Spirit was bringing conviction to the deep hidden areas of sin that many of us had held onto our entire lives. We began to have corporate times of intercessory prayer and worship nearly every night of the week. This went on for some time as God began sending us out into the streets to reach souls for Him. As He continued to work more deeply in our lives and bring revival to our congregation He then began to elevate the congregation in the region. Within a short period of time the senior pastor was placed as the head of our cities ministerial association and the young adult minister was given a position helping to spearhead a city-wide youth initiative.

City-level Move of God's Spirit

A city level move of God's Spirit later took place when the police department in our city came to the churches and asked for help. They were confounded by crime and violence in a particular area of the inner city. An off-duty police officer was recently shot and killed and this incident caused such desperation that God used it for His glory. A born-again police officer submitted a plan to the Chief of Police to institute 40 days of prayer in the most crime ridden area of the city. This initiative was entitled "Operation Armor All". Our congregation joined with 70 other ministries in going down during the 40 days to pray for this section of the city.

During these days we were waiting to see what God would do. It was around the 11th day that we saw the first newspaper headline, the main gang leader in that area of the city, a man that the police had been unable to catch for some time, was just arrested. As we read the report we saw God's hand at work in how he was turned in to the police. Another gang member who was his second in command had led the police right to his hiding place. This gang member said that he didn't know why he was doing it, but he said to the police that he "just had to turn him in."

A few days later a major drug bust took place in this same area of the city which resulted in hundreds being arrested and drugs being removed from the streets. This interesting story of a police department fighting crime through prayer even made national news. At the end of the 40 days the report came in that there were no murders during the days of prayer. This was truly unprecedented! Not only that, but crime began to drop following those days to such a degree that years after this initiative there are still tangible results.

Pursuing a National Level Revival

In time God began to burden us to believe Him for a national level revival. As our relatively small ministry began to organize for a national conference, we received favor from a large organization which was willing to send out the invitation to their entire database. We were blessed that they were willing to do this and we were relying on them to get people there. As we were closing in on the timing of the retreat, there were less than 10 people signed up. Because we had booked a hotel for these meetings we had already signed a contract to pay for a large number of hotel rooms, so there were financial implications in the conference becoming a failure.

We began to pray with a greater sense of desperation but nothing that we were doing was causing people to sign up. It was at this time that we sought to corporately humble ourselves and wait upon God in silence. During this season of waiting before Him, one evening God spoke clearly to us and said, "You are asking Me to open the nation to you, but the idols of the land are still in your own hearts. Only as you allow Me to deal with these idols will I open the nation to you."

It is hard to express just how humbling this message was to our little core group. Here we were, a small band of about 20 people, fasting, praying, and believing God to move in our nation. We thought that we were fully with God. Our sense was that we were way out in front, forerunning for God in a nation that was far from Him. We thought we were surrendered. We thought we were radical. We were praying into the night, weeping and asking God to change our nation. But to hear God's perspective cut through all of the external fervency, and revealed our hearts. This is a clear illustration that we may be seeking to humble ourselves, we may be praying and seeking God, but without His kind of repentance there is still a hindrance.

At first we were in stunned silence as this message traveled across our small band of believers. But amazingly enough, God began to reveal to person after person the idols of their hearts. I personally watched as God corporately dealt with a group of people. For each of us the idols of our hearts were different, but He carefully and graciously began to walk us through this new level of repentance.

What was God's response to our repentance? Did He wait until we had gotten ourselves perfected before responding? Absolutely not! From the moment we began to humble ourselves, there was a Heavenly response. One by one, influential leaders from various parts of the country began to sign up for the retreat. We had not done anything different in our attempt to publicize the event, but suddenly people were being led by God's Spirit to travel across the country and come for the conference. Out of that conference, key cities across the nation began to open up to partner together for a national move of God's Spirit.

What is my point in sharing this testimony? If nothing else, it is to make it abundantly clear that God is more than able to move at every level of society: In an individual, in a family, in a local congregation, in a city, and in a nation. It is also to share that often times, if we are not seeing God move in this way, it has to do with the depth and sincerity of our humility, of our seeking of Him, of our prayer, and of our repentance. If we are lacking in any of these four components, then we should recognize immediately, our lack of seeing God at work has nothing to do with His lack of desire or ability, but there must still be something in us that is hindering Him from moving in power. I believe that if we will allow God to change our default setting, and instead of thinking that we are waiting on God to move, we begin to realize that He is waiting on us to align ourselves more closely to Him before He moves, then we can save ourselves a great deal of unnecessary pain.

God's Ministry or "My Ministry"

FOR NO MAN CAN LAY A FOUNDATION OTHER THAN THE ONE WHICH IS LAID, WHICH IS JESUS CHRIST. NOW IF ANY MAN BUILDS ON THE FOUNDATION WITH GOLD, SILVER, PRECIOUS STONES, WOOD, HAY, STRAW, EACH MAN'S WORK WILL BECOME EVIDENT; FOR THE DAY WILL SHOW IT BECAUSE IT IS TO BE REVEALED WITH FIRE, AND THE FIRE

ITSELF WILL TEST THE QUALITY OF EACH MAN'S WORK.

1 COR. 3:11-13

Most of the time, we may come to find out that one of the greatest hindrances in our seeing a move of God is that we have still been operating as though we need to do something for God, when He is waiting for us to recognize that He will do everything through us if we will simply surrender our labors to Him. There is much discussion in the global Body of Christ in our day about doing "ministry" for God. It should be clarified that the highest form of ministry, and the only form of service that God Himself recognizes as true ministry, is that which is done in service to His will. All other "ministry" is done in the religious flesh and will be burned up on the final day.

FOR SINCE THERE IS JEALOUSY AND STRIFE AMONG YOU, ARE YOU NOT FLESHLY, AND ARE YOU NOT WALKING LIKE MERE MEN? FOR WHEN ONE SAYS, "I AM OF PAUL," AND ANOTHER, "I AM OF APOLLOS," ARE YOU NOT MERE MEN? 1 COR. 3:3-4

If there is a motive for our ministry that is not simply to see the will of God accomplished, then we are on very dangerous ground. There is a tremendous warning in this spiritual truth. We must check our heart motives in any service to see if we are truly doing what we are doing because we have heard God say that this is what He wants, as opposed to us doing "ministry" for some motive of our own. Let us avoid doing any form of service simply to be approved by our fellowman.

We must be very careful that we do not waste the limited time God has entrusted to us by giving ourselves to things that may appear very religious, and even good on the outside, but are not the specific will of our Father. We would be wise to have ministry decisions flow out of times of interaction with the Spirit of God in which we have asked, and waited for the answer to these simple questions, "What is Your will? What is your way to accomplish Your will?" Only as we are certain that we have His answer to these questions, are we in a position to do ministry that will bear lasting fruit.

God's ways vs. Our Ways

"FOR AS THE HEAVENS ARE HIGHER THAN THE EARTH, SO ARE MY WAYS HIGHER THAN YOUR WAYS AND MY THOUGHTS THAN YOUR THOUGHTS." ISAIAH 55:9

God's ways are as far above our ways as the heavens are above the earth. Therefore, even when the will of God is revealed to us, if we simply run out and seek to accomplish this in our human understanding, we will fail. Many servants of God are diligently seeking to see souls saved, discipled, and sent out to save others, but because they have not inquired of God's ways, they are failing to bear lasting fruit.

The truth of the matter is that God is waiting on us. He is waiting for us to humble ourselves in the depths of our hearts. He is waiting on us to seek Him more deeply than we have in the past. He is waiting for us to allow Him to teach us what He means by prayer. And He is waiting for us to repent of every way in which the idols of our nation are still in our own hearts. If we will do our part, He will do His. And when He moves in power, in our individual lives, in our marriages and families, in our local congregation, and in our city and region, we will wonder why we did not seek to do this sooner!

260

Discussion Questions:

1. Have you ever been a part of, and/or read about a regional revival in which God's Spirit moved across a whole area? If so, what stands out to you about this?

2. Do you believe that there is anything we can do to prepare our lives for a regional move of God's Spirit? If so, what?

3. What stood out to you from the testimonies that were shared in this chapter?

Action Step:

Based on the four keys to Renewal: Humility, Prayer, Seeking God's Face, and Repentance, what is God's Spirit speaking to you? Take time to ask Him how He would have you respond to what His Spirit is placing on your heart. Wait on Him to speak to you. Write down what He reveals and put it into practice.

Humility:

_____

_____

_____

Prayer:

_____

_____

_____

Seeking God's face:

_____

_____

_____

Areas of your life in need of repentance:

_____

_____

_____

Prayer Focus:

We want to pray for a revival to take place in our nation:

Father, I thank You that You desire to move in my nation even more than I desire You to move. I ask that You would reveal to me any way in which my life is presently hindering You from moving in the way that You desire. I thank You that You are more than able to move powerfully in my nation. Use me as part of Your solution. (Keep praying as God's Spirit directs you.)

Note: Disciple Nations International partners with various cities and nations in order to serve them as they pursue corporate renewal. If you are interested in any of the resources that we have available you can contact us at: office@dninternational.org or visit us on the web: www.dninternational.org

Chapter 13: Establishing Christ's Kingdom in the Workplace

In previous chapters, we have looked at the impact that God's Spirit can make in an individual life and in a marriage and family. The next step is to begin to seek God for wisdom as to how He wants to transform our sphere of influence. Let us prayerfully join with other Jesus–followers to help build a lifestyle of seeking God in our place of work and in our community. There are some workplaces that have been changed as even one Christ-follower began to start this process of inviting God's Spirit to move in their midst.

Imagine every business, every facet of government, and every school, being led by those who are seeking to walk out a Spirit-Empowered lifestyle. Imagine regular strategic prayer piercing the darkness at the local bank, restaurant, engineering firm, college campus, elementary school, television station, and police department. Imagine co-workers coming to Christ, teachers and students seeing the power of the Living God, open doors to share the Gospel where there had been only hardness. Imagine whole businesses experiencing the transformation of God's Spirit. The possibilities are endless!

HE HAS SENT ME TO BIND UP THE BROKENHEARTED, TO PROCLAIM FREEDOM FOR THE CAPTIVES AND RELEASE FROM DARKNESS FOR THE PRISONERS.

ISAIAH 61:1

Testimony of Establishing Christ's Kingdom in Business

In a technological hub in East Asia, a businessman who had begun to establish a Spirit-Empowered lifestyle in his family recently felt compelled to take this same lifestyle into his workplace. As the division head of one facet of a manufacturing plant, he had a considerable level of responsibility. Though his office was predominantly Buddhist, he began a corporate gathering with several other Christ-followers, in order to read the Word of God aloud, worship God, and pray on behalf of their workplace.

Within a short period of time, God's Spirit began to show him unethical practices in their business activity that he was still engaged in. Here he was asking the Holy Spirit to move in his workplace, while he himself was still contributing to the ungodliness of the office. As he repented for allowing financial compromise, God's Spirit began to move in the office bringing more and more souls into a saving faith in Jesus Christ. He risked his job to obey God, but before long their small group had grown from a handful to 10, 20, 30 and eventually 40-50 people gathering on a regular basis to seek Jesus.

God's Spirit then began to reveal another area of sin. They were keeping the workers so late at the office in order to meet their quotas that there was no time for the workers to go home and help their families enter into a lifestyle of seeking God. Relationships with spouses and children were suffering.

This same man risked his job again by choosing to begin to let the employees go home at 6pm and no longer allowed overtime, in order to ensure that they had time with their families. If their production quota was not met, it would mean the loss of his job.

Within a short period of time his superior came and asked him, "What is going on in your department?" In simple honesty he explained that they were seeking to honor Jesus Christ in the workplace. At first his overseer did not think he was being serious but eventually stated, "Your department has become the most productive department in the entire company. Whatever you are doing here, we want you to share it with all the other department heads. We have scheduled a meeting for you to share with them for one hour."

At this one hour meeting the man shared a five point presentation beginning with a slide which stated, "The fear of the Lord is the beginning of knowledge." (Proverbs 1:7) and concluded with a slide which stated, "Jesus Christ is the solution to all of our problems". Though some of the other department heads were coming from a Buddhist background, one stated, "I may not understand all this, but there's something about this Jesus man!" The Christ-followers now have a vision to establish a lifestyle of seeking God in every department in the entire company!

Just one person with a vision for establishing Christ's Kingdom at their workplace has had an impact on an entire company!

This is just one example of thousands around the world. In Taiwan alone, they have seen hundreds of marketplace professionals beginning to take their workplaces for Jesus, as they have established a corporate lifestyle of seeking God. Testimonies are coming from the government, film and television studios, small businesses, and doctor's offices. It is truly amazing what God is able to accomplish when we come in faith and simply give Him room to live His Life in and through us.

Uganda is now at the point where virtually every business in the capital city of Kampala has established a corporate gathering of Christ-followers who are seeking Him for their place of work. Believers from different congregations, join together to read the Word, worship, pray and invite God to come and have His way in their workplace. These fellowships strategically pray for their workplace environments and they have seen dramatic answers to prayer. In this way, marketplace fellowships have spread into the President's office, the Parliament, banks, hotels, and virtually every sector of life. They now have many businesses with names that give praise to God (for example, Hosanna Reality, Hallelujah Video Rental).

Part of what it means to see the Kingdom of God manifested in the marketplace, is that the economic resources of the land begin to be reallocated and placed towards the establishment of Christ's Kingdom. Whereas before the resources of the land were being put towards ever increasing darkness, now we can see a shift that causes the financial resources to be placed into the hands of the godly, for the purpose of being used for Christ's purposes in the land.

Do you believe that such a thing can take place in your nation? More importantly, do you believe that God thinks this is possible? Do you believe that God wants this to happen where you work? If so, then let us link our hearts with His faith and trust Him to give specific guidance as to how to see this take place in our sphere of influence.

A Scientist Invites God into His Workplace

Dr. George Washington Carver was born into slavery in the United States of America in the 1860's. Even though the Civil War was coming to an end at that time, he was still denied education due to his skin color. This did not stop George from pursuing his passion to understand God's creation.

Later in life George eventually went to high school and graduated college with a degree in agricultural science. At one point in his career he had a conversation with God in which He asked Jesus to show Him the secrets of the universe. God responded to his request by saying, "Your mind is too small to perceive this." Eventually George asked God, "Then teach me the mysteries of the peanut."

What was the result of his taking the time to hear from God?

George's research eventually resulted in the creation of more than 300 products from peanuts. From paint, peanut butter, cooking oil, to using peanuts as a medicine for respiratory illnesses. In addition, he created hundreds of other products from sweet potatoes, soybeans, pecans and sweet potatoes. It should be noted, that George's goal was not to become rich and famous but to help the poor people whose lives were improved through these inventions. He did not patent peanut butter because he believed that food was a gift from God. On his grave was written, *He could have added fortune to fame, but caring for neither, he found happiness and honor in being helpful to the world.*

It is said that George would often state that God is the One who guided Him and without Jesus he was nothing. Here was a man who was a servant of Jesus Christ. He spent time waiting on God to hear His wisdom, and when just one small facet of God's creation was unlocked to him, it provided hundreds of solutions to everyday needs.

Could it be that God is looking for men and women today who will take the time to invite Him into their fields of labor so that He can receive similar glory through their lives? How many other secrets does God desire to disclose for the advancement of His Kingdom on the earth?

Biblical Basis for Marketplace Ministry

NOW THEN, IF YOU WILL INDEED OBEY MY VOICE AND KEEP MY COVENANT, THEN YOU SHALL BE MY OWN POSSESSION AMONG ALL THE PEOPLES, FOR ALL THE EARTH IS MINE; AND YOU SHALL BE TO ME A KINGDOM OF PRIESTS AND A HOLY NATION.' THESE ARE THE WORDS THAT YOU SHALL SPEAK TO THE SONS OF ISRAEL."

EXODUS 19:5-6

God spoke to sons of Israel, that a day would come when they would become a "kingdom of priests". This was referring to the kingdom that would come through Jesus, in which every believer would be made a priest of God.

Every Christ-Follower Is a Priest and the Workplace is Our Mission Field

Sadly in many areas of the world, the Body of Christ has not been properly taught and empowered to view the marketplace as their mission field. Reaching the marketplace with the Gospel of the Kingdom is critically important if we are to bring our nation into the fullness of the purposes of God. Based on Peter's writing it is evident that every born again believer is a priest of God.

AND COMING TO HIM AS TO A LIVING STONE WHICH HAS BEEN REJECTED BY MEN, BUT IS CHOICE AND PRECIOUS IN THE SIGHT OF GOD, YOU ALSO, AS LIVING STONES, ARE BEING BUILT UP AS A SPIRITUAL HOUSE FOR A HOLY PRIESTHOOD, TO OFFER UP SPIRITUAL SACRIFICES ACCEPTABLE TO GOD THROUGH JESUS CHRIST...YOU ARE A CHOSEN RACE, A ROYAL PRIESTHOOD, A HOLY NATION, A PEOPLE FOR GOD'S OWN POSSESSION, SO THAT YOU MAY PROCLAIM THE EXCELLENCIES OF HIM WHO HAS CALLED YOU OUT OF DARKNESS INTO HIS MARVELOUS LIGHT.

1 PETER 2:4-5, 9

Do you believe that there are any people who are not full time ministers in Christ's Church? Do you believe that you are a full-time minister of the Gospel?

AND THEY SANG A NEW SONG, SAYING, "WORTHY ARE YOU TO TAKE THE BOOK AND TO BREAK ITS SEALS; FOR YOU WERE SLAIN, AND PURCHASED FOR GOD WITH YOUR BLOOD MEN FROM EVERY TRIBE AND TONGUE AND PEOPLE AND NATION. YOU HAVE MADE THEM TO BE

*A KINGDOM AND PRIESTS TO OUR GOD; AND THEY WILL REIGN UPON
THE EARTH." REVELATION 5:9-10*

God's Word teaches us that every born again believer is a minister, no matter what field of labor they are in. While there are levels of spiritual maturity (1 Cor. 3:1) and while there are those who through their faithful lives have been given a role of serving as overseers and teachers within the Church (Acts 14:23, Titus 1:5, James 3:1), we must never allow this to pull us away from the truth that every truly born again believer is a minister of the Gospel.

Does the global Body of Christ recognize that most people spend the majority of their time in the workplace?

Do we realize that the Church is the people who have a covenant relationship with Jesus Christ and not a specific type of religious building? Do we realize that all Christ-followers have been called to be priests of God, right where they live and work?

Can the Body of Christ afford to ignore the workplace? Do we as the Church recognize the tremendous opportunity and responsibility that Jesus Christ has given to His followers, to disciple the souls that He has placed in our workplace? If we fail to realize that the workplace is one of the primary mission fields for the Body of Christ, we miss the perspective God has for us to daily serve as His ambassadors to a lost and dying world.

*NOW ALL THESE THINGS ARE FROM GOD, WHO RECONCILED US TO
HIMSELF THROUGH CHRIST AND GAVE US THE MINISTRY OF*

RECONCILIATION, NAMELY, THAT GOD WAS IN CHRIST RECONCILING THE WORLD TO HIMSELF, NOT COUNTING THEIR TRESPASSES AGAINST THEM, AND HE HAS COMMITTED TO US THE WORD OF RECONCILIATION. THEREFORE, WE ARE AMBASSADORS FOR CHRIST, AS THOUGH GOD WERE MAKING AN APPEAL THROUGH US.

2 COR. 5:18-20

What if those in positions of influence in government, business, education, media and the arts used their influence for Jesus Christ? What kind of impact would this begin to have on all facets of life in our society? Could we see whole cities literally turned upside down as the Kingdom of God is established? (Acts 17:6)

Discussion Questions:

1. Have you viewed yourself as a full-time minister of the Gospel in the past?

2. Do you now believe that you are in full-time ministry? Why or why not?

3. 2 Corinthians 5 states that we are "ambassadors" for Christ and that we have been given a "word of reconciliation". What do you think this means?

4. How did this chapter cause you to rethink or confirm your understanding of "full-time ministry"?

5. What difference does it make to recognize that you are a missionary in your sphere of influence? How should this affect your lifestyle?

Action Steps:

Coming to realize that God sees you as a missionary ought to cause you to rethink how you are approaching your workplace/sphere of influence. Ask God's Holy Spirit for a specific action step that He wants you to take regarding your sphere of influence. Prayerfully consider writing down any way that God may ask you to begin a corporate gathering of believers at your workplace.

_____

_____

_____

For those who are at a workplace, prayerfully begin to ask God's Spirit for His wisdom as to how you can begin to invite Him to move in your workplace. Often times the first step is to begin to allow God's Spirit to work more deeply in your own heart and life. As we have mentioned, some of those who were unaware of any other believers had to begin alone, but in time God blessed their labors. We hope and pray that the testimonies of entire workplaces being transformed as one Christ-follower stepped out in faith, will be an encouragement to push past any obstacles that the enemy may seek to throw at you and to simply begin to trust God to use your life to establish His Kingdom in your workplace.

Prayer Focus:

We want to pray into this truth that every born again believer in Jesus Christ is a priest and minister of the Living God.

Father, I thank You for calling me into Your service. I ask that You would help me to see that I am Your priest in my sphere of influence and that my lifestyle will either cause others to be drawn to You or to be pushed away from You. I desire to be a faithful ambassador of Your Kingdom in my sphere of influence. Help me to hear from You and know how You want me to make a difference right where You have placed me. I thank You in advance for the fruit that You will bear in and through my life, as I trust You to use me for Your Glory. (Keep praying into this as God leads.)

For further workplace resources visit the **Marketplace Revolution** section of our website:

www.dninternational.org/marketplace

Chapter 14: Establishing Christ's Kingdom in a Region

THE GLORY WHICH YOU HAVE GIVEN ME I HAVE GIVEN TO THEM, THAT THEY MAY BE ONE, JUST AS WE ARE ONE; I IN THEM AND YOU IN ME, THAT THEY MAY BE PERFECTED IN UNITY, SO THAT THE WORLD MAY KNOW THAT YOU SENT ME, AND LOVED THEM, EVEN AS YOU HAVE LOVED ME.

JOHN 17:22-23

Imagine spiritual leaders gathering every week across a region to seek God's intervention. Imagine 50-100 congregations uniting together every month to bring God's Kingdom into their area. Imagine if each participating congregation had already encouraged all their membership to establish a Spirit-Empowered Lifestyle in every marriage, family, workplace, and sphere of influence. Picture thousands of Christ-followers from many different denominations gathered together on a regular basis to establish a regional time of seeking God.

Whole communities could be transformed in less than a year. Whole cities could be overtaken by the Gospel of Jesus Christ. Marriages restored across a whole society. Not just an individual but a whole school or a whole community of youths rescued from destructive lifestyles and given a new purpose in life. The collective spiritual power of such a contingency of believers, united in living out a lifestyle of radical abandonment to Jesus Christ could literally transform a nation! This is not an exaggeration.

In recent years, establishing a Spirit-Empowered lifestyle in the regional Church has literally begun to shift the course of entire nations. For instance, the national level gathering of ministries in Uganda paved the way for God's Spirit to urge the President to hand the flag of the nation over to the Body of Christ. Those who lived during that time stated that this moment was the turning point in seeing the Gospel spread into every facet of society.

Is such a thing possible in your nation? What about the areas of the world where there are only a handful of believers in the entire region; is this possible even there?

THEN THE DISCIPLES CAME TO JESUS PRIVATELY AND SAID, "WHY COULD WE NOT DRIVE IT OUT?" AND HE SAID TO THEM, "BECAUSE OF THE LITTLENESS OF YOUR FAITH; FOR TRULY I SAY TO YOU, IF YOU HAVE FAITH THE SIZE OF A MUSTARD SEED, YOU WILL SAY TO THIS MOUNTAIN, 'MOVE FROM HERE TO THERE,' AND IT WILL MOVE; AND NOTHING WILL BE IMPOSSIBLE TO YOU.

MATTHEW 17:19-20

Jesus states that if we have faith the size of a mustard seed that nothing will be impossible for us. Therefore we hope that the testimonies in this book have served to encourage you to believe that our God is able to do this work in any nation, if we will simply step out and begin building with those that God has placed around us.

275

God Sees One Church in Our Region

To see this type of lifestyle established within a local congregation is a wonderful thing and can have great impact at the local level. But if we wish to see our entire region or nation transformed we must begin to see the Church as God sees it. We must begin to ask hard questions that will challenge the status quo of how the Church has operated in the past.

Did God really intend for there to be over 40,000 different denominations?

When God looks at our region does He see all the divisions that we have placed there with our various ministry names, titles and positions, or does He see only One Church?

AND KNOWING THEIR THOUGHTS JESUS SAID TO THEM, "ANY KINGDOM DIVIDED AGAINST ITSELF IS LAID WASTE; AND ANY CITY OR HOUSE DIVIDED AGAINST ITSELF WILL NOT STAND."

MATTHEW 12:25

Jesus made it clear that if any kingdom was divided against itself that it would be laid waste and not be able to stand. If we see that the Church is failing to have the impact that Jesus said that it would we would be wise to check our hearts to see if there is any way that we are walking in unforgiveness and division. It is absolutely essential in our labors to establish God's Kingdom to maintain a heart of love and unity with the rest of the Body of Christ.

THEREFORE IF YOU ARE PRESENTING YOUR OFFERING AT THE ALTAR, AND THERE REMEMBER THAT YOUR BROTHER HAS SOMETHING AGAINST YOU, LEAVE YOUR OFFERING THERE BEFORE THE ALTAR AND

GO; FIRST BE RECONCILED TO YOUR BROTHER, AND THEN COME AND PRESENT YOUR OFFERING. MATTHEW 5:23-24

Breaking A "My Kingdom" Mentality

Does God have a greater vision than simply the growth of our own ministry?

DO NOTHING FROM SELFISHNESS OR EMPTY CONCEIT, BUT WITH HUMILITY OF MIND REGARD ONE ANOTHER AS MORE IMPORTANT THAN YOURSELVES; DO NOT MERELY LOOK OUT FOR YOUR OWN PERSONAL INTERESTS, BUT ALSO FOR THE INTERESTS OF OTHERS.

PHILIPPIANS 2:3-4

In far too many locations around the world there is a "my kingdom" mentality that stifles partnership within the Body of Christ and creates untold divisions. Rather than loving and supporting the Body of Christ in the region where God has placed us, a spirit of religious pride keeps many from working with each other. This mentality has been supported and exported by some of the largest ministries in the world who knowingly or unknowingly foster division, jealousy, and competition. Whenever we find ourselves talking about "my ministry", "my people", "our building, our programs, our successes..." we miss the point completely. All of these are not "ours" but His. Jesus is ministry. If it is not His Life flowing through us, it is simply our religious flesh, which is useless to the true purposes of God.

FOR WHO REGARDS YOU AS SUPERIOR? WHAT DO YOU HAVE THAT YOU DID NOT RECEIVE? AND IF YOU DID RECEIVE IT, WHY DO YOU BOAST AS IF YOU HAD NOT RECEIVED IT? 1 COR. 4:7

Fellow servant of God, if there is anything of true eternal value flowing in or through your life it is not you but Him. It is not your life producing this fruit it is Jesus Christ Himself producing this fruit. Therefore when we make statements like "my church, my ministry, my successes..." we are walking on very precarious ground. None of these are ours. They are all His. May we be very careful to never seek to touch His Glory!

BEHOLD, TO THE LORD YOUR GOD BELONG HEAVEN AND THE HIGHEST HEAVENS, THE EARTH AND ALL THAT IS IN IT.

DEUT 10: 14

"I AM THE LORD, THAT IS MY NAME; I WILL NOT GIVE MY GLORY TO ANOTHER, NOR MY PRAISE TO GRAVEN IMAGES.

ISAIAH 42:8

Fellow servant of the cross, I do not know how you may have been infected with the idea that something is your ministry, your church, or your people, but I stand to tell you definitively that Jesus Christ does not view things in this way. It is time for the global Body of Christ to begin to humble ourselves and submit our way of doing things to God. We must begin to do things in His way and not ours. It is His ministry, it is His Church, and it is His people. It has been and will always be His.

The global church culture has literally been saturated with a false ideology that we are to seek to establish and grow our own ministries. But Jesus Christ said that there is only One Church and it is His. He said that His people were to be One, as

He and the Father are One! Have we walked in this depth of unity?

This unity is what Jesus Himself prayed for us. The same unity that exists between Father and Son is to be our unity in the Body of Christ. Why? Jesus said that it is out of this unity of heart and mind among His people that the world would know that the Father has sent Him.

> *THE GLORY WHICH YOU HAVE GIVEN ME I HAVE GIVEN TO THEM, THAT THEY MAY BE ONE, JUST AS WE ARE ONE; I IN THEM AND YOU IN ME, THAT THEY MAY BE PERFECTED IN UNITY, SO THAT THE WORLD MAY KNOW THAT YOU SENT ME, AND LOVED THEM, EVEN AS YOU HAVE LOVED ME.*
>
> *JOHN 17:22-23*

> *BEHOLD, HOW GOOD AND HOW PLEASANT IT IS FOR BROTHERS TO DWELL TOGETHER IN UNITY! IT IS LIKE THE PRECIOUS OIL UPON THE HEAD, COMING DOWN UPON THE BEARD, EVEN AARON'S BEARD, COMING DOWN UPON THE EDGE OF HIS ROBES. IT IS LIKE THE DEW OF HERMON COMING DOWN UPON THE MOUNTAINS OF ZION; FOR THERE THE LORD COMMANDED THE BLESSING—LIFE FOREVER.*
>
> *PSALM 133:1-3*

When the people of God walk in a depth of unity, the world will know that God sent Jesus. The Psalmist states that in the place of unity there is a commanded blessing. Therefore do you think that the enemy of our souls, knowing that deep unity in the Body of Christ causes people to know that Jesus is for real, has sought to deceive the church into viewing ministry as being ours? Do you think Satan has deceived the Church into thinking that it is normal and acceptable when we claim our ministries and our people as our own and aid and abet the division of Christ's One Church?

Instead, why not acknowledge from this day forward that it is not our Church, it is His. May our lives testify that they are not our people, they are His people, and may we choose to never touch His Glory again in this matter. I assure you, this decision will so radically change the way we do ministry that God Himself will teach us what it means to care for other parts of the Body more than we care about ourselves.

Imagine ministries in a city or region who have so entered into this reality that they serve, give and support the other local congregations in their area even more than they care for themselves. Do you think that such a local congregation would be blessed by the Lord? Do you think that they would begin to see God do in and through them things that they have never seen before?

This is what it means to begin to enter into the reality of a true Regional Church. Where we love and care for the rest of the Body of Christ around us even more than we care for ourselves. As this attitude of heart and mind begins to breakdown every element of the "my Kingdom" mentality, the Kingdom of Jesus Christ will begin to be ushered into our region in greater and greater measure! Hallelujah!

The Importance of Recognizing We Are Priests of God

SO THE LORD SAID TO AARON, "YOU AND YOUR SONS AND YOUR FATHER'S HOUSEHOLD WITH YOU SHALL BEAR THE GUILT IN CONNECTION WITH THE SANCTUARY, AND YOU AND YOUR SONS WITH

YOU SHALL BEAR THE GUILT IN CONNECTION WITH YOUR
PRIESTHOOD." NUMBERS 18:1

The Word of God indicates that the Old Testament priests were responsible both for their own personal sin, as well as for the sins that take place in connection with the sanctuary. In this way, they needed to atone for both their personal sin, but also for the sins of all the people of God.

In the New Covenant, part of our role as a member of the Kingdom of priests is that we must bear the responsibility for what happens in the courts of the Lord. Suddenly we realize that their struggles are not just someone else's problem, but they are our problem. Any sin going on in the Body of Christ is part of our collective sin as the Church in the region. It is not enough for us, as priests of God, to just be saddened when we hear news of compromise or corruption that has come into another section of the Body of Christ. If we truly understand our role as a priest of the Lord, then we realize that the responsibility for the sins committed in the community of believers is our responsibility.

BUT IF THE WATCHMAN SEES THE SWORD COMING AND DOES NOT
BLOW THE TRUMPET AND THE PEOPLE ARE NOT WARNED, AND A
SWORD COMES AND TAKES A PERSON FROM THEM, HE IS TAKEN AWAY
IN HIS INIQUITY; BUT HIS BLOOD I WILL REQUIRE FROM THE
WATCHMAN'S HAND.

EZEKIEL 33:6

There ought to be great gravity and sobriety in this truth. It is our responsibility as priests of God to deal with the sin in the corporate Body of Christ by bringing repentance to God on

281

behalf of it, and by proactively seeking to be a vessel of cleansing to the Lord's Church. This may be in the form of warning those involved in the particular sin, or it may be in coming alongside them as a friend and helping them move beyond the sin and compromise that has taken place.

After entering into the reality of being a priest of God, we may find ourselves groaning and in deep agony over sins we see in the larger Body of Christ that before we had no burden for. Previously we may have simply dismissed this as someone else's problem. As we see their sin as part of our own sin, this creates an entirely different mindset, and stirs urgency in our hearts to see sin dealt with in prayer, and through practical action. In this way, we are beginning to take up our role as a priest of God in the land.

I PRAYED TO THE LORD MY GOD AND CONFESSED AND SAID, "ALAS, O LORD, THE GREAT AND AWESOME GOD, WHO KEEPS HIS COVENANT AND LOVINGKINDNESS FOR THOSE WHO LOVE HIM AND KEEP HIS COMMANDMENTS, WE HAVE SINNED, COMMITTED INIQUITY, ACTED WICKEDLY AND REBELLED, EVEN TURNING ASIDE FROM YOUR COMMANDMENTS AND ORDINANCES. MOREOVER, WE HAVE NOT LISTENED TO YOUR SERVANTS THE PROPHETS, WHO SPOKE IN YOUR NAME TO OUR KINGS, OUR PRINCES, OUR FATHERS AND ALL THE PEOPLE OF THE LAND.

DANIEL 9:4-6

Another element of our role as a priest goes beyond just repentance for the sins in the Church. God also wants to show us that as priests of God, we are spiritual gatekeepers for every element of life in the nation. As priests we are responsible to bring repentance to Him on behalf of all the sin that is going on in the nation. Only the Holy Spirit can truly lead us individually and corporately to a place where we do this effectively, but we must first see the responsibility that God has given us as the holy priesthood in the land. We are to repent on behalf of sin in the families, in the businesses, in the government, in education and media, as well as the sin taking place among the unholy priesthood of the land.

Just as Daniel modeled for us, though we may not have committed these sins ourselves, we are to take responsibility for them as though we did. Having this understanding of being a priest of God, creates a deep burden in our hearts for the Spirit of God to breakthrough and deliver our nation. No longer can we look at the sin and corruption taking place in our society and feel apathetic about it. As a spiritual gatekeeper of the Living God, their sin is part of our sin. As this revelation dawns on us, a burden for an intervention from God will come upon us as never before. It is one thing to be aware of the grievous sins going on in our nation, but it is quite another thing to realize that God expects us as priests of the land to bring repentance on behalf of those sins, to cleanse the land of all defilement, and to bring healing, and deliverance into every area of society.

Isaiah chapters 58 and 59 provide a detailed description of the sinful ways of the nation of Judah at that time. These Scriptures discuss how the people of God were living in sin, as well as how the land itself had become defiled as the people shed innocent blood and gave themselves over to corruption. God states, *"The Lord's hand is not so short that it cannot save; nor is His ear so dull that it cannot hear. But your iniquities have made a separation between you and your God."* (Isaiah

59:1-2) Only as the people of God bring repentance for the sins of the land can a nation be rebuilt.

THOSE FROM AMONG YOU WILL REBUILD THE ANCIENT RUINS; YOU WILL RAISE UP THE AGE-OLD FOUNDATIONS; AND YOU WILL BE CALLED THE REPAIRER OF THE BREACH, THE RESTORER OF THE STREETS IN WHICH TO DWELL.

ISAIAH 58:12

As priests of God, the first level of repentance required is to divorce ourselves from any way that the sin of the land is still at work in our own hearts and lives. Only after we have allowed God's Spirit to set us apart from the sin of the land, will we have true authority to bring repentance on behalf of others who are still living in sin.

Seeing Sin in Others When We Seek to Unite

As we see sin and compromise in others, rather than going to judgment and cutting off fellowship, take these failings that you see to God and plead for that person before the Throne of Grace. Ask for God's mercy to be upon them to change them and to make them into the person that He created them to be. Join God in believing for the fulfillment of His destiny in their lives.

The fact is, God already knew about the areas of failure in their lives even before you met them. Rather than judging them and writing them off, ask God's Spirit to give you His heart for them. If you are seeing something in them that needs to change, the Holy Spirit may very well have placed you in their life for this very reason. He may be asking you to pray for them and love them through to a place of victory. Whether they are a new believer or a minister of 70 years, you may very well be the one that God has entrusted with the task of seeing them restored to His way of life. Don't underestimate the power of God through the prayers of His saints and don't judge them. Seek to partner with the Person of the Holy Spirit in seeing Christ's Kingdom will and ways come into that situation. In this way, you will be a true child of your Father in heaven who sends His rain on the godly and sinner (Matthew 5:43-45).

Summary of a Regional Priesthood

As priests of God it is part of our role to take responsibility for the sin of the land, beginning in our own hearts, then to the house of God, and continuing out into society as a whole. As we realize the burden we have to cleanse the land and bring the Kingdom of God into all facets of society, unity with the rest of the Body of Christ is no longer optional but essential. As we seek to unify we will see faults and failings in others, just as they may see failings in us. God has not called us to work together in order to judge one another but to be about His Kingdom purposes together. If we see failings in them, recognize God knew these things were there even before you and that instead of judging them He expects you to pray for them and come alongside them so that they will be ushered closer and closer to the destiny God purposed for them even before the Creation of the earth. In this way, as we unite and help to strengthen Christ's Church we are helping to proactively disciple our region in the will and ways of Jesus Christ.

Having a True Kingdom Mindset regarding Christ's Church

Did you know that the early church considered every follower of Christ in their city to be a part of the same church? Even though they met in different locations, they believed that they were a part of One Church.

THE LORD'S HAND WAS WITH THEM, AND A GREAT NUMBER OF PEOPLE BELIEVED AND TURNED TO THE LORD. NEWS OF THIS REACHED THE CHURCH IN JERUSALEM.

ACTS 11:21-22

NOW IN THE CHURCH AT ANTIOCH THERE WERE PROPHETS AND TEACHERS...

ACTS 13:1 (NIV)

Luke speaks of one church in Jerusalem and Antioch though the believers were meeting in many different locations across those cities.

Look at Paul's writing to the Church in the cities of Corinth and Ephesus:

TO THE CHURCH OF GOD IN CORINTH, TO THOSE SANCTIFIED IN CHRIST JESUS AND CALLED TO BE HIS HOLY PEOPLE.

1 CORINTHIANS 1:2

PAUL, AN APOSTLE OF CHRIST JESUS BY THE WILL OF GOD, AND TIMOTHY OUR BROTHER, TO THE CHURCH OF GOD IN CORINTH...

2 CORINTHIANS 1:1

PAUL, AN APOSTLE OF CHRIST JESUS BY THE WILL OF GOD, TO GOD'S HOLY PEOPLE IN EPHESUS, THE FAITHFUL IN CHRIST JESUS.

EPHESIANS 1:1

Even more importantly, what is Jesus' perspective on His Church in a region? This is His Church after all. Does He honor all our distinctions? Does He see as we see? Is it possible that He looks past our banners, and our titles, and wants something much greater than we are presently modeling?

Jesus speaking:

Rev. 2:1 "To the angel of the church in Ephesus write:

2:8 "To the angel of the church in Smyrna write:

2:12 "To the angel of the church in Pergamum write:

2:18 ""To the angel of the church in Thyatira write:"

3:1 – "the church in Sardis"

3:7 – "the church in Philadelphia"

3:14 – "the church in Laodicea"

Jesus sees One Church in our city, One Church in our nation, and One Church in the nations. We would be wise to begin to operate with His perspective, rather than the perspective that many in the current religious system have sought to portray as the way things are done.

Are there barriers due to the distortion that has taken place over time. Absolutely, there are obstacles to God's purposes in the area of unity. But you and I are called to model the Truth of the Kingdom of God. As others see us modeling this, it will help them break through into God's perspective of His Church. We are called to look past denominational barriers and different worship styles in order to realize what those in the early Church knew to be true. Though we may meet in different locations, there is only One Church. There was One Church in Corinth, Ephesus, Antioch and there is only One church in your city made up of everyone who is truly born again. Let us begin to operate in the Light of God's Word and not our religious tradition.

Seeing the Need for the Regional Body of Christ to Work Together

As we begin to see the tremendous task ahead of us in bringing God's Kingdom into all of life, we will begin to see our need for partnership with every other sector of the Body of Christ. If this is our task, to disciple every facet of our nation in the will and ways of Jesus Christ, then we no longer have time for factions. We no longer have time for petty doctrinal disputes. Suddenly we realize that unity with every other part of Christ's Body is absolutely essential if we are going to fulfill what is on His heart. This translates all the way down to every individual in the Body of Christ. We need their gifts, we need their calling, we need their prayers and assistance. Every part of the Body is essential if we are to be a fully functional Body that is capable of discipling our region.

WE ARE TO GROW UP IN ALL ASPECTS INTO HIM WHO IS THE HEAD, EVEN CHRIST, FROM WHOM THE WHOLE BODY, BEING FITTED AND HELD TOGETHER BY WHAT EVERY JOINT SUPPLIES, ACCORDING TO THE PROPER WORKING OF EACH INDIVIDUAL PART, CAUSES THE GROWTH

OF THE BODY FOR THE BUILDING UP OF ITSELF IN LOVE.

EPHESIANS 4:15-17

If all God was calling us to do was to attempt to plant a church in our city and give a small percentage of the people in the area an opportunity to hear the Gospel message, then perhaps one congregation could accomplish this task. If God is calling us to literally disciple every aspect of life that goes on in our region, then it would be virtually impossible for one local congregation to complete this task alone. If instead, God has called His Church to disciple every facet of society in our entire nation, then our eyes should be forever opened that no matter how big "our ministry" becomes, it can never single-handedly fulfill the task that God has given to us. We need all those who have truly given their lives to Jesus Christ to unite and work together.

By entering more deeply into this reality, our hearts will begin to long for the unity that Jesus prayed for in John 17:22-23. We will begin to be burdened to go across town and meet with the other ministries in our region. We will make the time for this to take place. We will begin to see in deeper and deeper ways how we need each part of the Body of Christ in order to fulfill God's purposes.

The Challenge to Begin Building

I WILL NOT DRIVE THEM OUT IN A SINGLE YEAR, BECAUSE THE LAND WOULD BECOME DESOLATE AND THE WILD ANIMALS TOO NUMEROUS FOR YOU. LITTLE BY LITTLE I WILL DRIVE THEM OUT BEFORE YOU, UNTIL YOU HAVE INCREASED ENOUGH TO TAKE POSSESSION OF THE

LAND. EXODUS 23:29, 30

"WHAT SHALL WE SAY THE KINGDOM OF GOD IS LIKE, OR WHAT PARABLE SHALL WE USE TO DESCRIBE IT? IT IS LIKE A MUSTARD SEED, WHICH IS THE SMALLEST SEED YOU PLANT IN THE GROUND. YET WHEN PLANTED, IT GROWS AND BECOMES THE LARGEST OF ALL GARDEN PLANTS, WITH SUCH BIG BRANCHES THAT THE BIRDS OF THE AIR CAN PERCH IN ITS SHADE."

MARK 4:30-32 (NIV)

It may not appear significant at first, but God will use the steps of obedience we take to bring glory and honor to His Name. Will you step out to build Christ's Kingdom in your nation through establishing a Spirit-Empowered Lifestyle in your personal life, family and sphere of influence? If so, choose to begin today, while there is still time.

Discussion Questions

1. What do you think would change if you began to function as One Church in your region rather than as many separate entities? What could this look like? Allow God's Spirit to birth His Vision for this in your heart.

2. In what way have you allowed a lack of love in your heart towards other members or segments in the Body of Christ? Why do you think you have allowed this lack of love towards them?

3. Since we know that God asks us to love even our enemies, how would God's Spirit have you change your heart towards that member or segment of His Body?

Action Points

Ask God's Spirit how you can begin to unite with other local congregations in your region, in order to see this Spirit-Empowered Lifestyle spread across the area. Write down anything that He speaks to you.

_____

_____

_____

As the Body of Christ begins to unite in humility, prayer, seeking of God and repentance, you can believe that these regional fellowships will begin to uproot the powers of darkness that have been holding back the purposes of God in your territory. As you remain in a place of total dependency upon the Spirit of God, believe that He will use these regional gatherings of His Church to bring great glory to His Name.

Prayer Focus

Take time to wait on God and allow His Spirit the opportunity to bring to your mind any lack of love that you have had towards family, friends, and others within the Body of Christ. For each of these areas, wait until a revelation comes from Him regarding the true state of your heart. Write down what He reveals to you regarding your lack of love.

- Family members:

_____

_____

- Friends:

_____

_____

- Other members of the local congregation where you
  fellowship:

_____

_____

- Other sections of the Body of Christ in your
  community/city/nation:

_____

_____

- Now, for each person or section of His Body that He
  reveals to you, ask God to give you His heart for them.
- Allow Him to remove any unforgiveness from your heart
  that has caused you to fail to love them as God has
  commanded you.
- Be obedient to anything His Spirit asks you to do in order
  to right the situation. (Trust Him to restore unity)

Chapter 15: Rebuilding the Walls and Gates in our Nation

As we begin the process of seeking to disciple our nation in the will and ways of Jesus Christ, Nehemiah is a wonderful visual picture of what can take place. At first, all hope appeared to be lost when Nehemiah realized the sad state of his nation. There were various stages that he was led through and not everything he faced was easy. But as we will see, when God is behind just one man, an entire region can be changed.

Stage 1: Situation Analysis – Deeper Awareness of Our Current State as a Nation

THEY SAID TO ME, "THE REMNANT THERE IN THE PROVINCE WHO SURVIVED THE CAPTIVITY ARE IN GREAT DISTRESS AND REPROACH, AND THE WALL OF JERUSALEM IS BROKEN DOWN AND ITS GATES ARE BURNED WITH FIRE."

NEHEMIAH 1:3

The first thing that took place in Nehemiah's ministry is that he learned that the people of Jerusalem were in great distress. He learned that the walls were broken down and the gates were burned with fire. The walls represented protection, and the gates represented the places of influence where decisions are made in regards to keeping evil out of the city or allowing good things into the city. A city without gates has no control over the evil that is rushing in and the good that is being taken out. A city without walls is defenseless against its enemies. Needless to say, this was not good news for the people of Jerusalem.

Stage 2: A Season of Weeping, Mourning, Fasting and Praying

When I heard these words, I sat down and wept and mourned for days; and I was fasting and praying before the God of heaven.

Nehemiah 1:4

Some of us may need to take the time to really look at just how far we are away from God's heart desires in our personal lives, in our families, in our sphere of influence, as well as in our nation. We may need a season to literally sit down and weep over the current state of things. We need God's Spirit to break our hearts with the things that break His heart. This will produce in us a heart that is desperate to see God bring about a change.

Stage 3: Determine to Begin Rebuilding

Then I said to them, "You see the bad situation we are in, that Jerusalem is desolate and its gates burned by fire. Come, let us rebuild the wall of Jerusalem so that we will no longer be a reproach." I told them how the hand of my God had been favorable to me and also about the king's words which he had spoken to me. Then they said, "Let us arise and build." So they put their hands to the good work.

Nehemiah 2:17-18

After processing through the bad news, Nehemiah determined to be part of the solution. Instead of dwelling on all the negative things that were going on, he purposed in his heart that things were going to change and he was going to fulfill his part of the work. Though it was an overwhelming task, he prayed and petitioned the King for his assistance. Then he literally walked around the city to inspect the destruction firsthand. After this, Nehemiah not only made the decision to begin rebuilding, but he rallied others from across the city to join with him in this "good work".

Stage 4: Opposition from the Enemy

BUT WHEN SANBALLAT THE HORONITE AND TOBIAH THE AMMONITE OFFICIAL, AND GESHEM THE ARAB HEARD IT, THEY MOCKED US AND DESPISED US AND SAID, "WHAT IS THIS THING YOU ARE DOING? ARE YOU REBELLING AGAINST THE KING?"

NEHEMIAH 2:19

THEN SANBALLAT AND GESHEM SENT A MESSAGE TO ME, SAYING, "COME, LET US MEET TOGETHER AT CHEPHIRIM IN THE PLAIN OF ONO." BUT THEY WERE PLANNING TO HARM ME. SO I SENT MESSENGERS TO THEM, SAYING, "I AM DOING A GREAT WORK AND I CANNOT COME DOWN. WHY SHOULD THE WORK STOP WHILE I LEAVE IT AND COME DOWN TO YOU?" THEY SENT MESSAGES TO ME FOUR TIMES IN THIS MANNER, AND I ANSWERED THEM IN THE SAME WAY.

NEHEMIAH 6:2-4

Nehemiah's bold decision to partner with God did not go without opposition. His enemies rose up almost immediately to attack the good work that had been started. In the same way, our decision to begin to walk out a Spirit-Empowered Lifestyle will not go without opposition.

Nehemiah's enemies rose up and sought to get him to fear for his life. In fact, throughout the entire rebuilding project, his enemies continually sought to distract him and get him to stop the work. In a similar way, Satan will seek to get us to stop establishing this lifestyle in our lives, our families, and our sphere of influence. We too must choose to trust God and persevere.

BELOVED, DO NOT BE SURPRISED AT THE FIERY ORDEAL AMONG YOU, WHICH COMES UPON YOU FOR YOUR TESTING, AS THOUGH SOME STRANGE THING WERE HAPPENING TO YOU; BUT TO THE DEGREE THAT YOU SHARE THE SUFFERINGS OF CHRIST, KEEP ON REJOICING, SO THAT ALSO AT THE REVELATION OF HIS GLORY YOU MAY REJOICE WITH EXULTATION. IF YOU ARE REVILED FOR THE NAME OF CHRIST, YOU ARE BLESSED, BECAUSE THE SPIRIT OF GLORY AND OF GOD RESTS ON YOU. 1 PETER 4:12-14

Stage 5: Respond in Faith and Perseverance

SO I ANSWERED THEM AND SAID TO THEM, "THE GOD OF HEAVEN WILL GIVE US SUCCESS; THEREFORE WE HIS SERVANTS WILL ARISE AND BUILD, BUT YOU HAVE NO PORTION, RIGHT OR MEMORIAL IN JERUSALEM." NEHEMIAH 2:20

Nehemiah's response was one of unwavering confidence in God. He continually rebuffed his enemies and refused to fall victim to their attacks. We do not see the fiery darts of the enemy piercing through his armor. Instead, we see his resolve to rebuild the wall strengthened even further through their attacks. We too must respond to the attacks of the enemy with faith in God and a heart that chooses to persevere no matter what is coming against us.

Stage 6: Every Believer is Critical to the Rebuilding of a Nation

THEN ELIASHIB THE HIGH PRIEST AROSE WITH HIS BROTHERS THE PRIESTS AND BUILT THE SHEEP GATE; THEY CONSECRATED IT AND HUNG ITS DOORS. THEY CONSECRATED THE WALL TO THE TOWER OF THE HUNDRED AND THE TOWER OF HANANEL. NEXT TO HIM THE MEN OF JERICHO BUILT, AND NEXT TO THEM ZACCUR THE SON OF IMRI BUILT... NEXT TO HIM SHALLUM THE SON OF HALLOHESH, THE OFFICIAL OF HALF THE DISTRICT OF JERUSALEM, MADE REPAIRS, HE AND HIS DAUGHTERS...AFTER HIM NEHEMIAH THE SON OF AZBUK, OFFICIAL OF HALF THE DISTRICT OF BETH-ZUR, MADE REPAIRS AS FAR AS A POINT OPPOSITE THE TOMBS OF DAVID, AND AS FAR AS THE ARTIFICIAL POOL AND THE HOUSE OF THE MIGHTY MEN... AFTER HIM BARUCH THE SON OF ZABBAI ZEALOUSLY REPAIRED ANOTHER SECTION, FROM THE ANGLE TO THE DOORWAY OF THE HOUSE OF ELIASHIB THE HIGH PRIEST...AFTER THEM BENJAMIN AND HASSHUB CARRIED OUT REPAIRS IN FRONT OF THEIR HOUSE. AFTER THEM AZARIAH THE SON OF MAASEIAH, SON OF ANANIAH, CARRIED OUT REPAIRS BESIDE HIS HOUSE.

NEHEMIAH 3:1-2, 12, 16, 20, 23

When we read through Nehemiah chapter 3, we see that every single person in the region was vital to the work of rebuilding. In a similar way, when we see the size of the work that God wants to accomplish in our region, we will begin to realize that we must mobilize others to join with us if we are going to fulfill what is on His heart. Some worked on large sections of the wall (regional and congregational discipleship) and others just worked on the wall by their homes (family discipleship), but together the results were God-sized!

Stage 7: The Wall is Rebuilt and Surrounding Nations Are Impacted

SO THE WALL WAS COMPLETED ON THE TWENTY-FIFTH OF THE MONTH ELUL, IN FIFTY-TWO DAYS. WHEN ALL OUR ENEMIES HEARD OF IT, AND ALL THE NATIONS SURROUNDING US SAW IT, THEY LOST THEIR CONFIDENCE; FOR THEY RECOGNIZED THAT THIS WORK HAD BEEN ACCOMPLISHED WITH THE HELP OF OUR GOD. NEHEMIAH 6:15-16

After all of Nehemiah's hard labor and the battles that were fought, the wall was completed. Given the size of the work, it is truly amazing that the wall was rebuilt in just 52 days. The surrounding nations recognized that "this work had been accomplished with the help of our God."

In Summary

As we go before God to gain His broken heart for our current state, we are drawn to a place of desperation to see a move of His Spirit. As we determine to begin rebuilding we will face opposition which will require us to respond in faith and perseverance. As we help to activate each member of Christ's Body in our territory around a common vision and goal, we too can watch as things begin to happen that can only be explained by the fact that the Living God is moving on our behalf. As He moves in power in this way, even the surrounding nations will begin to see that our God is at work and they will desire Him to work there as well! Praise God!

Discussion Questions:

1. Have you ever experienced being broken over the state of your nation? If so, explain what you experienced.
2. Have you ever attempted to begin obeying something that God was asking of you only to encounter opposition in the process? What was your response to the opposition?
3. What type of faith and perseverance do you believe Nehemiah must have had to help oversee the rebuilding of the wall? (Explain)
4. What do you think it would look like if the Body of Christ rallied to work together for the common good of your nation?

Action Step:

We see in the life of Nehemiah, a man who overcame every obstacle in order for God's purposes to advance in his nation. Do you have a sense of what God is calling you to do in your nation? Take time to write down anything that He has been speaking to you as you have been going through this book. Then pray into what He has shared with you. Allow this vision He has given you to begin to shape your actions.

_____

_____

_____

_____

Prayer Focus:

We want to take time to pray for the nation where God has placed us. Just like Nehemiah, may we allow God to break our hearts over the state of our nation so that we will make ourselves available to Him however He chooses to use us as part of His solution.

Father, I thank You for placing me in this nation. I thank You that You have a plan and a purpose for me here. I ask that You would help me to see this nation through Your eyes. Help me to ache with the things that bring pain to Your heart. I want to see our national sin as You see it, so that I will have a desperation in my heart to see a breakthrough in this land. I trust You to use me here for Your glory in the days ahead.

Grant me Your faith and perseverance so that I will not grow weary in doing good. I choose to trust that in Your perfect timing there will be good fruit from my labors. Help me to see Your vision for my nation so that I will have the faith to believe what You believe. (Keep praying as God's Spirit leads you.)

Conclusion

A Vision to Equip and Send Spirit-Empowered Christ-Followers to Establish God's Kingdom in the Nations

THEN THE LORD ANSWERED ME AND SAID, "RECORD THE VISION AND INSCRIBE IT ON TABLETS, THAT THE ONE WHO READS IT MAY RUN. "FOR THE VISION IS YET FOR THE APPOINTED TIME; IT HASTENS TOWARD THE GOAL AND IT WILL NOT FAIL. THOUGH IT TARRIES, WAIT FOR IT; FOR IT WILL CERTAINLY COME, IT WILL NOT DELAY."

HABAKKUK 2:2-3

Would you consider being a part of helping to establish a Spirit-Empowered lifestyle in your nation? Would you share this vision with others within your sphere of influence? Our hope is to see every nation see some of the following goals take place. Should the Lord lead you to partner with us in this endeavor, please contact us so that we will be aware of your partnership in the Gospel.

National Goal

It is our hope that the Living God will cause many to participate in equipping Spirit-Empowered Christ-followers in each of our respective nations. Our hope is that each nation would see thousands of families take up the call to see God's Kingdom deeply established within their marriages and families. That thousands of marketplace leaders in every nation will choose to establish Christ's Kingdom in their position of business, government, education, media, and that thousands of local congregations will take up this call to a Spirit-Empowered lifestyle at the congregational level.

Through the establishment of this Spirit-Empowered Life in the Global Body of Christ, we believe for a mass harvest of souls coming into a saving relationship with Jesus Christ and that we will begin to see the Gospel of Jesus Christ transform entire regions. We believe that Jesus Christ is jealous for the over seven billion souls on the earth and that He has placed His Church here to be the salt and light of the earth (Matthew 5:13-14).

Final Encouragement – Keep Going until This Lifestyle Is Established in You

The goal of this book is not merely to cast a big vision and share some spiritual concepts that cause us to see them at a distance but not put them into practice. Our hope is for this book to be an aid in seeing this lifestyle literally established in every Christ-follower in every nation. We would encourage you to not simply read this book one time and then set it aside, but to continue to pour through this material until this has become a part of your lifestyle. Ask the Holy Spirit to lead you into a deeper lifestyle of abiding in Him. He cannot fail as you entrust yourself to Him. In time, as this becomes your lifestyle, then you will be in a position to share this with others.

Share This Lifestyle with Others

Even now you may begin to prayerfully ask Jesus if there are any specific people that He would have you share this lifestyle. He modeled for us a lifestyle of pouring what the Father gave to Him into the lives of 12 other people. From these 12, God began to multiply them in such a way that the Gospel has spread to the nations of the earth. If you begin to share this lifestyle with just 12 others, it could quickly spread across your region. Ask God for wisdom as to how He desires to use you to disciple others in this lifestyle.

Contact Us:

If you have been touched and inspired to enter more deeply into a Spirit-Empowered Lifestyle in your personal life, family, workplace, congregation or region, please contact us so that we will know of your decision and so that we can support you. We have further resources available online.

We would also love to hear any testimonies of how this resource has been used by God to speak to you. You can send testimonies to us via email. God bless you!

Information:

Website: www.dninternational.org/contact

Email: office@dninternational.org

Spirit Empowered For Life

Commitment Form

This form can be filled out online at: www.dninternational.org/SpiritEmpoweredForLife

If you fill this out online, it will allow us to send you relevant resources to assist you in your commitment.

- I commit to seek God to establish a deeper lifestyle of abiding in Christ in my personal life

- I commit to seek God to establish a deeper level of being empowered by God's Spirit in my marriage / family

- I commit to seek God to establish a deeper level of being empowered by His Spirit in my sphere of influence

Recognizing that there will be spiritual warfare against the establishment of this lifestyle:

- I am committed to persevere until this lifestyle has been thoroughly established. This may take 2 months, 6 months, or 2 years before it is established, but I am committed to seeing this take place.

(Questions for pastors/ministry leaders)

- I commit to seek God to establish this Spirit-Empowered lifestyle in the personal lives, families and sphere of influence of the ministry that God has entrusted to me.

- I commit to seek to stay regularly connected with other ministries in my region in order to stay encouraged in this vision, as well as to be an encouragement to others.

- I commit to seek God for the specific way that He would have this Spirit-Empowered lifestyle become established and I'm willing to make this lifestyle the focus of our congregational meetings (Providing teachings, times for sharing testimonies, sharing struggles, and offering ministry to those who are seeking to live out a Spirit-Empowered reality.)

Signature_____

Goals for pastors/ministry leaders: Prayerfully consider setting goals for how many lives you believe God to equip and empower in the Spirit-Empowered Life in next 6-12 months:

Goal for Spirit-Empowered Individuals: _____

Goal for Spirit-Empowered Marriages and Families:_____

Goal for Spirit-Empowered Believers reaching out to their sphere of influence with this lifestyle (Business, government, education...):_____

Goal for how many other ministries you will share this vision with:_____

If you took the time to fill out this form in the book rather than on our website please take a moment to contact us via email just to let us know that you have made a commitment: office@dninternational.org
If you contact us, we can provide you with further resources that can assist you in your commitment towards a Spirit-Empowered Life.

(If contacting us via email, please include your name, and physical location in the body of the email.)

The Spirit-Empowered Life
30 Day Challenge

The previous form is primarily for individuals who are committing to this lifestyle for a lifetime. The 30 day challenge is a simple way to jump start a lifestyle of being empowered by the Spirit of God in a corporate setting. This can be implemented in a marriage and family setting, a small group, a local congregation, or across an entire region.

Goal of the 30 day Challenge

O TASTE AND SEE THAT THE LORD IS GOOD; HOW BLESSED IS THE MAN WHO TAKES REFUGE IN HIM!

PSALM 34:8

Sometimes before we are willing to readjust our entire lives to come into conformity with God's ways, we need to first taste and see just how good it is to live in deep communion with Him. The goal for the 30 day challenge is to help provide an opportunity for God's people to taste and see the goodness of deep intimacy with God, with a long-term view towards sustainable lifestyle change.

The 30 Day Challenge can be done as an individual, in a marriage, in a family, in a local congregation, in a workplace, or even as the united Body of Christ in a region or nation. We encourage everyone who commits to the challenge to prayerfully ask at least one other person to serve as their accountability partner so that they can go through this together and help each other continue to grow after the challenge has concluded.

Lifestyle of the 30 Day Challenge

I HAVE BEEN CRUCIFIED WITH CHRIST; AND IT IS NO LONGER I WHO LIVE, BUT CHRIST LIVES IN ME; AND THE LIFE WHICH I NOW LIVE IN THE FLESH I LIVE BY FAITH IN THE SON OF GOD, WHO LOVED ME AND GAVE HIMSELF UP FOR ME.

GALATIANS 2:20

Over the course of the next 30 days I commit to pursue a deeper revelation of what it means to die to myself and allow the Spirit of God to live His glorious Life in and through me. Specifically I will seek to implement the following Spiritual Keys during the 30 days:

Spiritual Key: A Lifestyle of Praise and Worship

I commit to spend more time in daily worship, asking God's Spirit to take me deeper into what it means to worship Him in Spirit and in truth.

ENTER HIS GATES WITH THANKSGIVING AND HIS COURTS WITH PRAISE. GIVE THANKS TO HIM, BLESS HIS NAME.

PSALM 100:4

Spiritual Key: A Lifestyle of Waiting and Listening to God's Spirit

I commit to spend more time waiting before God's Spirit, and listening to what He has to say to me.

MY SHEEP HEAR MY VOICE, AND I KNOW THEM, AND THEY FOLLOW ME. JOHN 10:27

Spiritual Key: A Lifestyle of Being Filled with the Word of God

I commit to spend more time in the Word of God, asking God's Spirit to cause my interaction with His Word to be powerful and alive.

FOR THE WORD OF GOD IS LIVING AND ACTIVE AND SHARPER THAN ANY TWO-EDGED SWORD, AND PIERCING AS FAR AS THE DIVISION OF SOUL AND SPIRIT, OF BOTH JOINTS AND MARROW, AND ABLE TO JUDGE THE THOUGHTS AND INTENTIONS OF THE HEART.

HEBREWS 4:12

Spiritual Key: Lifestyle of Prayer and Intercession

I commit to spend more time in daily prayer, asking God's Spirit to give me His heart to pray for those around me

PRAY WITHOUT CEASING.

1 THES. 5:17

Spiritual Key: A Lifestyle of Accountability and Mutual Submission

I commit to connect more deeply with at least one or two other believers in order to be real with them and share what is going on in my relationship with God.

LET US CONSIDER HOW WE MAY SPUR ONE ANOTHER ON TOWARD

LOVE AND GOOD DEEDS, NOT GIVING UP MEETING TOGETHER, AS SOME ARE IN THE HABIT OF DOING, BUT ENCOURAGING ONE ANOTHER—AND ALL THE MORE AS YOU SEE THE DAY APPROACHING.

HEBREWS 10:24-25 (NIV)

Heart Attitude of the 30 Day Challenge

Heart attitude is very important in approaching God. Though we may seek to increase the amount of time we spend with God, if we do not address the state of our hearts we may labor in vain. Therefore, we encourage you to combine the spiritual keys with a heart attitude that is seeking to put 2 Chronicles 7:14 into practice. The combination of the two will be like a spiritual atomic bomb.

IF I SHUT UP THE HEAVENS SO THAT THERE IS NO RAIN, OR IF I COMMAND THE LOCUST TO DEVOUR THE LAND, OR IF I SEND PESTILENCE AMONG MY PEOPLE, AND MY PEOPLE WHO ARE CALLED BY MY NAME HUMBLE THEMSELVES AND PRAY AND SEEK MY FACE AND TURN FROM THEIR WICKED WAYS, THEN I WILL HEAR FROM HEAVEN, WILL FORGIVE THEIR SIN AND WILL HEAL THEIR LAND.

2 CHRONICLES 7:13-14

As I commit to implement the spiritual keys I am also seeking God's Spirit to take me deeper in:

- Humility
- Prayer/Seeking His face
- Repentance of every way my life has not been lived in
- His will and ways

I resolve to allow God's Spirit to have greater control during these 30 days. I willingly allow God's Spirit to take these 30 days to establish a new pattern of seeking Him that will remain with me for the rest of my life.

Signature:_____

Accountability Partner: We encourage you to do the 30 day challenge with at least one other person who will serve as your accountability partner during this time. We recommend connecting with your accountability partner at least once a week during the 30 days in order to share with each other how things have been going, pray through difficulties that have been faced, as well as celebrate victories together. We hope that you will remain in close connection after the challenge has concluded in order to continue to encourage each other in this lifestyle.

Name of accountability partner:_____

It is our prayer that this will be a life changing time which will forever instill in you the incredible value of seeking to live a Spirit-Empowered Life! At the end of the 30 days please do not stop what God has begun, but take this as the beginning of a new way of life that will not end until you see Him face to face in eternity.

For further resources related to *The Spirit Empowered Life - 30 Challenge* go to our website at:

www.dninternational.org/SpiritEmpowered30Days

Launch Journey into the Spirit-Empowered Life in a Local Congregation

In the section where I shared the testimony of God sending revival to the local congregation I was a part of, we have already seen the difference that a single Spirit-Empowered congregation can make in a city and even in a nation. If a congregation has grown in the understanding of being Kingdom minded and not just seeking to grow our own ministry, then one congregation can literally shift the course of a nation. In Taiwan, the current national level move of God's Spirit was started as two or three congregations completely devoted themselves to personal, family and workplace renewal. Today there are between 1,000-2,000 congregations involved with hundreds of thousands who have come to Christ!

For those interested in launching *Journey into the Spirit Empowered Life* in a local congregation we have various tools available to assist you:

For more information on launching Journey into the Spirit Empowered Life in a local congregation you can go to: www.dninternational.org/LaunchSpiritEmpoweredLife

For more information on a customized Church Renewal Strategy go to: www.dninternational.org/churchrenewal

DISCIPLE NATIONS

INTERNATIONAL

Disciple Nations International exists for two primary reasons:

1. To Renew the Already Existent Church
2. To Plant the Church Where There Is No Church

DNI was birthed out of a revelation that God truly desires to see entire nations discipled in the will and ways of Jesus Christ. Even as you read these words, there are some 500 communities around the world that have been experiencing God's Spirit impact all of society by the Kingdom of Jesus Christ.

If we truly desire to disciple the over 7 billion people on the earth, the starting point in any region or nation is the already existent Body of Christ. Even in nations, like China or India where entire people groups have no Gospel witness, an initial step is to gather the Body of Christ that is nearby and cause them to see the need and ask them to seek God's Spirit for His wisdom in how to reach the unreached.

Once we have had a revelation that the already existent Body of Christ is the key to the fulfillment of God's heart desire to see nations discipled, then we will be able to understand just how critical it is for us to Gather, Awaken, Equip, and Empower His Church to fulfill His purposes. We hope that you will prayerfully consider partnering with us to see the message of the Spirit Empowered Life taken to the nations!

Partner with Us

After learning about the heartbeat of Disciple Nations International, and in seeing the opportunity to be a part of equipping and empowering Spirit Empowered Christ-followers all across the earth, we hope that you will prayerfully consider joining with us in the discipleship of the nations.

Partnering with You for the Fulfillment of the Great Commission,

Chris Vennetti

Bond Slave (Mark 10:44)

Disciple Nations International

Donate today: www.dninternational.org/donate

Checks can be made out to "DNI" and mailed to:

Disciple Nations International
P.O. Box 771478
Orlando, FL 32877

Get Involved: www.dninternational.org/getinvolved

Email: office@dninternational.org

Made in the USA
Columbia, SC
16 November 2020